TWO IS ALWAYS BETTER THAN ONE

"Twins, Arthur, locked and intertwined, but the ewe has plenty of room. This shouldn't take long."

Nor did it, for basically all you do, in case, dear reader, you ever have to deliver twins is say to one, "Just you wait there a minute, my dear," and to the other, "up you come."

Putting it in more technical terms, you sort out the tangle of legs, then repel one lamb and advance the other, and in ten minutes the job is done. As I dried my arm I grinned at Arthur. This was the good bit, the job done, a healthy ewe already on her feet licking her offspring and giving that lovely, throaty chuckle which you get only from a sheep after lambing. It was a cold, damp night, but we waited to see the lambs stagger to their feet, heading for the milk bar for that first, all-important drink of mother's milk, finding their way with unerring, inborn instinct. This was the little miracle that made the toughest lambing worthwhile and that never palled on me or grew commonplace.

St. Martin's Paperbacks Titles
by Alexander Cameron

VET IN THE VESTRY
POULTRY IN THE PULPIT

Poultry in the Pulpit

Alexander Cameron

Further revelations of the Vet in the Vestry

ST. MARTIN'S PAPERBACKS

First published in Great Britain by Lochar Publishing.

POULTRY IN THE PULPIT

Copyright © 1988 by Alexander Cameron.

Cover photograph of the author courtesy of the author; inset photograph on cover courtesy Tony Stone Worldwide.

Library of Congress Catalog Card Number: 90-37242

ISBN: 0-312-92770-3

Printed in the United States of America

St. Martin's Press hardcover edition/December 1990
St. Martin's Paperbacks edition/April 1992

10 9 8 7 6 5 4 3 2 1

To My Family
Neil, Ian, David, Alan
and grandson Ross;
and to the wider family of the
congregations to whom I have
been privileged to minister.

CONTENTS

Prologue

ONE

"Mr. Cameron—can you tummle your wulkies?" asked young Stewart.

"Can I do what, Stewart?"

"Tummle your wulkies—look, like this" and he proceeded to do several somersaults.

"Oh, I see, Stewart. We called it tumlin' the cran at Glenafton where I was a boy, but I could never do it."

"What! Never?"

"Eh, no . . . I think it's something about not liking to be upside down."

"My, you're queer. I doot you were feart," he concluded.

Our lawns at Kilmarton were ideal for all sorts of games among our three lads, Neil, seven, Ian, five and young David, two. Almost every day in summer they were joined by the McPherson youngsters and sometimes their cousin Hugh, who lived in nearby Dunlop. The McPhersons had a family of boys, like us, Mure, Alastair, Ian, Stewart, just fractionally older than our brood. Bill McPherson was congregational minister at Kilmarton and he and Sheena were among our closest friends, then and now, and since their garden was small, their laddies came down to our wide expanse and played traditional games like hide-and-seek, cowboys, football and games of their own devising among the many bushes and trees on the lawns.

They were attired in a variety of gear from trousers, braces and big boots to shorts and bare feet.

In July of 1961 we had an addition to the family when baby Alan arrived, just months after Bill and Sheena had another boy, little Graham. Not many days after she returned from hospital, Janet was up in our bedroom attending to the new babe when she happened to glance out of the window which overlooked the lawns. Right at the window grew a beautiful gean tree, and Janet was petrified to see that one end of a rope had been slung over a branch and the other end was tied round David's midriff. His face was as red as a beetroot and he looked fit to burst as he fought back the tears while all the rest of the gang were hauling him up off the ground. The game had been cowboys, and David was being lynched! Janet gave a yell, hammered on the window, and with a thump David fell to the ground as the lynch mob realised the victim's mother was not too happy about the proceedings!

I had been preaching in the Laigh Kirk, Kilmarton, ever since I started my divinity studies at Glasgow Trinity. The weekly pulpit supply fee was a great help, and since the much-loved minister Andrew Hastie had died, the great, enormous but gracious manse had been empty, as negotiations dragged on and on for two years to unite the Laigh with the former United Presbyterian Kirk, Cairns. Eventually the Kirk Session of the Laigh suggested we live in the manse, and if I was willing to take the Bible Class, perhaps start a Youth Fellowship, do some visiting and take some funerals, as well as preach weekly, they would be willing to pay me practically a minister's full salary. This was truly manna from Heaven, for most of my share of the Bristacombe practice had gone to provide a home for my mother, my father having died just before I gave up practice, and mother finding herself in that cursed thing, a tied house. It was even more welcome manna with the addition to our family as money was in short supply. Nevertheless, looking back over the three years of study at Trinity with no kind of grant to assist, it was nothing short of marvellous at times the way we were provided for financially. It was hard work, of course, studying daily in Glasgow, preparing weekly sermons and practically running a Church, but the experience was invaluable, and our time at Kilmarton was a wonderful one for my first Charge at Moorton, the neighbouring parish, where, as recorded in my previous book, *Vet in the Vestry*, I was eventually appointed minister, succeeding the Revd Bruce Young who had been a great help to me at Kilmarton. It is customary to present a new minister with robes in his first Charge, but I had been given Andrew Hastie's practically new gowns by his sister, and I have been proud to wear them all my ministry.

Bill and Sheena were not spared their little lad, Graham, for long, as tragedy overtook him. When just a little fellow of two, Sheena found her little boy hanging on a nail in the wall at their back door, where, as he tried to climb the wall, his jersey had caught and been pulled round his neck. We mourned with, and for our friends, as did the whole of Kilmarton, in a so simple, yet tragic death. In time Bill left the Congregational Church and joined the Church of Scotland, maintaining a fine ministry in several places, particularly in the Gorbals where he saw a brand new Church built. In time he went to the quiet of the country until his recent retirement, a faithful ministry despite a life time of ill health and an artificial leg, both the result of his years in a Japanese prison camp where he, astonishingly, and despite his suffering, heard and obeyed the call to the ministry.

Looking back to these years at Kilmarton, two quite opposite events stick in my mind. One was crawling and weeding in the strawberry patch and listening on our portable radio to England thumping Scotland to the tune of nine goals, and poor Haffey the goalkeeper bearing the brunt of the nation's disgust. I am sure I pulled out more strawberries than weeds that day as the goals rattled in!

The other event was my first experience of the strange ways God guides. I had been visiting a very ill man called Mr. Stewart and though he always treated me with respect, he also held me at arm's length. I just could not get close to him. One day I set out to do a few visits at one end of the town and found myself to my utter amazement outside his door in a totally different direction. I was astonished to find myself there that day. I just seemed to have been carried and set down there, but I went in, and for the first time got close to Mr. Stewart. He was no more ill than usual, but he wanted to talk—and talk about life's basic things—so we did. We read the Psalm 23, had a word of prayer and I left, leaving a man who had clearly found peace of heart and mind. The next day when I got back from Trinity, I received a message to rush to Ballochmyle Hospital as Mr. Stewart, quite suddenly, had become worse and could not last long. I hurried as fast as I could, but was too late. I grieved with his wife, and yet marvelled too. We had not had any indication the day before when mysteriously I had been led to his home that this would be his last day on earth, but the great Father had known, and brought, even though at the very end, peace and calm to a wearied and troubled soul.

Many times since, such things have happened, as with all ministers but I first saw the marvellous and mysterious ways God works in Kilmarton. All my two and a half years there were clearly a preparation for Moorton, where this story begins, the vet back in the vestry, with many a look back to my days among pigs, pets, ponies and all the animal kingdom, and some comparisons with the life of a parson.

Thems As Knows Best

TWO

"Hello" said a female voice over the phone, "I'm looking for a brain."

"Have you lost one then?" I was tempted to ask, but instead said the rather flat, but certainly puzzled, "Beg pardon?"

"I suppose it does sound a bit queer, right enough" she went on, "I'd better start at the beginning."

"That might help," I agreed.

"My name's Helen Boyd and I'm Secretary of the Kilmaurs and District Young Farmer's Club. We have our first meeting of the new session two weeks tonight and it's to be a Brains Trust. We have three brains lined up . . ." I laughed "Queer picture. Are they sitting on a shelf?"

She laughed too, but went on, "We need a fourth brain and when I read about you in the paper, I thought "the very man."

"You certainly didn't read that I had a brain . . . maybe the Trust might be nearer it," I suggested.

"You are Mr. Cameron, the new minister of Moorton?"

"That's true . . . very new . . . two days to be exact."

"You were a real vet and you are a minister?"

"That's true too."

"Well, there you are then! The very man! I don't know what brains ministers need, I suppose they just get their sermons out of books, but I know vets have to think a fair bit, I mean animals can't talk and all that, and I thought 'kill two birds with one stone' . . . he can answer the animal questions and the holy ones . . . not that we're too holy in the Young Farmers" she added a bit doubtfully. "Say you'll come . . . please!"

I laughed again and replied, "Who could resist such a plea? OK. Where do you meet and when?"

So the details were settled and I was lined up for my first outside engagement almost before the furniture had settled properly in the Manse. I didn't know it then, but it was to prove the first of hundreds of requests, over the years, to give a talk, a slide show or be on a panel.

I duly turned up for the Brains Trust, found a surprisingly large crowd assembled, met Helen Boyd the brain researcher and also met my fellow "brains"—a pig breeder, a traveller for sheep dip, a lady apparently famous for her biting wit and campaign for Woman's Lib . . . and me, the total unknown of the company. The President of the Club was in the Chair and I was mightily impressed by the way he handled the whole evening, as I nearly always have been at YFCs up and down the country over the years. They could teach many of their seniors a thing or two about the conduct of a public meeting.

The questions had been handed in beforehand, and they varied from how to get blackcurrant jelly to set (about which I knew nothing) to the subsidy for hill cattle (where I knew little more). There were, however, many on animal diseases and a surprising number on Church affairs, and invariably the young Chairman would turn to me on such occasions and say "now we'll ask the man who knows best" or "now for the expert." After ten years as a vet I did not class myself as an expert, but I had learned a bit, and with two weeks in the ministry I did not consider myself anything in that field, but somehow got through the questions, which, among others, included:

"How can we prevent staggers . . . in cattle," added the Chairman amid laughter.

"How do you treat Orf in sheep?"

"What really causes Braxy?"

"Why can't ministers be more human?"

"What's the purpose of a Bishop's get up?"

"How can the Church attract young people?" How I wished I knew an answer to that last one as I looked out at these bright young faces!

The night flew past and I found I had thoroughly enjoyed myself. I do not know if much was learned from my answers, but, clearly, in their eyes, I was, for the night, in my departments, the expert. Later, as I wrote up my diary for the day, my mind kept turning to the Chairman's words . . . "the man who knows best," and I thought back to how I had been so classified on numbers of occasions in our vet practice at Bristacombe, and before the dying study fire, I drifted off on the wings of memory.

I was puzzled, on two counts. First of all, I wondered why I was there at all. I had passed the sprawling farm buildings of Meadway several times, knew the tenants were called Price, and with a dairy herd that size they must need a vet regularly. I had never before been called, therefore, they had another vet. I did not mind a bit. The practice was growing steadily and from what I had heard of the Price brothers, I reckoned I was better off without them. Why then had they called me out that cold January night to calve a cow?

With my calving coat on, arms scrubbed up and right arm inside the cow's uterus as far as I could reach, I was even more puzzled. What on earth had we here? I looked round the stony faces of the reception committee, three of them, standing watching me in complete silence. I thought they looked a bit like the three brass monkeys, "Hear no evil, speak no evil, see no evil," only much more villainous than the monkeys! I came out of the cow, took off my calving coat, stripped to the waist to gain a few extra inches, and re-inserted my arm. She was an old Friesian and very deep, and despite my six foot, one and a half inches, I felt I could do with a leg up to get far enough in. I could trace two front legs, but where was the head? I checked—yes—they were front legs, not rear, it was not a breech presentation. I had seen a calf with two heads, one with six legs, but never one with no head—and then I felt the loose flap of skin and the sharp edge of bone. I paused and thought a bit, then withdrew my arm, went to the bucket of water, carefully cleaned my arms and body, then dressed slowly and deliberately. I had my jacket on and was reaching for my coat when one of the surly crew shouted, "Where the devil are you going?"

I smiled a mirthless smile and retorted as coolly as I could.

"You're right about the Devil, but he's not going . . . He's been here already and I don't like his work or fancy his company!" Quite a speech, I thought, "So I'm off home," I added.

"What do you mean?" piped up brother Bill. The other was Joe.

"Look, Mr. Price, I don't like being made a fool of and I'm not in the habit of clearing up other people's messes. I'm going home for these very good reasons.

One, I am not your vet. Two, you never told me somebody had been at this cow before me, and three, whoever it was should be hung, drawn and quartered, but the most I can do is report him or you to the RSPCA. In my years as a vet I've never before examined a cow and found a headless calf inside, the head cut off a living calf and the skin and jagged edges of bone stuffed back in, and you hadn't the guts or common decency to tell me. The person who did this is a devil alright, for as well as killing the calf, he's probably condemned this cow to death.

Finally, I'm not going to have it said you had Cameron, the vet, out to one of your cows and he killed it. Good night to you. I'll send you my bill in due course," and I headed for the door. I was flaming mad.

But Joe Price reached the door before me, looking sheepish. When I heard his feet behind me, I half expected him to clobber me, but he was all remorse or seemed to be. At any rate he was barring my exit.

"Look, Mr. Cameron, us's done wrong in not tellin' 'ee like, but Sam Godber's a dab 'and at calvins, like, an' us thought he would manage but it bate 'im."

"So you're Sam Godber!" I glared at the third man present, a swarthy, unshaven, thick-necked individual, not unlike the Devil, I imagined. "I've heard of you and seen some of your work and taken the blame already for two cows you killed."

He stepped towards me, mouthing curses, and looking ugly. There's one in every parish, somebody reckoned to be a dab hand "when cows are bad to calve." He thrust his unshaven face close to mine. I kind of hoped he would hit me, for I was livid and spoiling to do something. I'm afraid I would have found it hard to turn the other cheek that night.

"I never killed no cows no-how," he muttered.

I looked through him; in fact, in retrospect, I thought my performance was worth an Oscar! Now he became more abusive still.

"Look, sonny," he sneered, "I've calved more cows than you've ever touched an' I reckon I've forgotten more than all that thar book learnin' they gives you at college." This was quite a speech for him, though actually it was somewhat longer than reported for every other word was an obscenity. I listened to his tirade and thought of two cows I'd seen, one with metritis (inflamation of the womb) and the other with a ruptured womb. I knew what some of the farming community had said . . . "we had Sam Godber, an' he calved them a'right, but vet lost them after." It was always the vet's fault, said thems as knows best.

"Well then, in that case, Mr. Godber, since you know

it all, and certainly more than me, I suggest you go ahead and finish this calving you started."

He really had no answer to that, except more curses. By now the other Price brother was beside me, pawing at my arm.

"Please, Mr. Cameron; Sam's done 'is best, like, but this thar's a job for them as knows best. (I was exalted in status, I thought.) We can't leave the poor beast like that."

"Then send for your own vet," I snapped. "Why didn't you anyway?"

"We didn't reckon Mr. Warman 'ad take it too well, like, to us 'avin 'ad a go." I bet he wouldn't. He'd have sworn at them for five minutes probably, without repeating himself, and then told them to send for the knacker. "We knew you was a bit of a preacher, like, an' we thought you'd take more kind to it, do you see?" Probably what they really meant was "he's a soft mark," for I confess I wasn't feeling very Christian just then, but I don't suppose Christ was the picture of gentleness when He took a whip to the rogues in His Father's house.

I looked at the two Price brothers, and the man Godber, tough nuts all of them. Then I glanced at the poor beast. Whatever else I was, Christian or no, I was supposed to relieve suffering.

"Alright," I said, "I'll do what I can on two conditions. First, that if this cow dies, you'll say you called the vet too late, and second, that Mr. Godber, who reckons he knows it all anyway, clears out."

This was rubbing it in a bit, but I was hanged if I was going to have a critic looking on, a sort of back seat driver, and equally determined I was going to give no secrets away to this fellow who badly wanted teaching a lesson. They hesitated, and the two Prices looked at Godber.

"A'right, I knows when I'm not wanted. I'll go." "Swine," he snarled as he passed me. I did not mind. I had been called worse.

It was no easy task delivering that headless torso. Clearly the calf had been coming head first with fore legs back, and unable to repeal the head or advance the legs to the normal chin on legs position, Godber had cut a living calf's head off, and pushed the stump inside. Then, with the vaginal wall swollen, oedematous and lacerated, he had taken fright and advised getting the vet. I got my calving chains on the forelegs. I used special chains rather than ropes, for they were stronger, easier to grip, less liable to lacerate the vaginal wall and more easily sterilised. Then I managed to put another chain round the flap of loose neck skin, more or less enclosing the jagged ends of the calf's neck bones. Then masses of lubrication was pumped into the womb and vagina, and while the brothers pulled on the leg chains as directed, I shielded the vaginal wall as best I could with one hand over the neck stump, and slowly advanced it with the neck chain. Then with the stump and legs outside, it was just a question of pulling. It was a big calf, but it could have been saved. "And it was a heifer too," murmured Joe. For the first time that night I began to feel a twinge of pity for any human present. I cleaned the cow there and then (removed the afterbirth), inserted some pessaries, gave a whacking dose of penicillin and intimated I would be back for the next two days to give more injections. She did fine, and I gained half a client. They evidently did not like to leave their own vet, but they were genuinely grateful, and came to us for some cases.

Godber? He went on acting as midwife. I sometimes think it takes about as long in remote country districts to counter this kind of quackery, as it did Mary Slessor to checkmate the witch doctors of Calabar, for in the minds of very many, it is only the likes of Godber with no book learning, but plenty of experience, "as knows best."

Frank Fowler was also reckoned to be in the ranks of "thems as knows best," but he was a different kettle of fish from Godber. Nature had endowed him with a small, narrow hand—or rather two of them—infinite patience and considerable know-how in the ways of sheep. Every lambing season, if the farmer was beaten, the first line of approach was usually the wife or daughter, smaller hands again. If they were beaten, you sent for Frank. He was good, there was no doubt about it. But sheep were valuable at that time in the early 1950s, a ewe with twins was potentially £20 anyway, so it was worth considering having a vet, at the very most two guineas a time, possibly less, and that was all the ewe would fetch for slaughter, again possibly less. So one triumphant day I was summoned to a case where Frank was stuck. He was there to watch proceedings, plus a few neighbours. Frank would never "bad use" a ewe, but if two or three hands have been there before yours, the uterine fluids are usually dried up, the ewe exhausted, and perhaps a lamb or lambs dead. The audience that day, with the exception of the farmer, probably hoped for a failure. What could this Scotsman do that their own Frank could not? What, indeed, that Scotsman was wondering himself?

I examined the ewe, trying to look assured and confident before this audience, and for that first case I was in luck. All I could feel was a multitude of legs, and no heads. I knew Frank would never be guilty of a Godber decapitation, so I patiently worked away, sorting out what were back and fore legs. The two essentials of lambing are undoubtedly patience and gentleness, and in multiple births, it can sometimes take time to get everything in position. Now the great disadvantage of spectators at a lambing is that they cannot see a thing, at any rate what the vet is doing inside. I got a pair of hind legs, eased them up gently, and felt the lamb come—a breech presentation. I grunted "this one will be dead" and I was proved an accurate prophet, which greatly enhanced my standing with the spectators, but I knew fine that a breech that had been so long in the delivery as this one had, would be dead, the lamb had suffocated. Then to appreciative murmurs I brought out two smaller lambs, normal front presentation. The heads had been twisted right back and their legs tangled with the big breech lamb, but no matter, the ewe had live twins, and as she nuzzled her lambs and "talked" to them in that lovely throaty way, I reckoned that her satisfaction and mine about matched.

I have always enjoyed lambings and constantly marvelled at this new, young life. To me lambs were the loveliest of all new born creatures, certainly far and away beating babies, though no mother would agree with that. Every lambing produced in me a sense of wonder and of achievement, even though the emotion was tempered with the knowledge that in a few short months that little bundle of life would end up on a plate with mint sauce. I always marvelled too at how quickly both mother and offspring were on their feet after the birth. I remember getting into trouble with my mother-in-law after Ian, our second son's birth. He arrived during the lambing season, and though not seeing his birth, that being frowned upon by the medical profession then, I was at the nursing home shortly afterwards. Having duly admired my new son, I kissed my wife and said, "Why are you still lying there? When are you getting up?" She spotted the twinkle in my eye, but her mother did not, and she rounded on me and retorted, "Up? Up? Oh, you big cruel brute. She's just given you a lovely son and you expect her to be up already. Ach, men!"

"Oh, I don't know," I replied. "I lambed a ewe at Martincombe just half an hour ago, and it'll be half way up Hangman Hill by now!"

I would not have been human at the lambing I've described to feel no gratification, succeeding where others had failed, but after all I was only doing my job. It was just a week later that I had an even greater sense of achievement. I was actually summoned by Frank Fowler himself to his own farm, to deliver a lamb. It could not have been easy for a man almost twice my age to admit that others knew best, but he did. I knew this was bound to be a corker, for Frank would never have summoned me to the very shrine of the sheep kingdom unless it was an exceptionally difficult case.

"Big lamb, head back," was all Frank said. Around the straw lay his ropes and bits of fine cord. Beside the ewe was a bottle of green oils, that famous remedy favoured by shepherds for all ills and an excellent lubricant. I was not too confident this time, as I looked at that Devon Closewool ewe lying with its neck stretched out, exhausted. But I had one secret weapon Frank had not and I used it that night. A lamb, as a calf, is normally born with front feet first, and head resting on them. It is impossible to deliver a lamb if the head is not coming with the feet, and perhaps the most common difficulty, especially if the lamb is big or the ewe small, is for the ewe, as it strains in labour to advance the forelegs, instead of the head sliding into the passage with them and pushed forwards with each contraction, because of the tightness is pushed backwards until it is turned right round in a looking-over-the-shoulder position.

That was the problem with Frank's ewe, and his lambing cords told me he had been trying, in traditional manner, to get a cord over the lower jaw, or even round the neck, to bring up the head. So I did not, after a quick examination, even try with cords, but produced my secret weapon. I saw Frank's eyes on me as I took it out of the steriliser. This was something new to him. It was, in fact, a blunt eye hook, with a long handle, available at that time, and just recently available, only to vets. It had to be used with considerable care. So, repelling the legs, I manipulated my hook into the bony eye socket, and as the ewe strained, ever so slowly I managed to bring the head round, until with a jerk it was in the correct position, following the legs. I unhooked my new toy before Frank could see what I had used it for, and then, by pulling the legs only, the lamb was delivered, alive, and with eye undamaged.

As I cleaned up, I could see Frank minutely examining my weapon. "Could you get me one of these?" he asked.

"Sorry, Frank, they're only available to vets. It's a dangerous toy, you know!"

"I can see that, but you know I'd be careful."

"I don't doubt it, Frank. I know you're good, none better round here at lambing a ewe. But once you had one, every Tom, Dick and Harry would be after one, and can you imagine the suffering that could be caused? Besides," I grinned at him, "I've got to earn a living too, you know."

"I dare say you're right," he replied, though clearly disappointed. "The likes of this is best handled by thems as knows best."

Of all the branches of the animal kingdom, none, like the equine, is so afflicted with experts, self-pronounced, or raised to the status of thems as knows best by a reputation, or sheer brass neck, developed over the years. The wide boys, the fly guys, the know-alls abound in the horsey world, especially in that of the competition or thoroughbred fraternity. We had only a few work horses left in Devon, but everybody kept at least one pony on his farm. Many had hunters, and there was the odd thoroughbred that had not made the grade. Horses went the rounds, and in their life-time might have a variety of owners, and here and there a seller would find a vet ignorant enough, genuinely deceived, or very occasionally unscrupulous enough to pass an animal as sound, when in fact it was not. It was my experience too, that for all the camaraderie that existed on the surface between horse breeders, there were plenty ready to pull a fast one. I liked the story of the horse dealer, who, having had a Christian unbringing, would always conclude a deal with a quotation from Holy Writ. On one occasion he had been guilty of a piece of sharp practice, having passed off an old broken-winded nag to an ignorant buyer, as sound in wind and limb. Coming in the house, gleefully pocketing the cheque, he was rebuked by his wife for what he had done, to which he replied readily, if quoting somewhat incorrectly, "he was a stranger and I took him in."

I knew that Fred Boothby was of this breed. He was the horsiest type for miles around, kept a few ponies, and what he lacked in farming skill, or willingness to work, he made up by his horse-dealing. It was therefore, with no great enthusiasm that I looked forward to my visit one afternoon to his farm of Greystones. He had recently bought a pony and wanted me to vet it, since he was somewhat suspicious of it. There had been a time clause in the bargain that if any fault was found within a week, the seller would take it back, or give a price reduction.

The uneven yard of Greystones seemed filled with horses and attendant males or females as I drove in. All the clever jacks were there, including, I noticed, Donald Tucker, his pointed chin and nose seeming to meet as ever, and his eyes always appearing to look past you. There had evidently been considerable discussion, debate and argument about this latest piece of horse-flesh to arrive at Greystones, and I realised at an early stage that my judgement was keenly awaited; maybe they had even been wagering on it, the "sounds" and "unsounds" being about equal in numbers. Now I was no horse expert, as I admit elsewhere, always feeling more at home with cattle, sheep or pigs, but I had been fortunate enough to grow up in the country, work on farms where horses were still the norm and a tractor a luxury, and I had seen practice in a part of the country famous for its breeding of Clydesdales. Even in my assistantship years at Mochrum, I suppose I treated a horse every second or third day. True, these had almost entirely been work horses, but the diseases and defects were the same in their loftier kin of the hunting field and the turf, so I had obtained rather more experience than the average general practitioner today.

I looked at Fred Boothby's pony. It was a handsome chestnut, with a bold carriage of the head, a lovely arched neck, and long flowing mane and tail. He had paid a pound or two for that, I reckoned, and clearly this was his hope to clean up some winnings at coming gymkhanas and country meets.

"That yer hoss is a rale topper, I reckon," announced Donald Tucker in a rare moment of speech. Usually he just communicated with grunts, nods and sly looks. His remark was greeted enthusiastically by many present, but others, including, I noticed, Fred Boothby himself, were silent. I did not like the man much, but he knew a horse. I had his daughter trot it up and down, then walk it, and suddenly make it break into a trot. Then I had it ridden round and round in circles. It seemed sound, yet there was just a suggestion of stiffness now and then, even a stumble on occasion. Then I examined him limb by limb, sounded his lungs, tested heart-beat and pulse, felt for any scars. I was sure there was a something but what? Suddenly I recalled an old Clydesdale I had seen as an assistant.

"Is he stiff when you take him out first thing?" Boothby nodded.

"And does it gradually wear off as he gets going?" Again he nodded. There were comments from various sources.

"Oi be stiff, like, mornings meself," said one old codger.

"But it don't wear off you, Bert," retorted a wag.

I went over the horse again minutely, running my fingers up and down his legs, feeling the joints, tendon sheaths, looking at the feet, until at last I got it.

"Your horse has a ringbone, what they call a high ringbone, Fred." I beckoned him over.

"Feel the pastern joint in that near foreleg." He obeyed, followed by Donald Tucker who was adamant there was nothing amiss with "this 'ere hoss."

"Danged if I can feel anythin' there," announced Donald.

"Shut up, Donald," said Boothby. "Vet's right, 'tis swollen there for sure." He looked at me somewhat belligerently as if I had done the dirty on him and demanded "What do we do then?"

"Oh, I can treat it for you alright, but you'll never have a winner here. The swelling might go away for a bit, but almost certainly will come back. I should think that whoever sold you this horse knew what was what, for a ringbone could easily be missed in the first week."

Half the company were looking at me suspiciously, as if I had put the ringbone there, but one or two, Boothby included, were looking with some respect, and I heard him speak of vets as "thems as knows best."

So I was moving in a mixed society. The Prices had said that of me, now Boothby, none of whom I would have trusted with a shilling. But Frank Fowler had said it too, and as I sat at the now dead study fire, I recalled the young President that night had also used more or less the same phrase. I felt a trifle smug, until I remembered that folk like Godber were so addressed too. Oh well, at least I was one of the élite!

The Rock Whence
Ye are Hewn

THREE

The Church at Moorton was old, built in 1643 during the Covenanting struggles of the 17th Century, cruciform in shape, whitewashed, with distinctive features like its crow step gables, an outside staircase to one of the galleries, sentry boxes at the gates where in the days of the body snatchers elders had stood guard at nights to guard the new graves, and where the office bearers still greet the flock on a Sunday. Beside the gates were two table-like erections for the offering and I used to feel it was typical of the caricature of the canny Scot. You had to pay at the gate before even reaching the Church doors! There was an outside bell-rope where the Beadle, Andrew Crombie, tolled the bell to summon the worshippers, protected on wet days by someone with an umbrella. Fastened to the outside of one wall was a metal collar, the jougs, where evil-doers in days gone by had been punished for such crimes, according to our old records, as

"Bleaching washing on the Sabbath day"
"Cursing, swearing and fighting with ye mother-in-law"
"Calling an Elder a slavery loon"
"Telling the Minister it was a black day he came to Moorton."

This last entry encouraged me no end, for the first minister, William Guthrie, was a saint, a preacher of great power whom folks walked twenty miles to hear. Moreover he was a kind, caring man who had presence about him, so that whether fishing for brown trout in the Moorton Burn, or black sinners in the parish, he always seemed to have his Lord by his side. He was a man much loved, a moderate man, a gentle man in hard, cruel days, but even he was expelled from his Church by order of the Bishop for preaching freedom of the faith and the one Head of the Church, no earthly monarch like Charles II or James II, but the King of Glory. I used to think that if such a man had, at least, one local critic, then it was to be expected I would have plenty more.

Inside the Church was beautiful in its simplicity, with its fine wood which positively shone, dusted and polished daily and lovingly by Andrew. The pulpit was central, on which there was a sand-glass like a large egg timer, which Andrew solemnly turned as the sermon commenced each Sunday. Every eye in the building following him up and down the steps. Only when the deed was done, I discovered, did the folks settle down to listen to the sermon, the shape of the Church making the congregation seem like a large family gathered around. I never preached the glass to its end, but one day when I was elsewhere, a visiting lady missionary did. Our boys did not know whether to be pleased or disappointed that Dad's record had gone to "yon wifey that preached the glass dry."

Surrounding the Church was the old graveyard, and since the Manse was just across the road, I thought that at night when the trees were rustling and the owls hooting, it would be somewhat eerie. Graveyard stories there were in plenty, like the one where a man the worse of drink, taking a shortcut one Saturday night fell into a newly dug grave waiting for a funeral on the Monday. He could not get out, and eventually fell asleep. At 6:00 am the next morning, a dairyman taking the same shortcut heard moans and groans coming from the bowels of the earth. He went over to investigate, saw the shivering and now sober figure at the bottom and demanded, "Whit's wrang wi ye, making a' that noise."

"Oh, I'm awful cauld," came the response.

"Nae wonder," said the dairyman, "you've kicked a' the dirt aff ye!"

There was another story, a definitely authentic one, of a Beadle who was going down the path of a Borders Church to light the coal fire in the boiler early one Sunday morning, when a voice called him from under one of the six-legged, flat-top gravestones. Another roisterer had evidently sought shelter there the night before. The Beadle was whistling as he walked when the voice from the dark, and apparently from the tomb hailed him, "Man, John, is it that time already?"

The terrified Beadle did not wait to enquire but fled for his life.

The tale was often told me of how one night in Moorton the Church bell had started to ring. The folks shivering in their houses were afraid to investigate, convinced it was a warning of some kind or the Devil himself. Eventually one brave spirit did go to the Church and in the darkness could just make out a white figure with horns and a tail tolling the bell. He fled, and reported his findings, whereupon everyone was convinced it was indeed "Auld Nick" himself. Only with daylight did the population head for the Churchyard where they found a white cow with the bell rope tied to its tail. Clearly some joker had enjoyed the night of his life.

But our graveyard was in no way "spooky." Indeed it had a calm atmosphere, as if those there, after life's fitful fever, slept well, and many nights I walked through it, savouring its tranquillity. It was a famous graveyard, for it had many headstones to Covenanting martyrs, sixteen in all, more than any other Church in Scotland.

Best known was Captain John Paton, farmer, elder of Moorton Kirk, and soldier of fortune under the great Swede, Gustavus Adolphus. He had a farm in the parish, and just a few miles from it was the Covenanters' cave, where many a time he, or some other hunted man found refuge. Early in my ministry, I visited the cave and climbed up into it. It was a poor place, cold, damp, big enough for maybe three men, but in its position a secure hiding place for many of the men of the Covenant when Scotland was divided between those who fought for religious liberty and those who took the part of the King as he sought to impose his will, his form of worship and Church government, and especially his Kingship of the Kirk. So for fifty long years the struggle for freedom of the faith was waged, claiming many lives, and leaving in its wake memorials all over lowland Scotland to those who gave their lives for what they held dear. Religious freedom came finally with the accession of William of Orange in 1688.

As an old man Paton was captured, tried and condemned to death. A petition was raised on his behalf, he was pardoned by the King, but legend has it that the Bishop kept back the news till after Paton's execution in Edinburgh's Grassmarket, with the story that the pardon had arrived too late. Paton handed his wife his Bible from the scaffold, and symbolically it ends with the words from Revelation 12, the last few chapters being missing,

"They overcame by the blood of the Lamb and by the word of their testimony, and they loved not their lives unto death."

This faith and courage was the motivating force of these men and women, and their gallant struggles "the rock whence we are hewn" in Scotland's Kirk today.

North of the village was the moor from which it took its name. It is quiet on the moor today. There you can lie on a clump of heather and watch the bog myrtle wave in the breeze, see a hare lope over the hill, hear the plaintive call of the curlew and perhaps the bark of a fox. It was not always so peaceful, for often the moor would resound to shouts, to the cries of hunted men and the

thunder of galloping horses, for right on top of the moor
is the farm of Lochgoin, where in the killing times of the
late 17th Century many a fugitive found refuge. The
tenants of the farm were the Howie family who had come
to Scotland in the 12th Century for religious freedom.
Often the farm was raided by dragoons, the cattle driven
off, the buildings set alight, but no Covenanter was ever
caught there.

On the Tope, (the top of the hill) stands a large monument to John Howie who in his *Scots Worthies* and other
books told the story of these days. The monument is to
him, but indeed to all the men of the Covenant, and for
years, like Moorton's little Kirk and Kirkyard, had been
a place of pilgrimage for those interested in Scotland's
storied past and keen to learn more of that rock from
which Scotland has been hewn. They came by busload
and car to see, to listen to talks I early found I was
expected to give, and to photograph the graves of the
martyrs.

One day, Duncan, my treasurer, a local Councillor and
no mean historian, came to me in a state of considerable
anxiety. He launched straight in.

"Tom Howie's been offered £2000 by an American for
the relics. We canna let them go oot o' the parish! Whit
can we dae?"

So we talked about it at length, decided we would form
a Trust and somehow try to raise £2000, a considerable
sum in those days. We got Tom (the last of the Howies
of Lochgoin) to agree to hold his hand and give us a
chance to buy the relics of Moorton—flag, drum, Paton's
Bible and sword and many others. We enlisted Sandy
Paton, a descendant of the famous Covenanter, and feeling very small, the three of us proceeded to launch appeals
the length and breadth of the land. Quite early we had a
great boost when Lord Rowallan, former Governor of
Tasmania and Chief Scout, and landlord of Lochgoin,
expressed an interest, and was promptly voted Chairman

of the Trust. Gradually money came in until one glorious day we had the total. Then, on an even more glorious day and in a magnificent gesture, Lord Rowallan said he would gift Lochgoin to the Trust, and have as tenants old Tom Howie's daughter and her husband at a modest rent, provided they made over one room of the little whitewashed farm in its ring of trees, as a museum room.

I was asked to produce booklets about Moorton's Covenanters, and on a shining July Sunday, with a detachment of the Cameronians on guard, (the regiment that rose from the Covenanters and took their name from Richard Cameron, the young Lion of the Covenant and who had stood guard at many a Conventicle in the hills) on that Sunday we held a never-to-be-forgotten Service, followed by a Conventicle at Lochgoin. The Captain of the Cameronians posted his men, then marched smartly up to me on my pulpit (a farm trailer) and announced in the words his forerunners had used many times

"Reverend Sir! The pickets are posted, there is no enemy in sight; the Service may proceed."

The Revd. Ronald Falconer, BBC Director of Religious Broadcasting led in prayer, we sang the old Psalms with a precentor as our forebears had on many hills, then Dr. Stewart Mechie, my old history lecturer from Trinity, gave the address, on, of course, "the Rock whence ye are hewn." There followed a moving ceremony as Lord Rowallan handed over the Title Deeds of Lochgoin to Duncan as Secretary of the Trust. As the sun beat down on the assembled vast throng of 600, and in the blue distance "Paddy's milestone" rose out of an azure sea, as the soldiers marched the boundaries and the sheep and curlews called, I felt, as others there, that we were making our own little bit of history. Ronnie Falconer evidently felt the same and said, "We must repeat this next year, for television."

But by the next year the Cameronians had been disbanded in the government's re-organisation of the various regiments, and instead I was asked to do a week's television talks on the Covenanters and the Cameronians, something that was achieved in much fear and trembling, as is recounted elsewhere.

Lord Rowallan and the faithful Duncan are long gone, Sandy Paton more recently, and I am the only survivor of the original trustees, but others have come forward. Lochgoin is visited by hundreds each year from all round the world, and Moorton's lovely little Kirk sits secure and solid amid its surrounding gravestones, slumbering the years away as the men of the Covenant slumber, waiting for the day of Resurrection.

Robert Louis Stevenson captured it perfectly when he wrote,

> Blows the wind today, and the sun and rain are
>   flying
> Blows the wind on the moor today, and now
> Where above the graves of the martyrs the whaups
>   are crying,
> My heart remembers how!

Sporting on the Green

FOUR

"Howzat!" came the stentorian voice of Neil, our eldest son. "You're out! That ball was hitting the middle stump if your big leg hadn't been in the road."

"No . . . a'm no oot," retorted Ronald the batsman.

"You was LWB," said David, aged five.

"It's no' LWB, you dopey," corrected young Billy, who bore the nickname of Miggermite, "it's ebberwub-bleyou."

"Och, you be quate, loon. Fit div' you ken," said the batsman, sticking to his guns.

"Definitely out," pronounced Trevor.

"Come on, Donian," said Ian the wicketkeeper, "the ball was hitting the wickets."

"Naw, it wisna."

"Him zoot," piped up baby Alan, aged three pointing, and determined not to be left out of things.

I sighed. The voices, getting louder by the minute, came floating in my open study window as I tried to concentrate on a sermon, no easy task when our lads and half the village were sporting on the green.

"LWB," reiterated young David.

"Och, you gommerel, fit div you ken," replied Aberdonian Ronald. "It's LBW but it's no LWB—och, you ken fit a mean."

I knew what would shortly happen, and sure enough it did. David Ferguson the policeman's son, and captain of the batting side, shouted above the increasing din.

"Get your daddy to decide!"

The cricket nearly always deteriorated into an argument and nearly always I was called on to mediate. I did not mind that particular night for it was a glorious summer evening, the sermon had stuck, and I thought I would rather be in the midst of a cheerful mêlée than scratching my head over my notes. So out I wandered, gravely listened to the claims and counter claims, and then with the wisdom of Solomon gave my verdict.

"A free shot at the wicket by the bowler to decide." That always seemed to calm the storm, and Neil duly ran up, aimed the tennis ball at the home-made stumps . . . and missed.

"That proves it," grinned the jubilant Donian. "I kenned I wisna oot," and so the game continued again till Mum called young David and Alan in for bed. The others gradually drifted off home, until only three boys were left. Another Test Match was over, and a draw was a favourable result for all concerned.

We did not have what you might call a lawn as such at Moorton. There was an immense stretch of grass in front of the Manse with a large clump of trees down one side where every spring the rooks built their nests and our children tried to provoke heart attacks in their parents by their antics up these trees, hanging upside down, climbing high, or swinging on overhanging branches. We kept the grass under control and reasonably short with a rotary grass cutter and as time went by, by dint of much hard labour, the grass had almost the consistency of a proper lawn. In one corner towards the Manse, Janet built a rockery, and beyond it we had a large patch of Hybrid Tea (HT) roses, which were annually our pride and joy. There were ten dozen of them, and we knew them all by name, treating them almost like members of the family.

"I see Papa's in bloom" (Papa Meilland),

"Ena's hanging her head as usual—a shy rose," (Ena Harkness).

"What a glorious scent has Shot Silk," and so on, round our floral family. Beyond the rose garden was a wide border stretching across the front of the Manse, just below the study window, and here too were roses of the Floribunda type. We got great pleasure from our garden, having seen it develop from a wilderness, not least the enormous walled vegetable garden which annually was ploughed and worked for us by my very willing farm elders, Jim Shankland and Jim Grant. When we first arrived, it was so wild you were in danger of being lost in it. Indeed when I first fought my way into it, I thought I might meet some former minister trying to find a way out, but over the years these two men worked wonders, so that everything was laid out neatly in beds and plots.

But our pleasure was nothing to that of our laddies. The lawn was their own private stamping ground, and the grass ideal for their football, cricket, cowboys, hide-and-seek and a variety of games of their own devising. The thing about our lawn was its versatility. It was, in rotation, Hampden Park, Lords or Wimbledon, depending on the season. Football was, however, without question number one, and regularly a host of village children would be sporting on the green with our brood of four. We had Jimmy Rodgerson, the joiner, erect a miniature set of goalposts at one side, and many a rousing battle was fought on our own "pitch," and there Dad and the boys would play a game of their own invention called Combi—short for Combination—when the ball had to be controlled and passed in two touches, thus developing skills at an early age which were to come to fruition later on as all four developed into really first-class players, even allowing for a father's natural pride. I had promised Neil, the eldest, a shilling at Bristacombe when he could kick with his left foot as well as his right, and he practised and practised to earn his shilling until he was, in fact, genuinely two-footed. The others got the same offer, no account being taken of inflation, and they all went at it day after day to earn the coveted award.

When Test matches were on television, as has already been indicated, they became Cowdrey, Sheppard, Statham, Laker and the like, and many a stern battle was fought, though, as fervent Scots, they were never very sure whether they wanted England to win. If a batsman was proving difficult to shift, Dad, if he was around, was called on to do his fiery Fred act, when, as Trueman, I would rush up and hurl the tennis ball down. Sometimes it got near the sticks which did duty as stumps! They played and played, seemingly oblivious to the midges, which on many nights, speedily drove me indoors.

One day my elder Jimmy Aitchison came to me and said "There's some saying you're no too parteecular who you let into your gairden to play wi' your boys."

"What do you mean, Jimmy?" I queried.

"Catholics!"

"What about Catholics?"

"There's two o' these weans are Catholics an' they're in the Manse gairden."

"Good!" I exploded.

"Good?"

"Good! The more youngsters are together, the less trouble and bigotry there would be in the world. I'm delighted these laddies want to play in the garden."

Jimmy's face broke into a big grin, he slapped me on the back, and said, "Man, I'm pleased to hear it. That's what I feel too, but you ken what some folk are like."

"More pity them," I responded, "there'll be no Catholics in Heaven and no Protestants either. It won't matter there," and the subject was closed. Roger Flynn, a wee Catholic boy, was, in fact, a close friend of Ian's and later on played regularly for our Bible Class team.

It seemed our lads had evolved their own code of conduct and behaviour and those allowed into their garden had to abide by it. This was made clear one evening when Janet was standing at the kitchen window which happened to be right at the Manse front gate. Outside the gate stood two tough wee fellows from two poor homes in the village. They watched the fun inside with envious eyes, at the same time not wanting to seem too interested, but clearly longing to join in what was going on. Eventually one said,

"Are you fur in?"

"I dinna ken; are you?"

"Och, we micht as weel."

"Weel, mind, if you go in there you canna sweir!"

So saying, they opened the gate, prepared to cut off swears in mid-flow for the sake of getting a game. I really felt quite a paternal pride when I heard that.

Our "lawn" was ideal for picnic teas in the summer, and Neil and Alan, forever dubbed through their lives as "big man" and "wee man" by others, though both are now over six feet, having summer birthdays, had birthday teas with their friends, when we erected our big, old, brown ex-army tent in case of rain in Moorton's fickle climate.

The great occasion of the year, however, was Guy Fawkes night. For weeks the boys would collect rubbish round the village and sticks from the wood and build a huge bonfire. On the great night they assembled with their special friends, each clutching his fireworks, and occasionally one of my twin brothers, Fergus or Graham and his five year old son, Hugh, would come up to join the fun. They let off their fireworks under careful supervision, then midst mounting excitement, the bonfire would be lit, and all sat round it for the feast. We sizzled sausages, roasted potatoes (and ate them half raw!) and Mum had always prepared delicacies like muffins, perkins, ginger cake and treacle toffee. Then, as the fire died down, Dad had to tell a ghost story.

One night, after a particularly creepy one, the friends of the boys all mustered together to go home *en masse*, feeling that a crowd was more security against ghoulies and sinister women in black who beckoned from the tomb and said "Come with me, come with me." My brother Fergus thought he would add a touch of realism, and draped in a sheet, he nipped into the old churchyard just across the way, intending to leap out at the kids as they reached the end of the wall. It seemed a good idea but something obviously miscarried for no phantom appeared. Eventually he came hirpling back, carrying his sheet, having in the dark tripped over one of the flat topped grave stones raised on its six legs, and banged his leg good and proper which is enough, of course, to discourage any sensitive ghost. On another occasion, I told a story about vampires.

"Och, that's not true," bragged Ian to the others with great bravado. "I don't believe in vampires," and somewhat hesitantly, the others agreed. They did, however, just to be safe, hurry home, their walk breaking into a trot, and finally a mad gallop to reach their respective houses. I had a little luminous cross which sat on the study desk and the next morning it had disappeared. It was found eventually beside Ian's bed, that, of course being the recognised preventative for vampires. He who did not believe was taking no chances! Yes, the Manse garden saw quite a few stirring scenes.

Moorton Church, like most country churches, had to have fund-raising events from time to time, and it was decided one year to hold a Garden Fête in the Manse grounds, with various stalls in the Church hall. The fête was to be opened by Frank Beattie, captain of Kilmarnock FC, and the great attraction was Campbell Forsyth, Kilmarnock and Scotland's goalkeeper, who was to be in the boys' little goalposts, and at a penny a shot, all and sundry were to try to beat him. Our football-mad sons were in a fever of excitement at the prospect, especially Ian who supported Kilmarnock, but even little Alan, an avowed Celtic fan, condescended to allow players of another team in his garden. (Many years later, when we had left Moorton and when Ian was himself a star, having played for

Aberdeen, then Kilmarnock and gained a Scottish League cap, he went back and opened the then fête).

The great day dawned fair; the village folks came in droves, and farmers and farm workers travelled in from the country. The fête was duly declared open by Frank, then there was a mad stampede by the ladies for the baking and produce stalls where some of the attendants like Kathleen Sturrock, Babs Aitchison, Jean McKinnon and many others were on duty, but from the beginning a queue of both sexes and all ages formed to try to beat Scotland's goalie. Dressed in a track suit and trainers, he leapt and dived across the goals and not a ball went past him. I had a few tries, hit it my hardest and a giant paw just plucked the ball from the air. Then Neil, aged about eleven at the time, had a go, and lo and behold scored— a *bona fide* goal too, not a put up job, the ball going in at the post. Young David also later succeeded. The various stalls were kept busy, most people had a go at the many other games in the garden where men like Harold Lambie, Tom McMichael, Jim Davidson and John Brown were calling out their wares in true showman fashion. The pony rides of Jimmy English were popular with the little ones, and a good time was had by all, the Church also benefiting with a large amount of money.

While Duncan, the treasurer, and others counted the takings Joe Gibson, John Andrews and many other willing hands cleared up. The Woman's Guild and Mothers' Circle tidied up the remains of their stalls, auctioning any left-overs. Campbell Forsyth, hot, dirty and sweating had a bath in the Manse which completed Ian's bliss and put him into his own seventh Heaven. Scotland's goalkeeper had bathed in his bath. Why, the very dirt was precious!

Thus does a little community rally round to support its Church, enjoying much fun and fellowship in the process.

In some ways our fête took me back twelve years to my first Gymkhana at Bristacombe, held annually out in the

country at the curiously named village of Upper Down.
I was asked to be the vet in attendance, my badge of office
and free tickets for two duly arrived and eventually that
day also dawned fair. All morning floats laden with cattle
and sheep and Land Rovers hauling horse-boxes had been
heading for the field from near and far, for many of the
competitors went the rounds of the various gymkhanas.
Those taking part also included a number of young, semi-
professional riders who were destined to make their marks
at the Horse of the Year Show and other prestigious
gatherings in years to come.

One gymkhana is much like another, and I imagine
most country vets have been asked to be in attendance.
James Herriot in one of his books describes his hilarious
adventures and gives a comprehensive picture of the proceedings.

First I had a quick walk through the marquees to see
the flower arrangements, knitting, sewing and dressmak-
ing of the women, marvelled at the enormous onions,
leeks, carrots, beans and the rest, but hurried to the animal
pens, for animals were my real interest. There husky men
in smocks or shirt sleeves were busily engaged with
brushes, curry combs, buckets of water and whitening
powder, preparing their charges for the ring, in which at
that moment was a parade of magnificent Clydesdale and
Shire horses, their harness gleaming. Suddenly the loud-
speaker crackled into life:

"Would Mr. Cameron the vet go to the cattle pens?"

I collected my two black cases, having loaded my car
with everything I thought I might need, and feeling ten
feet tall that my name had, for the first time, been broadcast to the world, or at any rate to Upper Down! At the
cattle pens a little crowd was gathered around a recently
calved Shorthorn cow which was just barely standing,
wobbling about on its feet. One glance gave the diagnosis—Milk Fever—so calcium was duly administered in-
travenously and under the skin, being careful not to leave
any lumps or bumps which would have told against it in

the ring. I had just put my cases away when I was again called on the tannoy to go to the dog show. There the judge said to me, "Would you examine this dog? I don't like the look of it." Neither did I when I saw it. There were little globules of pus in the corner of its eyes, eyes it kept half shut against the light, occasional shivers and a generally miserable appearance. In short, one very unhappy Springer Spaniel.

"There be nowt wrong wi' him oi'm zertain zure," said the owner.

"We'll soon see, sir," I responded in my best vet-client manner, though it was abundantly clear we had one very sick dog. I took the temperature which was well raised, listened to the stertorous breathing in the chest and gave my verdict to the owner.

"Sorry! You can't go in the Show. Your dog's got Distemper or Hard Pad (we still believed in the latter then) and the sooner you get him home and to your own vet the better." The dog's owner had appeared a bit aggressive at first, but at the mention of Hard Pad, he blanched, and asked pathetically,

"Are you sure?"

"Certain," and he departed with his sick pet.

"Mr. Cameron to the measuring stand for ponies," came the next call, so I went to the Secretary's tent, collected my measuring rod, and headed for the queue of ponies that had already formed. Each pony had to pass under the rod which consists of an upright pole with a horizontal bar which slides up and down the pole, the pole measures in hands, each hand being four inches.

I began badly. The first rider was a helmeted, breeched and booted young woman waving a piece of paper.

"This is a certificate from the vet at Tillietudlem testifying my horse is under fourteen hands."

"Sorry, miss, I'm not allowed to accept any certificates. Each horse must go under the rod."

So she stretched her horse out to its full length and I

eased the cross piece down on to the withers, or highest
point of the horse's body . . . but all the stretching in
the world could not make that horse under fourteen
hands.

"Sorry! You'll need to go up to the next class."

"But you've *got* to accept this vet's certificate."

"No, I haven't. You'll have to see the stewards if you're
not satisfied."

She fetched her father, a big, blustering, prosperous
looking character wearing a multi-coloured waistcoat
and a large scowl. We had a rare old argument while
the queue got longer and more impatient, but I was
determined "they shall not pass if not eligible," and muttering threats and imprecations and waving their certificate, they eventually stumped off, the pony rearing and
kicking out in my direction to show it had the same
opinion of me as its owners. It took some time to measure all the entrants, and while most passed alright, the
odd one had to move up a class but generally the rider
took it philosophically. I had never seen so many horsey
types in one group before, and it was quite an education. The locals, entering for the fun of it and with little
thought of winning, took it all in good part, particularly
as I was vet to many of them. It was the visitors and
semi-professionals who treated this "still wet behind the
ears—Scotsman—not a proper vetnary," as one described me, with derision.

I breathed a sigh of relief when that task was done, had
my tea, then went and listened to the band who were
giving somewhat modified versions of Gilbert and Sulli-
van, tuneful if not always strictly in tune. Next came the
judging of the Pets' Corner, a motley collection of dogs,
cats, budgerigars, parrots, rabbits, hamsters, guinea pigs,
tortoises and so on, all gathered for what was meant to
be a fun event. How on earth do you compare a tortoise
with a Golden Retriever, a rabbit with a parrot, I wondered? I did the best I could, though really I would like

to have given them all a prize for virtually all the owners were children. If I may quote my famous colleague of the Yorkshire Dales again, this fun event got him into big trouble and produced a sparkling story. I was more fortunate. Most of the crowd clapped the winners, and I escaped in one piece.

The rest of the day was given over to the pony events and jumping, and I had to wait to the bitter end in case of accidents, for nestling in my car was a humane killer which I fervently hoped I would not have to use. The day which had started so fair had deteriorated, it being now cold and damp. Many cattle floats were taking their charges home, and to keep out of the way and to keep warm, I eventually sat in the car.

There were fun games with the ponies, like the potato race when each rider had to grab a potato from the top of a pole and drop it in a bucket, dismounting if he missed. There was a version of musical chairs, but the evening finally became concerned with the serious side of the jumps. I noticed all styles of riders, some very upright in the saddle, some very hard on their horses, tugging at reins and bit, some riding with taut reins, others with slack—but despite all the grand horse experts from miles away, the star of the show and undoubted champion was young Kingsley Tucker, one of the famous rough and ready family I described on another occasion and who were particular favourites of mine. Where other riders sat very upright in the saddle and kept tight control of the horse's head, Kingsley had no saddle, riding bareback, and crouched low over his mount's neck, he gave the horse his head so that horse and rider seemed fused into one. He raced up to each jump on his old grey pony, and again and again had a clear round, beating all the "fancy" riders from "away," to the mounting excitement of the home crowd. He was a natural horseman, his riding a delight to behold, and no one clapped louder than me when he was finally awarded the cup.

* * *

After I came into the ministry, of course, I lost touch with most of my former clients, and it was about thirty years later I saw Kingsley, when Janet and I were holidaying in 'Combe with Bernard and Ann. It was in Brookfield Free Church, where we had worshipped weekly all these years before. Sitting beside our life-long friends Lil and Cath, Lil whispered, "That's Kingsley Tucker." I was surprised to see Kingy, for Church had not been a regular part of his schedule when I knew him last, but I was also deeply concerned, for I would scarcely have recognised him. He looked an old man, was clearly very ill, pale, drawn, in pain as he slouched in the Church chair. He would, at that time, be about forty-seven. I had a few words with him at the close of the Service and he gave me a great welcome, the old Kingsley smile lighting up his face. He told me quite calmly he had cancer and it was a struggle now to get to Church.

I could not get him out of my mind, and determined to go and see him in his home, particularly as Brookfield was without a Pastor at the time. His wife welcomed me warmly and showed me into the bedroom where Kingsley lay, looking more ill than ever, but despite his weakness and the fact he was clearly a dying man, he seemed delighted to see me and eager to talk. We relived the old days and I reminded him of his success at my first Gymkhana all these years before.

"Aar—them was grand days, Mr. Cameron," he said, and for a moment he was that brilliant young rider again on his old, grey, working pony. He told me that three of the five Tucker boys were dead, all young, and he spoke quite naturally, and indeed enthusiastically of the faith he had found, and of the tremendous strength this had been to him. Beside him in bed was a well-thumbed Bible. Here was no temporary conversion, no passing thing, but a deep lasting experience, a strong anchor, that had held him in many misfortunes and I was confident it would see him through to the end.

He was on his last ride, taking the jumps one by one

as cleanly as before. He was heading for the winning post in style.

I never saw him again. He died shortly afterwards, but I was confident the verdict of the Judge would be—"Clear Round."

Rejected

FIVE

During my three years training for the ministry, I returned to my original trade in the summer holidays, and acted as *locum tenens* for vets on holiday, for money was tight, and with a wife and family to keep, and no kind of student grant, I had to earn as much as possible. I worked in various places but three come to mind.

In Cirencester I was greeted by the vet's secretary with the words,

"Pity you weren't here last week. You would have had some fun."

"Oh? Why was that?"

"We had a travelling circus passing through for a few days, and the boss was asked to visit, not knowing what kind of animal he had to treat. He was met by the elephant trainer who informed him that one of the elephants, the fifth in a line of six, had a large abscess on the leg which required lancing and draining and said, 'She's quiet, but just watch the one next to her,' and left him to get on with it."

"Well, I like elephants—but preferably from a distance, so I'm mighty glad this was last week," I replied.

I was then conducted to the house where I was to stay for a fortnight. It was a stately mansion belonging to a retired dentist and his wife, and my corduroys and sports jacket seemed very humble and considerably out of place in that opulent setting. Carefully minding my Ps and Qs, I got through the evening meal and subsequent conversation, but it appeared next morning I had literally put my foot in it. I was informed by one of the two elderly maids that I had omitted to leave my shoes outside the door for polishing. I looked at my scuffed old brogues, said "Oh-ah-sorry-must have slipped my memory," as if the procedure was my usual nightly ritual. Though the owners were kind enough, meals were very formal affairs, conversation exactly correct—in fact I was miserable, the more so as the practice was very quiet and I had little to do. I remember spending hours with a book on trees in my hand, wandering the lanes, studying the various varieties in that lush, gracious part of old England. Anything to escape from the house where I had to wait impatiently for the phone to ring, and during that fortnight I became quite an expert on leaves, bark, seeds and the various varieties of trees they signified.

After a lazy two weeks for which I felt I had not earned my fee, my next port of call was Stroud in Gloucestershire. It was a busy little town and proved to be a busy practice. This was normally a two-man affair, a youngish man and an elderly semi-retired vet, and I was, of course, taking the place of the younger man for two weeks. Now I am not a good map reader (my wife is always the navigator, and an excellent one, on car journeys, except for her propensity suddenly to explore unmarked, single track roads with a gradient of about 1 in 3!) and consequently looking up farms on a strange map, in a district where I did not know a single road, was time-consuming, especially if it was an urgent case. So the old boy would regularly direct me.

"You go along the main road south to the *Beetle and Wedge*, then you swing on to a B-class road till you come to *The Fox and Grapes*. Follow that to *The Merry Huntsman*, where you take a left on to an uncharted road till you reach *The Cricketers*, where you'd better ask your way."

It was the same each day and I got to know every pub around Stroud, of which there seemed to be a remarkable number! The old vet had the high colour of a heavy whisky drinker and each day he had a fair load aboard. He was never under the weather, however, always neatly dressed in the pre-war vet costume of breeches and matching jacket one of the many who had come through the hard times in practice between the wars, and in his day had been, I imagine, a very competent vet, with still his love for the old remedies on which I too, as an immediately post-war student, had been nurtured. The surgery had that lovely smell of our trade of *nux vom, ammon carb*, gentian, ginger and the other ingredients of the many stomach powders that were dispensed, a smell that is absent from the modern vet's dispensary. His wife told me one day, to my surprise, that her husband was a high churchman of the Church of England and always gave up whisky for Lent, which must really have been a considerable sacrifice. His other love was roses of which he had a great variety in his fine garden where he pottered away the days. The only rose I knew in those days was Peace, but he immediately snorted and said; "Terrible rose—not one thing or another—give me whole colour. HTs all the time, and none of these blasted bi-colours and hybrids."

If I had learned about trees at Cirencester (all of which I have forgotten), I gained a love for roses at Stroud which has stayed with me, and in our three homes since then we have always had many roses, mostly HTs, and yes, mostly whole colours. Thus are the ignorant initiated in their formative years! All in all, life in Stroud was full of colour, busy, and the time flew past, concluding with a fascinating visit to Peter Scott's bird sanctuary at Slimbridge on my way home.

But my favourite port of call was Windermere in the Lake District, where I stood in for the then vet, Mr. Bell, on several occasions. These were glorious days amid the magnificent scenery. Janet and I have always loved the Highlands and this was the English equivalent. Fortunately, Janet was able to be with me some of the time. I explored lakes large and small and steep valleys, on my way to cases in a Land Rover, and grew to love the area, the only snag being the amount of visitor traffic on the roads, making it impossible to hurry to any case. While I had my share of farm cases, in the many large houses fringing the lakes or little ones perched precariously on ledges, I treated dogs and cats, and the days passed happily and smoothly enough, with no deaths or tragedies.

One day however, I was asked to collect a cat to be put to sleep in Windermere itself. I found the poor animal, which apparently had just become redundant, (the kind of euthanasia I have always hated), popped it in a cat basket, deposited it in the back of the car and set off for the surgery. It was a warm day and the Land Rover windows were open. There was a constant miaowing and scratching coming from the basket, but I drove on regardless, when suddenly a cat shot over my shoulder and out the window of the moving car. Now it is considerably humiliating to lose a patient, and although I had thought the basket escape proof, it was apparently not so for that determined feline. Mind you, if I was going to my death, I should have struggled a bit too. There was nothing for it but to go back to the owner's house, explain what had happened, and tell them if it returned, to get in touch with me. I never heard any more, so presumably the cat had gone wild or found another home, at least a better fate than than planned for it.

Just after I got back to the surgery, the police arrived with a little dog that had been run over and badly hurt. It was a terrier cross, a little mongrel—but I have a soft spot for mongrels, and of course promised I would treat it as best I could, though it appeared in a bad way. The police departed, promising on their part to try to find the owner of the dog, which was collarless, with nothing to identify it. I had nobody to assist me in the surgery at Windermere, but laid the unconscious little form gently on the table. There were many cuts and lacerations, one leg was hanging limply, its membranes were pale, so clearly it was in shock with perhaps internal haemorrhage. I carefully felt it all over, but could find no fractures except its useless rear leg, though without X-rays to assist, it is possible some ribs were gone. I injected it with various drugs to control the shock, and hopefully arrest any internal bleeding, then set to work on the visible damage.

By now he had stirred, so I put him under a light anaesthetic, set the fractured leg in plaster, and then began the long process of clipping hair, cleaning wounds, dressing with sulphanilamide powder and suturing. It took a considerable time and I realised all the while that there was a fair chance the police would not find the owner and I was spending quite a bit of Mr. Bell's supplies on an unidentified dog. But what else could be done? "Put it down," a voice had whispered to me early—save yourself a lot of work—"besides it might well die anyway." I could not put a helpless creature down, condemned without at least a trial. There were no kennels at the Windermere premises, but there were some dog baskets, so laying him gently on a blanket in one, I switched on the electric fire to warm him and counteract shock, fitted up a primitive drip into a vein, and generally made him as comfortable as I could.

The surgery at Windermere was attached to the house, so all that evening I kept popping through and looking at him. He was still under the combined effects of anaesthetic and shock. No owner appeared. I got up through the night and had a look at my patient, who was now wide awake, yawning prodigiously, so I tried him with water and a little food which he did not even look at. Nor did he look at me. He was just a lost wee dog, wrapped in his own misery and loneliness.

The next day and night passed, and the next. Other patients came into the surgery, were treated and departed, their owners looking wonderingly at the little dog in his hospital bed. He was really an attractive little fellow, a little gamin, normally, I was sure, full of fun, mischief and the joy of living. Still he pointedly disdained to look at food or water, even when held under his nose or when meat was smeared on his mouth. He ignored me, taking his further injections without a movement or a murmur. Obviously a one man dog, I thought, and I was not that man. Then, on the third day the police came in to say they had found the owner and he would be looking in shortly. I was delighted and relieved. The wee dog would be going home. I was in the surgery when I heard the outer door of the waiting room open, and immediately there was a transformation. My patient came alive at the sound of recognised footsteps. He sat up in his basket, licked his lips, gave a little whimper of excitement and waited. So did I. But the steps came no further. I went out into the adjoining room and there was a big, rough looking man with a young man, obviously his son, along with him.

"You've got my dog," he launched straight in. "Well, you can keep him. He's nowt but a blasted nuisance, more trouble than he's worth. I don't want the beggar back."

"But your dog trusts you, and needs you. You should have seen the way he came alive when you arrived. He's had a fair old knock, but nothing that time won't heal. You won't even have any more expense, he's pretty well patched up now."

"I expect you think I'll pay for what you done," he sneered. "Well, you can think again. I never asked for no treatment. Get rid of him for he's nowt but a pest."

I talked to him, I reasoned with him, I even pleaded with him, but to no avail. He refused even to open the door and look at his dog, and eventually stumped out. The matter was closed.

With a heavy, sinking heart, I opened the surgery door. The little dog had dragged himself from his basket despite his useless leg, and was immediately behind the door, tail thumping the floor, head erect, eyes bright.

"All would be well now, master had come and would take him home."

But the master had come and gone, and as it heard the footsteps recede, the little dog's head went down. Why had master left him? Why? Why?

There was but one thing I could do, put the little creature down. There were no facilities in the town for keeping an injured dog. The RSPCA, I was sure, would not board such an animal with an uncertain future, as under the leadership of Mrs. Gorman at Bristacombe they had done. I lifted him slowly on to the table. He did not cry or move. Life held nothing for him now, and as I gently patted the little head and smoothed the rough coat, with a heart heavier than I have seldom known, I pressed the plunger and he was gone, and oddly, like an echo from the past, I seemed to hear the words:

"Away with this man! We don't want Him! He's just a source of trouble—Crucify! Crucify! Crucify!"—even though, like the little dog, He went on loving to the last.

"Having loved His own, He loved them to the end."

The Call that Costs

SIX

"Where will it be this year?" asked Tom the Polis.

"How about Majorca?" suggested Jimmy, the tattie merchant, with a grin.

"Weel, I've been workin' it oot," says Bobby, the Car Convenor, and proceeds to elaborate on roads A class, B class and no class at all, and manages to lose us all in the process. Bobby had a wonderful gift for confusion, but was an invaluable member of our committee. As the local milkman he knew everybody in the village, and acted as the news carrier from house to house, always with his hearty laugh.

"Whit aboot tea; will it be sausage rolls or gammon salad?" asks Margaret Gibson, one of our food convenors.

"Will we go to a Kirk hall or Agnes's canteen?" queries the other food lady, Margaret Harrison.

The Guild of Friendship committee was in full swing, and while the Secretary, John Brown, tried to keep a minute, I, as Chairman, endeavoured to keep us to the point, for we all had a tendency to go off at a tangent and discuss the price of beasts at the mart, or wee Jeannie Jones' appendix. The Guild of Friendship was perhaps one of the most practical things I ever did in a sermon, when, concerned about the number of elderly folks living alone, I suggested we should form an organisation which would provide a concert and knife and fork meal every six weeks in the winter, a car outing and meal in the summer, and have a list of our younger people "twinned" to some old person, whom they would visit regularly. It had proved to be a resounding success, and it was sometimes difficult to decide whether the organisers or the senior citizens had most pleasure from the Guild's work. It was really a heart-warming sight to see so many old folks tucking into their meal, the tongues wagging merrily, while in the background the two Margarets, aided by many others like Renée Lindsay, Margaret Berry, Nancy Murchison, Babs Aitchison and many more cooked and served the dinner. Then it was over to little Mrs. Hill, who, though only a half pint in size, was a half pint of good nature and fun, and organised the concert. Equally impressive was the sight of twenty or thirty cars setting out in convoy on a summer day, their drivers giving up an afternoon and evening to provide such happiness to so many as year after year they completed a mystery tour. The minister was tucked into the middle of the procession, "for he goes ower quick tae be in front," and in the rear car our mechanic, Jock, ready for any emergency. These committee meetings of the Guild of Friendship maybe lacked something in orderliness, but were more than compensated for by the degree of real camaraderie and fellowship. I sighed contentedly as I made for the Manse, another meeting over, blissfully unaware that the next morning's post was to bring a letter which would have far-reaching consequences, and eventually remove the close relationship with these good folks I had come to love.

When I opened the letter marked BBC, I gulped. Me to do this? I was being asked to do a TV series, linking the Covenanters to the Cameronians, with a history of both. I was honoured and flattered, of course, but also terrified, for the letter specified that there would be no autocue or other moving screen with the words printed on it, such as newsreaders and other speakers use. Furthermore the talks were to be delivered without notes, and a week's lectures were all to be recorded in one afternoon. I immediately yelled for Janet.

"Read this, lass! I could never do what they want." She read the missive carefully and coolly, and then with a confidence in her man he certainly did not feel, she said,

"That's great, Alec. You'll do it fine."

"But . . . but . . . no autocue to read off, and if possible, no notes! How could I remember all the details they'll want, especially crammed into one afternoon?"

"You could record it on tape, and listen to it played back again and again till it is fixed in your memory."

"Och, you remember what happened to Andrew Eastham when he tried that with his sermon. He was so bored he fell asleep in the middle of it."

"One thing's certain," I went on, "Moorton's fairly getting on the map now. The Late Call series on STV, but they had a moving screen; the Covenanter's Trust; the Conventicle, the pages in *Life and Work* (the Church of Scotland's magazine), and now this. You would think we were St. Giles or something. I never expected all this palaver."

I sweated and worried over that BBC letter all day. Should I say "yes"? These talks were to be considerably longer than my five minute epilogues, and would need a great deal of swotting up of the Cameronian Regimental history. I pretty well knew enough about the Covenanting side, but the story of a regiment from its foundation to its amalgamation was something different and I shivered when I thought of all the dates and names I would have to remember. However, at last it was decided, I would have a try. After all, unless I made a complete botch of the whole thing, it could only help our Covenanter Trust, our lovely wee Kirk, and maybe the gospel, so feeling as important as Cliff Michelmore or some other seasoned TV reporter, I wrote accepting the invitation.

Then followed several afternoons in the Mitchell Library swotting up history. The old library was still the same, earnest students poring over notes, business men hurriedly turning pages of works of reference, old men dosing the afternoon away over their book, and in the alcoves, young couples, mainly students, sitting together, whispering surreptitiously as they watched out for the prowling attendant who had frequently told Janet and I in the 1940s to stop talking. I wondered if they were still dubbed "The Gestapo" by the students of the 1960s?

Having noted down reams of background material, I eventually decided I had enough and there followed the composition of it all in spare moments between my normal Church duties, usually in the "wee sma' oors" when everyone was abed and the house silent. It had to be made into an interesting series so that folk would not switch off in the first minute, and yet do justice equally to the Covenanters and Cameronians. It was a bit like making up the various concoctions I had brewed in my vet days, putting the ingredients into a mortar, mixing and grinding them together with a pestle, and looking with interest at the end product. Having written out my script, it had to be typed in my usual dashing two finger style, and submitted to the producers for approval.

So step by step things progressed. As it neared the afternoon for recording, I was a bundle of nerves, and felt I would break down in the middle, gibbering with fright. Well, I did not do that. In fact I nearly did not get started, for when I saw the studio, my little desk and three moving cameras with cameramen sitting on them, I almost turned tail and bolted. How on earth did these stars look so cool before the cameras? Why three cameras? Oh, mother I wonder if my tie is straight? Is my hair still shed? Where's the nearest toilet?

I said a prayer, swallowed a few times and marched to my desk and my doom. I got a dab of powder on my shiny nose, looked down at my notes (I was allowed them after all but told to try not to use them, just to keep looking into a camera) and we began, voice tests, lighting adjustments, conferences between the various technicians involved, me being told to try to look relaxed (Huh!)

and at last we were off. Fortunately the cameras only photographed my upper half, so my knocking knees did not show. I found it considerably difficult to concentrate on my talks with cameras advancing and retiring, lights beating down making the small studio like an oven, and all the time, as I had been urged, I had to look pleasant as if I was enjoying the whole thing. I found it a help to imagine an interested listener sitting in his armchair at home, and I talked to him. Before I knew it, the first address was over without any need for a re-take. My confidence grew somewhat. Then the second talk and still no re-take. My confidence soared. Soon I was in full flow—who's Cliff Michelmore or Richard Baker anyway—anybody can do this! Eventually all the talks were delivered and I staggered out to be congratulated by a generous producer, and with the father and mother of all my headaches from my effort of concentration, the lights and camera lenses. But it was done, hooray, praise the Lord!

I drove back slowly to the quiet of Moorton from the Glasgow studio, as limp as a wet rag, but feeling good. I knew now what Shadrach, Meshach and Abednego had felt in the burning, fiery furnace and the relief of delivery. Indeed I was inclined to think mine was an even greater miracle than that in the old Book, and suddenly it dawned on me, I was also getting paid for it.

I received numerous comments afterwards when the series went out, many asking me if I had only one tie, and what state was my shirt in at the end of a week! But the tangible result, among others, was that Moorton was now known nationwide. The numbers attending Lochgoin and visiting our old Church increased, sale of Covenanter booklets went up, we had increased requests from many quarters for visits to the Church and lectures. But there was another side effect which gradually showed up.

I spotted them as soon as Andrew showed me up to the pulpit that Sunday in late autumn, a group of four all sitting together. "Ah-ha," I thought, "a scouting party

from another Church." They had already been spotted by
the congregation and were getting long looks, for in our
wee country Kirk we had few Sunday visitors, especially
at that time of the year, and any stranger stood out like
a sore thumb. Had these folk come to steal away their
minister, the congregation was clearly wondering? After
the Service the itinerant four were shown into the vestry
by my faithful old Beadle. "Some people to see you, Mr.
Cameron. They would like a wee word with you, but I
hope you dinna listen," he whispered. The deputation
was from Glasgow and they would like me to consider
their Church, a fine Church, they emphasised, with a lot
of young people about it and a great choir. I thanked
them and said an emphatic "No." A few weeks later the
business was repeated, this time the deputation, from
another city Church, being crafty and seeking to hide by
sitting separately in different parts of the Church. I was
highly amused by the intense scrutiny I received for everything I said or did; one even was jotting notes in a book.
The Moortonites were hardly welcoming to their visitors,
treating them to hard stares and scowls. Again I said
"No." So it went on. Groups appeared uninvited for I
had applied for no other Charge, being completely content where I was. I had letters and phone calls, each it
seemed, outdoing the previous one in the desirability of
their Kirk. It seemed I was known and wanted, and while
it was flattering, it was unsettling. We asked the boys
how they would like to live in Glasgow, Aberdeen, Edinburgh or Timbuktoo to be met by emphatic negatives.

It is required of a minister that he shall stay at least five
years in his first Charge. I was in my sixth year, had seen
the Church grow a little as new people came into the
private development on the edge of the village, some of
them like John Andrews (later Session Clerk) and Colonel
Bill Munro (now Secretary of the Lochgoin Trust) outstanding folk with much to offer. There were those, already elders, like Gibby Anderson whom we welcomed to
our Session. The Sunday School, Bible Class and Youth

Fellowship were flourishing, not only on the spiritual side, but in their respective football teams. Every boy in the village wanted to be a Cub, run magnificently by Joe Gibson and Ian Brown, and Guides and Brownies were very much alive. Our oldest two boys were performing with considerable skill in the Bible Class team, young David equally so in the Cub eleven, while baby Alan could not wait to be old enough to join in. In addition to our greatly appreciated Guild of Friendship for the elderly, we had started a Study Group. Janet was happy with her home and Women's organisations and we felt part of a warm-hearted community where people seemed to like us and where I was welcome in every home. Why shift? We were near our relatives in Ayrshire, my mother and brother Fergus in Prestwick, other brother Graham, an elder in Andrew Eastham's Church at Dunlop. Janet's parents were near at hand in Maryshall, her brother Alec and wife Helen in Ayr, and there were other relations in Mochrum, where I had started my vet career with Ian Buchan. In short, we were at home, and there we meant to stay.

Then in February, returning about 2:00 am from the induction of my friend Jimmy Duncanson to his second Charge at Methil, we found in the front porch the magazine of Aldermouth Old Church and a cutting from *The Scotsman* advertising the vacancy. Not knowing the place at all, I looked it up, out of curiosity, in the Church yearbook. It was about twice the membership of Moorton—they were getting bigger! We discovered eventually the literature had been left by Andrew and Nan Archibald, two friends with Moorton connections who now lived in Aldermouth. In fact the whole Archibald family had visited little Moorton on several occasions, for grandfather Archibald had ministered there for a long period years ago. It was clear Nan and Andrew were now dropping hints. But I did nothing about it. It was still a definite "No." Then a curious thing happened. This one would not go away. It niggled on in my mind. It was not the size, or the pleasant area of the Moray Firth, or an increased salary. It was, what? I could not explain it, it just jolly well would not go away, a kind of jagging in my mind by, I believe, in retrospect, God's Holy Spirit. I had a phone call from the Archibalds urging me to apply, but still I did nothing till one evening in May I came in from a Communion Service and had an over-mastering feeling that unless I got rid of this prickling, I would never be comfortable again, and somehow I felt I had to phone there and then. So I looked up the original advert, found the name and phone number of the Interim Moderator (supervising minister) and rang him.

"Er . . . hello . . . eh . . . ahem . . . my name's Cameron and you'll think this a queer kind of call, but you see, it was suggested I might be interested in Aldermouth Old. I wasn't, but it just won't go away, and I'm phoning to find out if you have now settled on a minister, as I imagine you will by this time."

"Ah, Mr. Cameron," came the reply, "I know your name well. We've discussed you in our meeting, and no, we haven't fixed on anyone. Would you be willing to come up and preach before the Vacancy Committee?"

Here was a shock. I had been phoning up to clear my mind and get peace again and found myself asked to preach for the place. Oh blow! What did one do? I gulped and stuttered a bit.

"Oh, I'm not sure I'm ready for that."

"Well, why not put it to the test. I know exactly how you feel for I eventually had to leave a place I loved." He was a wise man, was dear old John, and was destined to become a very close friend. So we talked, and eventually I agreed to preach before their committee in three weeks' time, though on the strict understanding that I was far from sure, and even if they selected me, I might still say "No."

"That's alright," John replied, "I understand. No commitment either way."

So we travelled north, stayed overnight in Elgin, and

I preached morning and evening there before the
Aldermouth Vacancy Committee. We were given a five-
star lunch and afterwards a tour of the parish by the
kindly Archibalds, then a visit to Church and Manse. In
both we gasped and looked at each other. They were built
in the grand manner, magnificent buildings. The Church
was immense and after little Moorton's Kirk it looked
like a cathedral. But it was beautiful, with superb stained
glass windows, especially one of the Last Supper which
I was told was illuminated in the evening by a spot-light
and looked, with its mellow colours, like an old master
painting. There was a fine pipe organ and we were told
of the outstanding organist, Jim McMichael who, though
blind, with his wife Jean trained a choir of thirty and a
Junior Choir of forty. The pulpit was central and
equipped with two microphones, one for the congregation and one for deaf aids in certain pews. The font was
huge, of Sicilian marble but what perhaps impressed me
most was the fine old wood of the pulpit, pews and
gallery, wood that was highly polished and clearly lovingly tended.

"John keeps the Church beautifully," said Nan Archibald, "he's the full-time Church Officer, teaches in Sunday
School, keeps the grounds, arranges communion duties
and I don't know what else. He and his wife Elizabeth
are in the Church working every day—a great man—a
great pair."

There was a Hall and Boys Brigade (BB) hut and when
we came to the Manse, built of the same stone as the
Church, we counted thirteen rooms, plus, of all things, a
butler's pantry. I thought back to my boyhood in a council house and felt I was being offered a peerage!

We left on the Sunday evening for the long trip back
to Moorton and after a short distance, I stopped the car,
went behind a hedge and changed from my best suit
to flannels and sports jacket. We had been on our best
behaviour for twenty-four hours and in our best clothes,

now we relaxed, and as we journeyed talked over our experience of the weekend, but despite all we had seen, and the kindness of the people we had met, we were far from certain we wanted to move from our humble wee Ayrshire Kirk. But then we had not yet been asked by the congregation of Aldermouth and deep inside me was a hope that we would not be asked, for I loved my Moorton folks and the little white-washed Kirk with its storied past. But we were asked! In a few days I had a phone call. Would I be the sole nominee, preach before the whole congregation in Aldermouth, and would I give my decision about this in four days? I was honoured; I was flattered; I was being asked to be minister of one of the largest churches in the north, for I had discovered that in addition to the 1000 plus members, there were a further 500 adherents. I should have been over the moon, but I was miserable.

There is a hackneyed old story of a Manse couple who had received such an invitation and, so the story goes, while the minister went into his study to pray for guidance, the wife was already packing. Well, it is a crafty wee tale, but it was far from like that with us. My four days deadline passed and I had to phone the Revd John and tell him I was not sure and would need longer. Night after night I walked Bruce, our Boxer dog away out into the country and looked back at the lights of the village. In that house at the top were two sisters, one with a stroke who always looked forward to my visits. Below them were Mr. and Mrs. Crombie, my faithful Beadle and his wife, leal, loyal, true. Along the road a little way was a woman recently widowed. I had been involved with all these folks, with almost every home in the village. How could I go and leave them all? Besides, the family were unhappy about leaving the place they knew.

"What about our Bible Class team, Dad?" said Neil.

"Yes, we can't leave that," piped up Ian. Both were really promising footballers. David joined in,

"I'm not leaving the Cubs." He too was in their team and an equally good wee player, and baby Alan chimed in,

"Will there be a swingy where we go?" The swingy was the play park.

A week of uncertainty, indeed rank misery, passed and I had to phone Aldermouth once more, cap in hand and say, "I'm terribly sorry, I can't decide. I'll understand it if you're fed up with this fellow and go ahead with someone else, but we are going tomorrow on holiday with our caravan to Dornoch. We'll come via Aldermouth and I'll definitely give an answer then. If still uncertain, I'll say 'No' and you can proceed with another candidate."

Friends who knew about my invitation could not understand me. The challenge of a Church in size about three times my present, a Sunday congregation of maybe 600, a beautiful part of the country in the dry Moray Firth area, a larger stipend, a stately home—what was holding me up? I prayed and prayed for guidance. Someone said to me "darkness about going means light about staying," but someone else said "darkness about staying means light about going," so that was stalemate. That was still the state of affairs when we drove into Aldermouth two days later. We arrived in a thunderstorm which matched the storm within me. However, soon the sun came out, and as a family we walked up towards the Church, whose massive square tower was visible for miles, and as we walked the most wonderful peace came stealing over me, and by the time we reached the huge, majestic building and its adjacent Manse, my doubts had been laid to rest, or almost.

Our boys were thrilled, if somewhat over-awed by what they saw. There was a field next to, and belonging to, the Manse, and it had goalposts in it—their own private park for my football-mad sons. That settled it for them! In the well-tended garden was John the Beadle, who welcomed us with his quiet smile, a smile I was to get to know well in twelve marvellous years without a word of difference between us.

But that night I did something that was absolute cheek. I put down a Gideon's fleece, so to speak. I made one proviso, but told no one about it, not even Janet, only God. If even one person voted against me in their secret ballot, I would take that as a sign I was not meant to go. I was fighting against things right to the last but it seemed the Almighty was determined to show me once and for all, for it certainly could not have been my preaching, but the vote was 100 per cent "yes." I had no excuses left.

That call was, next to my decision to give up vet practice for the ministry, the hardest decision I have had to take in life. It was now clear that all the time my jagging, my restlessness, my pull towards the north had been the Holy Spirit at work, and sometimes the Spirit can make us profoundly uncomfortable, a call that costs. Later, the Revd John told me that the first time I had phoned all these weeks before, that night when an inner voice told me to ring then, he had actually had the Vacancy Committee with him telling him they were hopelessly split over three candidates, and not too happy with any, and my call when it came, though many would say chance or coincidence, was clearly God working in His own way.

Everything did not move smoothly after our decision, for Janet, completely out of the blue, took ill, requiring major surgery. What was to be done? Call off Aldermouth? But I had already told Moorton I was leaving in September. Have the operation and arrive in an ambulance? That was not on. Mercifully, we had an understanding surgeon who really decided it for us; he would keep my poor wife going on various medicines till we had settled in at Aldermouth, and then she would travel south for surgery.

So, bit by bit, the pieces fell into place and after some very tearful farewells to my Moorton people, we embarked on the next stage of the voyage, but comforted by a word ringing in our ears and hearts.

"Jesus Christ, *the same*, yesterday, today and forever." The same Lord would be at Aldermouth and I remembered that He too had had a call that cost, a far more awful choice than any other human has had to face, in Gethsemane, and He had made his choice and conquered for the sake of all mankind. To compare my struggles with Gethsemane was almost blasphemy, but my, they hurt, and yet why should I be so reluctant?

I had merely been asked to change houses and Churches, and indeed move to a delightful place with wonderful, kindly people. It would be the same job I had done at Moorton, and in a sense as a vet, only the flock would be different.

The Golden Years

SEVEN

We flitted to Aldermouth one glorious September day in 1968, pulling our caravan behind us. The furniture van had beaten us to it and the men had started to unload. Our next door neighbour was also a minister, Gordon McRae, minister of the High Church, and over the years he and his wife Winnie were to become good friends. Like us, they had four children, and naturally the bairns were curious, like all children, as to their new neighbours, and Jean, the eldest, from her bedroom window overlooking our doors, gave a running commentary to the rest on the proceedings, which apparently produced several surprises for the girl.

The first things the furniture men unloaded were several tea chests and a roll of netting wire, which latter they proceeded to erect in our back garden, and from the tea chests fluttered hens and bantams. Jean called in astonishment, "They've got hens!," which, incidentally, had laid us our tea *en route* from Moorton. Then we pulled up with our caravan, from which leapt our Boxer dog, Bruce, which, like all Boxers, looked as if his bite would be worse than his bark. From the car tumbled four boys and a somewhat stiff mum and dad, and Jean became more and more amazed, calling out, "They've got a big fierce looking dog, and it came out of a caravan, and there are four boys." The poor girl must have thought a tribe of tinkers was taking root just over the wall from her.

We had come a few days before I was due to start work, to allow us to get settled in. Andrew Eastham and his wife came up on the Saturday for Andrew was "preaching me in" and introducing me to the congregation at morning service. Now Andrew had been my parents' minister, and was considerably older than me and a wise counsellor and guide in my Moorton days, and while the Easthams were a delightful couple, we held them in veneration. They had no children so our brood were warned to be on their best behaviour, and for such honoured visitors Janet had made a big effort in the house and the kitchen— best china, table beautifully spread and everything ship-shape. During the meal Mrs. Eastham was admiring the crockery and cutlery when young David, aged nine, piped up, "Mummy, are these the spoons you got with Green Shield stamps?" Collapse of parents, and great hilarity from the Easthams! We had a thoroughly happy weekend with a delightful couple, and on their departure, I felt my new ministry had truly begun, same vet, different vestry.

Now, in most ways I am a fairly traditional minister of the Kirk, some would say old-fashioned. At any rate I have always felt visiting one's flock to be important, and while I realised that in a congregation of over 1000 homes it was a very large task along with the many other duties, I was determined at least to try to get round. So week by week, on two or three evenings a week, I would go with one of the elders and be introduced to his district, while on several afternoons a week I visited the sick, sorrowing, handicapped elderly and housebound, trying to make them feel they were still very much part of the Old Parish family and the family of God. Willie Barclay had said to us at Trinity College, "Get round your people as often as you can. You will learn so much from them, and a great deal of your preaching will come out of these visits. You mustn't be a stranger to your flock."

Now while I am certain Dr. Barclay was right, there

has never yet been a minister who has, in the estimation of all his congregation measured up, like the young minister, a keen botanist, who went to his first charge. Bit by bit he got round in visitation until one day he arrived at the door of a formidable female who met him, hands on his hips, the light of battle in her eye, convinced he should have been to her long since.

"Weel, you've come," she said in a voice singularly lacking in sweetness and light, "if I had been some kind o' fancy puddock stool you'd have been here long since!"

But quite apart from feeling that I ought to be out and about as other duties allowed, I enjoyed this part of my work and still do, and feel my life and ministry have been greatly enriched by meeting people in their homes, particularly those walking in the golden glow of evening. So it certainly was at Aldermouth.

There was Mrs. Laurie whom I first saw in the Northern Infirmary the day after she had had a leg amputated. She was sitting up in bed smacking her lips at a plate of broth and saying "My, that soup's guid. They're awfu' kind to you in here. You'll be the new minister, pleased to meet ye, I hope you'll like it in Aldermouth."

She had never been in hospital before in her eighty-two years and she did not have a word of complaint about herself or the loss of her leg. In due course she was sent home with a temporary leg, a wooden peg leg, and then got her permanent one. Visiting her one day some time later in her home, I found her wearing the old wooden one again.

"Mrs. Laurie," I demanded, "what are you doing with that old thing on again?"

"Ach, Mr. Cameron," she replied, "gang into the bedroom; ma 'ither leg's there."

Wondering somewhat, I did as she asked, and there on the bed lay the proper leg. "Bring it through," she called to me. So I picked up the leg and carried it through, wondering ever more.

"Pit it doon there," she commanded, and I set it upright

in the middle of the floor, where it stood up, a weird looking object, but not to Mrs. Laurie.

"It's a bonny leg," she enthused, "far nicer than ony leg I ever had," (I wondered if she had been a centipede!) "but it's too ticht." She was perfectly serious but I was doubled up in mirth at the picture of two people contemplating seriously one detached leg.

One evening some time later, Dr. John, one of our much loved team of GPs phoned me to inform me, "I've just sent Mrs. Laurie into hospital; her other leg's gone gangrenous. I don't think they'll operate and I'm afraid she won't last more than two days."

So I visited her that evening. By now Mrs. Laurie and I were firm friends; I could say anything to her, and, by golly, she said anything to me. I sat with her for a little and as we talked I marvelled at her spirit, courage, yes, and faith, and thought, "You know, John, I think you could be surprised. She'll cheat the doctors yet." We had a simple word of prayer and I left. They did operate; they did remove her other leg; she did pull through and eventually came home again to her little two room house, destined forever to sit in a wheel chair. She had a home-help and her granddaughter looked in daily, but Mrs. Laurie was independent, wheeled herself around her little home, cooked, dusted, and lived a more or less normal life. I visited her often and never once did I hear her bemoan her fate, nor, blunt woman though she was, did I ever hear her speak ill of anyone. She had the same code as my father, "if you can't speak well of anyone, stay silent."

Mrs. McDonald was another of independent spirit. She was ninety-five when I first knew her, lived in the old Fishertown part of the town, for her husband had been one of Aldermouth's many fishermen at the beginning of the century when the town was a thriving fishing port. It was a hard, hard life for the men, and for the women who followed the fleet to gut the herring. She had been a widow sixty long years. Often she would talk of the old days, bringing up a family on her own "an' no help frae the Government either!" The great fear of her generation was to get into debt. One week she had not a scrap of food in the house and not a penny in her purse. She wandered up the street, bowed down with anxiety, wondering what to do, and on the way met an old fisherman. He knew by her face something was far from right.

"What ails ye, quine?" he enquired, so she poured out her story.

"Do you know what he did?" she asked me.

"No, you tell me."

"He went into his purse an' took oot ten shillings—ten shillings, mind you! That seemed a fortune an' I didna ken whit to say."

"Noo, quine," he said, "dinna worry. Just you pay me back when you can afford it. There's nae hurry."

Mrs. McDonald looked away back over the years.

"Ye ken, it was the only time I owed onybody money, an' I never rested till I paid him back. He was a gran' man, and kind." I thought of our modern age of buy now, pay later, hire purchase, young folks who must have everything in their homes from the beginning, and the era of Mrs. McDonald when nothing was bought till it could be paid. Mostly we just went over "the clash o' the toon," but one day she told me of her husband.

He had lain ill for a long time in the box-bed in the living room. He was a fisherman of the old school to whom the most important things in life were his home and family, his work, and his Church, for none of the boats put out on a Sunday and all the fisher families were to be found at worship, the men in their thick blue jerseys. This particular day he gave thanks for a good wife and bairns, then suddenly sat up in his bed, his face shining.

"Look!" he called, "above Maggie Ralph's shop!"

His wife looked, but saw nothing, but her man was seeing with an inner eye, something hid from his wife. What? A band of angels comin' after me, or like Stephen the martyr, a glimpse of Heaven and his Lord?

"Oh, you've missed it," he said.

Then he lay back on his bed, sang a stave of an old Sankey hymn beloved by fishermen, "O happy day, when Jesus washed my sins away," then murmuring the name of his trusted friend, "Jesus . . . Christ," he was gone.

To many the story of his passing would seem like something from a Victorian melodrama, embarrassing to modern ears, but for the couple it was terribly real and unforgettable, an experience that can be paralleled many times over by those of our calling who attend the sick and dying. Then Mrs. McDonald went on, "He was awfu sair done to," and I thought she was still talking of her husband, but she continued, "A' thae sodgers, an' that muckle croon o' thorns, an' that wound in His side." She gave a great sigh, paused, and then her old blue eyes shining she said "An' it was a' for us!" That mark you, from a woman who was an adherent of the Church, who did not consider herself good enough to join or come to the Lord's table.

I was asked to be present at a meal one day, a quiet little celebration for Mr. and Mrs. McIntosh who were celebrating their seventieth wedding anniversary, a remarkable couple. Mr. McIntosh at ninety-six was still in Church every Sunday and down the street daily for the shopping, but his wife at eighty-nine was more frail. Only the family were present, and their minister. What a privilege to share in such an occasion, a Royal Wedding indeed. I was asked to say a few words. Not having been at a seventieth anniversary before, I had no suitable stories, and I knew from experience of them they liked a joke. After congratulating them, the best I could do as a lighter touch was to tell of the couple on their Golden Wedding day. They had lived all their lives in the one place, were highly respected, and both hale and hearty, and the young reporter sent to interview them for the local paper and get a photograph asked the old man what was the secret of their long, happy and healthy life together. The old man replied,

"Weel, son, it's like this. When Jean and I were wed we agreed we would never fa' oot, that if ever a row was comin' on, one o' us would just go a walk, and the reason we've lived so long and been so happy is plenty of exercise and fresh air."

Old Mr. McIntosh smacked the table in glee at the story so I told another Golden Wedding one which I had heard my friend John Baker, minister of Rosebank Church tell. A certain couple on their great day went back to Arran where they had spent their honeymoon fifty years before. It was a glorious day, and passed all too quickly, but at last it was time to go and get the boat. They found it had gone, so they were forced to stay the night on the island, and managed to get fixed up in the hotel where they had honeymooned. As the wife was preparing for bed and combing out her hair, now silvered, she said to her man,

"Aye, John, the winter's in my hair but the summer is still in my heart," to which her gallant swain replied:

"Mary, the winter's in your hair richt enough, and the summer micht be in your heart, but if the spring had been in your step, we wouldna' hae missed the boat."

It was a delight to see Mr. and Mrs. McIntosh, twenty years on from those in my stories, laugh heartily as if I had said something clever. It was a wonderful experience to hear them recount some of the happenings of their long lives together, walking side by side down the years, and now in the golden glow of evening, still, indeed even more one, dependent on the other.

Then there was Mrs. Gilchrist, her old face wrinkled like a ripe pippin, in her eighties looking after her grandson Alan, a terribly mentally and physically handicapped lad. He was in his twenties but had the mental age of an infant, always happy and smiling, and dearly loved by his parents and Granny who had brought him up from a child so that his parents would be free to live and work normally. Alan could not speak, had to be spoon-fed, and have absolutely everything done for him. I early discovered he loved music, especially a good-going tune, and every time I called I had to play "She'll be comin' round the mountain" and "Daisy, Daisy," while Alan kept time with his hand. About half way through my ministry in Aldermouth Alan died, and while most would have said it was a merciful release, Mrs. Gilchrist grieved for her "boy." On the face of it, one would think of such a life as a tragedy, but there were no happier home to enter in the whole town.

The oldest person in the town, and the oldest in any of the Church's Eventide Homes at the time was Miss Catherine Grant, aged 105. I visited her many times, and over the years had many yarns, for she could go back to the 1870s. She told me of her girlhood as a shepherdess in the hills above Loch Ness. She talked of the Battle of Culloden as if it was yesterday, and told tales of "the Bonnie Prince" she had heard from her great-grandfather. She recalled filling the "kist" with its supply of oatmeal for the winter, and of how a sheep would be killed for a celebration. It was incredible to think of the changes she had seen. No anaesthetics when she was a girl, no electricity, no cars.

"What about hospital?" I asked her. She was aghast.

"Och now, to go to hospital was a terrible thing, chust a place to die." She remembered well stories of how after a burial the relatives or Church elders had to guard the grave and the people built a sentry box at the gates, "for the doctors used to come to take the bodies away to study the internals." Sometimes the watchers would let the grave-robbers into the Churchyard, then shut the gate on them so that they could not get out again, and her eyes twinkled at the recollection. She had survived three leg breaks since her seventies, the last when she was a mere youngster of 102. I never thought it would heal, but it did and she walked again.

Always in her room, beside her bed, was the Bible, several individual books in very large print given her by the Bible Society for whom she had been a collector for many years. The books were well thumbed, she could recite many passages by heart, and treated "The Book" with the reverence of a bygone age. One day she surprised me by an apparent criticism of a Bible character, "You know, Mr. Cameron, I sometimes think that St. Paul was chust a little hard on the ladies," then, as if she had gone too far she added, "but likely they would be needing it."

I asked her what was her favourite chapter. She had no doubt, John 14! "In my Father's house are many mansions. I go to prepare a place for you."

So on her 105th birthday we celebrated, just a few of us, the matron and Superintendent of the Home, the Provost, the senior doctor, my wife and I and one or two others. In the middle sat the grand old lady, surrounded by cards, flowers, telegrams ("and one from the Queen no less"). She was resplendent in a frilly blouse and black hat, 1900 style, her face powdered, but a little bemused by the popping of flash bulbs, yet regal in her bearing, a queen in her own right, in full control of her life, body, mind and spirit.

Then there were the Campbells, a grand old couple who had, like so many of their generation, raised a large family on very little. They too had been spared to one another well beyond the three score years and ten, and to enter their snug little cottage was to be treated like a prince. Immediately I would be shown to the best chair, mother would give a nod, and the two unmarried girls would immediately rise to put the kettle on and prepare a cup of tea which was really a sumptious feast of home baked scones, pancakes, gingerbread, currant cake and a host of other delicacies. They too were adherents, but in Church twice a Sunday, a humble, gracious, God-fearing family whose like are the salt of the earth. Every Christmas, knowing their minister's sweet tooth and special delights, the two daughters, Grace and Mary, would arrive at the Manse door laden with good things, all their own marvellous baking.

So one could go on. Our senior elder was Mr. Ham-

mond, also in his nineties, who had had a family of daughters, and then lastly one boy, Sandy who was the former
Session Clerk and my dentist—a wonderful, talented,
generous, welcoming family. The first time I called, old
Mr. Hammond was in bed, but his violin was handed
down to him, and he entertained his new minister to a
selection. Great folks! There were our near neighbours,
Jim and Jean McLennan, who had a special interest in
the Manse boys growing up, and who put up with a ball
often landing over the wall in their garden.

One of our old folk we had known before coming
to Aldermouth was Mrs. Burns, Granny to everybody,
especially a succession of young doctors who rented the
house next to her. She was the mother of Nan Archibald,
whose contact had first turned my thoughts from Moorton to Aldermouth and who had visited us with far flung
members of the family, home for a visit to their native
Ayrshire from Canada. They included a call at Moorton
Kirk, where Granny Burns' father had been minister for
many years. She was a wonderfully bright, indomitable
soul, interesting and interested in all that was going on.
A similar "character" was Mrs. Mackenzie, again over the
ninety mark, who lived with her daughter Helen, and
whose other daughter was married to our marvellous
organist, Jim McMichael. She was always as bright as a
new pin, alert, informed, and regularly with a twinkle in
her eye informing me of course she was English and
proud of it, proud too that her late husband had at one
time been Provost.

There were well over 200 really elderly folks on our
Church roll, and one could speak of them all, but space
does not permit. To know them was a privilege and a
delight.

Mind you, age does not of itself bring goodness or
sanctity. I have known some awkward, difficult and bitter
old folks, demanding too, like the old boy who asked me
to visit him in hospital. The visit consisted of a list of
instructions from him of things he wanted me to see to,

including an enquiry about his investments. He was not seriously ill, had no Church connection, but like many another, alas, did not hesitate to use the Church for his own ends when needed. "Not bad," I thought as I left his bed "for one who usually has not a good word to say about Kirks or Kirky folk."

But for the most part, I have greatly enjoyed my contact with our older folks and still do, and look back over the years to some wonderful people I have known, who, though twice my age, accepted me without hesitation as their minister and friend, and from very many of whom, goodness simply shone out. The golden years indeed!

Years ago there were three famous Methodist ministers—Weatherhead, Sangster and Soper, all spiritual giants, close friends with the redoubtable Lord Soper still, at eighty five in 1988, alive and active. It was said of them, "Weatherhead loves the people, Sangster loves the Lord and Soper loves an argument!" Sangster was a really saintly man, other wordly, deeply spiritual, a man who was used to point many on the pilgrim pathway, a man just plain good right through. Pulling his leg one day, Weatherhead said to him, "Suppose you had to interview either an old wrinkled woman or a dashing young blonde in a low cut dress, which would you choose?" Sangster thought seriously for a time, then replied, "I think the older lady, for she would have seen so much more of life and could teach me so much."

I can well understand Sangster's choice, and like him I too, though far, far short of his saintliness, have been taught so much about life, in sunshine and in shadow, from those walking in the soft, fading light of evening.

Of course I knew many old folks in my years as a vet too but my relationship with them was different, for it was their animals that concerned me then, but one could not treat the pets or farm animals without getting to know the owners.

My partner of the early years at Bristacombe, Major

Kenneth Davidson, was on holiday and I was holding the fort on my own. The summer months saw a reduction in farm work, but this was balanced, as visitors flooded into the town, by a rise in the small animal side of things and in cases at the zoo, so one was never idle.

My first visit of the morning was a very easy one, I thought, to call at the home of a Miss Huxtable and clip the nails of her dog. I duly found the house and an elderly lady came to the door.

"Yes?" she enquired.

"I'm the veterinary surgeon. I've come to clip your dog's nails."

"Oh—oh my—well, I suppose you better come in."

I wondered at the hesitation, but followed the old lady into a very comfortably furnished sitting room, where another elderly lady was sitting nursing a Pomeranian, which, at the sight of me leapt from her lap, made for my ankles and caught hold of the bottom of my trousers.

"Oh dear, isn't he the little monkey?" said lady number one. "This is my sister," she went on, "but we were expecting Major Davidson."

"I'm sorry, he's off on holiday at present. I'm his partner."

"Oh, but I'm afraid," spoke up the seated sister, "we always have the Major. You see, he really understands Peter and Peter is used to him. He is such a sensitive little fellow."

"I understand, but I think I could manage to clip Peter's claws."

"Oh no!" said the dominant sister, "Peter gets so excited with strangers. I'm afraid it will have to be the Major. We will just wait till he gets back. Good day to you, Mr. er . . . er,"

"Cameron."

"Mr. Cameron," and before I knew it I was being shown out, pursued by a yelping Pomeranian.

Some years rolled on, Kenneth Davidson moved to Kenya, and Bernard Paterson became my partner. Here was a problem for the sisters, but it seemed it was not so much the Major they demanded, as always the senior partner, for when next summoned to the Huxtable abode, I was welcomed like a long lost cousin.

"Ah—Mr. Cameron! How nice to see you! It is Peter's usual problem of his nails and we have heard *such* good reports of you. Now the Major has gone we had no hesitation in sending for you. But you'll always come yourself, won't you?" Peter was a spoiled little lap dog, and yap dog, but while one sister held him and the other murmured endearments, I managed successfully to do the job.

"Now come and wash your hands," I was commanded, and ushered into a very luxurious bathroom with a brand new bar of Lux toilet soap and a white, fluffy, expensive towel laid out for my use. That operation completed, I was handed, on my way out, a parcel, "for Mrs. Cameron and your dear little boys." It proved to be a large box of chocolates, something I received on every visit thereafter, for Peter had regular problems of a minor nature in addition to the nails which needed frequent clipping, for he never walked on hard roads, only being allowed a little romp in their enclosed garden. A new bar of soap and my special towel always awaited me. Poor Bernard never got a look in until I left for the ministry, but there was always rejoicing with our laddies, Neil and Ian, whenever I visited there. They even got to asking,

"Is Peter not sick yet, Daddy?"

"When do you go to cut Peter's nails again?"

Many old folks keep pets of different kinds, and particularly for someone living alone, they can be a great boon. Sometimes it is astonishing to what lengths people will go for the sake of their companions, be it budgerigar or Boxer, cat or canary. I visited a lonely old soul at Martincombe one day. She lived in a little one-apartment house, a bed-sitter, and was possessed of a bad-tempered large Collie cross dog of which she was clearly distinctly nervous. She was no help at all in restraining it as I prepared to give it a distemper innoculation, so I had to muzzle it and continue to hold it tightly by the scruff of the neck while I slipped the needle in. I looked around the little room and asked where the dog slept.

"Oh, it sleeps with me," she explained rather shame-facedly.

"There can't be much room," I suggested, looking at the small single bed.

"No, there isn't," she acknowledged, "sometimes when he turns over bed I'm frightened to touch him and push him back, so I end up sleeping on the floor." That, I felt, was carrying one's devotion and self-sacrifice for a pet a bit far, but clearly this little woman was more frightened of intruders than her fierce dog, for no one would have dared beard that hound in its den.

But this kind of thing is the exception. Most pets, particularly dogs and cats, give back all they receive in love with interest, and some unexpected people, I found, lavished a great deal of tender loving care on their animals. Miss Inglewood, for example, was an elderly, man-ish, no nonsense spinster who had an old cat. It had a heart condition, was deaf, subject to eczema, was troubled by its kidneys and had not a tooth left in its head. But she loved her sixteen-year old cat with a passionate love. She was never away from the surgery with it for the least thing, or for a restock of its many pills, and there was no more precious feline in Bristacombe. A famous, well known, world renowned author was another who unex-pectedly showered extravagant devotion on his dog, a Dachsund. He and his wife lived in a lovely house above the dunes at the far end of Mortecombe's famous beach, three miles of clean, golden sand. He was very much a man's man, an old soldier who had a great hole in his leg from shrapnel in the First World War. Twice every day he waded in the sea to keep that old wound clean from which came periodically a sliver of diseased bone. He doted on that dog, and like Miss Inglewood, at the least sign of trouble was on the phone. Aunty Violet, as she was, and is to our boys, for she often thirty years ago baby sat for us, was another who lived for her cats and any strays in the area, and after her husband's death, and particularly after suffering a stroke herself, it was her cats alone, who by their affection gave her the will to live. That is the great thing about domestic pets; they normally ask for so little and give so much in return, and in my years in practice I saw many folks in the evening of life who were given an interest (sometimes it seemed the sole interest in living), by their little companions.

Of course the trouble is that animals do not live so long as people, and there can be great heartbreak when a loved companion dies. I have seen it so often and normally encourage the owner to get another pet as soon as possible. Nearly always they would initially say, "No! No other dog could take the place of Rex, or Tiger or Trixie or whatever," but I tried to point out that while that was true, in time the new animal would make its own place.

I remember the phone going about 9:30 pm one evening and a voice telling me she was phoning for Mr. Chugg, 21, Fore Street, and could I come as soon as possible as his dog had collapsed. Fore Street was a steep street leading down to the harbour and made up of cheaper class Guest Houses and old dwellings of the terrace type. An elderly man opened the door of number 21 and ushered me into a very humble abode. There, on a mat before a meagre coal fire was an old dog, lying on its side, its breathing very fast and laboured.

"I hope you can do summat for Rover, sir," said the old man. "He seems far through. He be nought but a little mongrel but you see, sir, since missus died last year, he's been ma only friend."

"We'll see what we can do, Mr. Chugg. How old would he be?"

"Ah! Rover be a good age, bout 15 an' a've had 'im since a pup."

I bent down and took the old dog's temperature. Rover scarcely moved, only his eyes following me around, and at the sound of his master's voice, his tail giving a half-hearted little thump on the worn old carpet.

"Can't make it out," the old chap went on, "he had 'is tea as usual, like, bout 7, then us 'ad 'is little walk down to t' harbour. He comed in an' just kind of fell down where ee be lyin' now." The old dog's temperature was subnormal, his pulse fast, thready and irregular. I had a listen at the chest with my stethoscope. There was fluid on the lungs, the heart-beat was weak, and of course, irregular. Just then the little dog gave a whimper and the old man was down on his knees cradling its head in his hands, and stroking it gently.

I straightened up. This was always the hard bit.

"I'm very sorry, but your dog's had a heart attack, Mr. Chugg, and he's very ill."

"Do ee mean he's dyin'?"

"I'm afraid so, Mr. Chugg."

"Can nuthin' be done, like?"

"Not really, I'm very sorry. If he had been a younger dog, and just had a kind of heart spasm, bit like angina in people, we could have treated him. But he's had a proper heart attack and his heart's very weak. There's fluid in his lungs too which means his heart is failing fast. It's just like a pump—but a very wonderful pump—but it's come to the end of its working life."

"What do ee advise then, sir?" the old man asked.

"Well, I don't think he's suffering too much pain, but he's very distressed. I think I should give him a little jag which will take away all discomfort and he'll just go to sleep."

"You mean he won't waken up?" the little man quavered. I hesitated to choose my words.

"He might, but I think it likely he'll just sleep quietly away. It's a painkiller, you see, I'm giving him, what we call a sedative, which will quieten his breathing and ease his distress. We can't allow him to go on fighting for breath like that, can we?"

The old man looked at his companion of the years,

tears coursing down his cheeks, then he got down on the
rug beside his friend and buried his face in its coat while
the dog's tail gave a few weak little thumps on the floor.

"Aar, you'm there, old fellow. You've been a wonderful
pal. You and me's had some great times, us 'ave."

Slowly he straightened up and said with a catch in his
voice.

"Alright, sir—give 'im 'is jag now."

I gave the dog a shot of omnopon and scopolamine
which would make him drowsy and comfortable, and in
sleep would most probably just pass on. It was not really
euthanasia, just making an animal as much at ease as I
could, but I was certain he would not waken up. The old
man was fumbling with a purse.

"What do I owe you, sir?" he asked.

"Oh—that's alright, Mr. Chugg. Let's just see how
Rover gets on, shall we?"

So I left the little old man, a quiet dignity about him,
as he got down on the carpet again, stroking his friend
of the years. I called the next morning, and Rover had,
indeed, quietly slept away in the night. I asked Mr. Chugg
if he would not consider having another dog and offered
to get him one, but his lip trembled and he said, "Ah,
but it wouldn't be Rover."

It so happened that several times in the next fortnight
I saw old Mr. Chugg out doing his bits of shopping, for
Fore Street was just round the corner from our surgery.
He looked forlorn, lost, desolate. Then I remembered a
Border terrier bitch I had whelped about three months
before and thought there might just be a chance. I called
at the Border's home, whose owner I knew well.

"How are the pups going?" I enquired after a bit.

"They've been slow this time, Mr. Cameron, and we're
left with one still which we just can't get rid of. We may
have to get you to put it down."

"Dog or bitch?"

"Oh, dog." I thought this was all providential.

"Would you consider giving it away to a good home?"

I quizzed, and told them about the lonely old man. They listened carefully and to my great delight agreed. Now for the difficult part. I called on Mr. Chugg that evening just at the darkening, perhaps the loneliest part of the day for an old person living alone.

"Ah, Mr. Cameron!" he greeted me, "it's nice to see you. Come in so that I can square up what I owe you." I went in, sat down and chatted for a bit. Eventually he rose and took his purse out of a drawer. The purse looked pretty empty.

"No, Mr. Chugg, I haven't come for that. As a matter of fact I've come to ask you if you could help me. You see, I have two friends whose bitch had pups and there's one they can't get rid of. If they don't find a good home for it, they're talking of having it put to sleep, and I thought maybe you could do me a favour and give the wee fellow a try. It's a pedigree Border terrier, just about the same size as Rover."

"Oh, Mr. Cameron, I couldn't, no, it wouldn't be Rover."

"Seems a shame to have it put to sleep, though, don't you think?"

"Aye, it be a right shame."

"Tell you what," I rushed on, "have a look at it. It's out in the car. You can always say 'No'."

It was a kind of blackmail, I realised, but I thought the end justified the means. So I went out to the car, carried in the little pup, which promptly did a puddle on the floor.

"That's torn it," I thought, but Mr. Chugg laughed.

"Rover did that the moment I brought him home too," he said. The bright little bundle of mischief went over to where the old man was sitting in an ancient broken springed chair, looked up at him, then leapt on his knee and licked his face, and I felt certain I had won.

And so it proved. A lonely old man got a new companion, and being a puppy, the training kept him busy, and in due course I saw him proudly going along the High

Street with the little dog on a brand new lead. I called one day to see how things were going for he had promised initially he would just give it a try. The dog was curled up at his chair, its chin resting on his foot, a picture of contentment.

"Well, Mr. Chugg, how about it? Will he do?"

"Aar, Mr. Cameron, he be a right topper, an' pedigreed an' all. Never had a pedigreed dog before. I've called him Mac, because he and you are Scotch. I hope you don't mind."

"Mr. Chugg," I said in all sincerity, "I'm highly honoured."

I thought, as I drove home, of the contrast of the old man that first night I had seen him and of the change wrought by a four legged bundle of mischief. Of course the dog could not replace the close companionship of his recently deceased wife, but in their own innocent way, many an animal has brought gladness, joy and all the love of its heart to someone in the golden years, providing its own kind of companionship. Indeed more than once someone has said to me something like "I'd rather have a dog than a husband/wife, for you can depend on a dog. It's loyal, always the same, and doesn't talk back to you."

That may be true of some relationships, but much as I love animals, I cannot agree that a dog or cat can take the place of a deceased partner. I can think of nothing more beautiful than an old couple, who have weathered many a storm together on the way, still walking hand in hand in the golden glow of evening, one through the years, one for ever.

When I was signing copies of my first book *Vet in the Vestry* a couple came·up to me clutching their book and said, "You won't remember us, but you played the organ at our wedding in Crosshill Church forty-four years ago, and as we went out at the end you played *I'll walk beside you*. It has been our favourite song since."

I would only have been a laddie of seventeen when I played at their marriage, but I could well understand why the song had remained a favourite, and it sums up all I've tried to say in this chapter.

"I'll walk beside you through the passing years;
Through days of cloud and sunshine, joy and tears;
And when the great call comes, the sunset gleams,
I'll walk beside you to the land of dreams."

And like a great echo, I hear the voice of *the* constant companion and friend say from that land of dreams, "Lo, I am with you alway, even to the end of the world."

The Least of These,
My Brothers

EIGHT

Years ago I read in *Reader's Digest* an article about a family in Canada who were seemingly untameable, living in their own style, and for the most part a law unto themselves. They were called McKie. On the very night of my induction to the Old Parish Church of Aldermouth, I was warned by a ministerial colleague about a local family who would plague the life out of me if I did not choke them off right at the start. They too were called McKie, their notoriety had spread far and wide, and sure enough they were at the Manse door within days.

The father was dead, but there were five sons and five daughters and the mother who was the head of the clan in no uncertain terms. She always dressed in black and looked somewhat sinister, but she had a gentle face and manner. However, I soon learned that looks deceived for she had led the family to ruin after the father's death, prior to which they had been law-abiding citizens. Their affection for mother and attachment to her was astonishing and in its way, admirable, but under her leadership they had gone to complete wreck and ruin. Her every wish was obeyed. The Police Sergeant told me that Mrs. McKie had been overheard issuing her instructions about which house to burgle, and they would go out and do it. Never have I known a family, alas, more attached to their mother, whose every desire was paramount. The eldest son, Dan, had been in prison more than a hundred times, could be violent, and indeed most of the family had a "record." One of the exceptions was a girl who had married early and got out of the tight-knit family circle. She was living a perfectly respectable, humble life in a local council house. The rest of the family, male and female, were almost constantly under the combined influence of drink and various forms of tranquillisers which a compassionate local doctor, who clearly did not know what to do with them, dished out freely.

They had been evicted from several houses because of the disturbance to the neighbours, and when I first knew them, were living in a large caravan down by the harbour. From the beginning there was scarcely a week we did not have them at the door pleading for help. Early on I realised that to give them money was fatal, for with a scarcely concealed grin of triumph they simply headed for the nearest pub.

One evening, in my first months, the steady member of the family came to see me.

"I'm worried about our Bobby," she said.

"Bobby? I haven't met him yet."

"No, he's just coming out of a young offenders' institution and he's sure to go the way of the rest unless somebody helps him."

"He's really got to help himself, Agnes."

"Oh, I know—but I thought if somehow he could get a job away from here, he might, since he's young, go straight."

I thought for a bit. Agnes was a caring girl, and clearly very fond of the baby of the family, and finally I agreed to try to help. I wrote to a Roman Catholic group in the south of Scotland that specialised in helping lads like Bobby, they generously agreed to have him, and the day he came out of the Institution I met him, told him all about it and the lad, a fine, big, good looking fellow in his mid teens agreed to give it a try. I paid his fare south and off he went.

Meantime the rest of the family were going from bad to worse. They ripped out most saleable items from their rented caravan to sell in exchange for drink, and were to be seen daily lurching along the streets, and very frequently at our door. We sometimes gave them a meal, but refused, apart from the occasional bus fare, to give them money. They had relations in Elgin and Inverness, and would periodically disappear for a time, to the infinite relief of the citizens of Aldermouth. There was peace for the harried folks of the town only when the McKies were away, usually in prison. I visited Dan in jail for although my common sense told me it was a losing battle, my conscience kept jagging me to try to help such pathetic human beings. I was told Dan, indeed all the McKies were model prisoners, and really they seemed happiest when "inside"—well clad and fed, clean, sober and human again. But their sentences were normally short and always they drifted back to mother, seeming docilely to obey her every wish and command. Bye and bye there was no caravan left, somehow they set fire to it, and they were out on the street.

They arrived *en masse* at the Manse one summer evening. I was picking raspberries in the garden and hidden from their view, and I could hear them making their plan of attack as they came along the path.

"Ask for £5!"

"Too much."

"Try for it anyway."

They were somewhat startled when I leapt out at them from between the high rows of raspberries and asked them what they wanted.

"Oh, Mr. Cameron! . . . er . . . it's a grand nicht."

It's that alright, and as you can see, I'm busy in the garden. What's the problem tonight?"

"Well, you see, Mr. Cameron, you've been awful good

to us and we don't like to ask you again, but there's this big tent we can get to stay in—eh—for £5."

I laughed. "Where do you think I'd get £5? I've a wife and family to keep, and ministers have not a great pay."

"Oh, we ken, Mr. Cameron—it's a crying shame, so it is—aye, a richt shame, but if you could just give us £5, we won't bother you again."

"For a tent, you say?"

"Aye, that's richt."

"Well, tell you what. If you tell the man who has the tent to contact me, I'll see what I can do, or better still, tell me who he is and I'll go and see him and get it for you."

"Oh no! That wouldna' dae at a', Mr. Cameron. The man's no there the noo but he's promised tae keep it for us. If you could just give us the money, you see!"

"No money!"

"£4?"

"No!"

"£3?"

"Not a penny."

So it worked down till they were asking for ten shillings, but despite the lovely night, the grand crop of rasps *and* my conscience, there was no money forthcoming, and at last, with mutterings and long looks, the deputation departed. Of course it was all a fabricated story, but some time later they did, in fact, somehow acquire a large bell tent, pitched it beside the burned out caravan, and there they lived. It was shocking that any family, however difficult, should live like that and I constantly badgered the Social Work Department to try to house them, preferably away out in the country which I felt was the only hope, with no neighbours to disturb with their wild drinking bouts and fights, but nothing seemed to be done.

In the midst of one of their many crises, young Bobby arrived home. He came to the Manse looking fit, well, sober, an upstanding young man, and announced that he was changed, had got religion, and was going to live a different life. We rejoiced with him and for him. Alas, within a week he was back in jail.

We tried again with Sandy, who was the smallest of the family—a quiet, subdued, shauchly, pathetic little creature, the one we saw most often. I managed to get him fixed up with the Salvation Army in Glasgow, and as the months passed and Sandy did not return, I began to hope. However, one day after nearly a year, a year of happiness for Sandy among the good folks of the "Sally Army" where he had helped in the canteen, he arrived back and went to stay with Aunt Mary, who, though a humble woman, was honest, kindly and straight.

Aunt Mary, like the McKies originally in their father's time, earned her living as a kind of hawker, but she was a decent soul, and deeply concerned about her nephews and nieces. She surprised Janet one day and showed that the giving was not all one way when she arrived at the door with a large, green, three cornered fruit dish "to show my thanks for all you've done for the boys." The dish has graced our dining table annually at harvest thanksgivings filled with fruit, and a token forever that even in the wildest and worst, as my father maintained all his life, there is some good. There was an even bigger surprise one day when Mrs. McKie herself, who had often been at our door pleading for bus fares to Inverness and been given the latest one on condition that she paid it back (something she always promised), actually paid it back. Janet nearly dropped the money in amazement, but took it and said, "I'll lay this aside for you and when you need it, it'll be here waiting for you." Mrs. McKie thanked her and departed. She was always most gracious in her thanks. Two days later she was back for her money!

Sandy struggled to keep his head above water for a time, but eventually, to the great sorrow of Aunt Mary, he was sucked back into the vortex of the family and their way of life, and before long, bruised and battered, for they were forever in fights, he was back at our door looking for money. Neither of us was in at the time, but he was given short shrift by Ian, for by now all our boys knew the family well and had been involved in their own way in our attempts to reform and rehabilitate.

Then came tragedy of a high order. On Games Day in Aldermouth when crowds flocked into the town from near and far, old natives of the area came home for the annual big event and there was general festivity and rejoicing, two of the McKie boys were found lying helpless in the street. I suppose, in retrospect, they should have been taken to hospital but being the McKies, the police, who found them, took them to the lock-up where one, the one least known to us, Billy, died in the police cell of that lethal mixture of alcohol and drugs, choking on his own vomit. There was an immediate outcry from the rest of the family about police brutality, one of the popular "dailies" got hold of the story, published an interview with the sorrowing mother and there was general indignation in the rest of Scotland which knew nothing of the family and cries of "why doesn't the Church do something for this poor neglected family," for whom nobody seemed to care. A post mortem confirmed the diagnosis, the brother was buried by me amid tremendous wailing, many of the mourners, who seemed to have flocked from all over the north, being drunk. Dan was escorted to the graveside by two prison warders, for he was undergoing one of his frequent stays in Inverness prison. I felt deeply sorry at the waste of Billy's life, and also felt keenly the tragedy of a life lived without God. How different, I felt, not for the first time, is the funeral of one where there has been faith. I thought back as one always does, should I have done more for the family? Eventually the episode passed. Though somewhat sobered for a time, the death of one son made no real difference to the lifestyle of mother or family.

So the weeks and months passed. One night in the dead of winter, mother and three of the family arrived at the Manse door "drookit" to the skin and with nowhere to sleep. I had greatly hardened my heart by this time, for we had helped as best we could so often, but I simply could not turn anyone away in such a state on such a night. So we bedded them down in the BB hut, gave them dry clothes, blankets and food, with instructions to be out early in the morning or the Kirk Session would have my head. They kept their bargain, apparently sleeping soundly all night long, which was more than I had done, for I was up umpteen times parading over to the hut to make sure it was not on fire, for in addition to their other "gifts," the McKies had quite a record as fire raisers. They still had the remains of the tent for their home, for it too had been damaged by fire, but very frequently practically the whole family, including finally the old mother too, were guests of Her Majesty in prison.

Then came a telegram to every clergyman in the town from the Director of the Social Work Department, which read "For the sake of Jesus Christ, do something about housing and helping the McKies."

With one accord, the brethren felt highly indignant at that, when we thought of what *had* been done, and how indeed we over the years had been doing things which we felt were the responsibility of that same Director. In time the furore died down, nothing was done by the authorities, another brother Sammy died in the same tragic way as Billy—drink and drugs—and I had a terrible feeling of utter helplessness. Of course the answer was a change of lifestyle, but that could only come from a change of heart, and yet could one continually preach the Gospel which could change, to those with empty stomachs and no roof over their heads? So things just drifted on. I kept vowing this was the last help they would get for almost everything went on drink. I regularly told them to go and work, go out and earn a living. But I knew in my heart that work was really out of the question for two reasons.

One, they were so weakened and drained mentally and physically, they simply could not work and two, no one in the area would employ them.

Usually it was the sons we saw. The girls, for the most part had other fish to fry and went their own ways, always however reporting back to mother. Oddly enough, women did not enter into the boys' scheme of things at all, except mother. If ever I saw a mother's influence for wrongdoing in her family, it was in Mrs. McKie. Yet their concern for her was deep and basic, and without her, they felt lost.

After wee Sandy, Dan was our most frequent visitor, a Dan whose face was now battered almost beyond recognition. Every now and then he would break into a house, but his method of operation was always the same. He would take out the light bulb, leaving his fingerprints on it, then burn newspapers for torches, escaping with £5 or a brooch. The police simply went and picked him up without difficulty or resistance, and for a while again, he was at least warm and well fed "inside."

Many times I told them there would be no more assistance, but one day Bobby arrived at the Manse, a different Bobby, well dressed, polite, sober, clean and with an independent air about him, a Bobby who could look the world in the eye. He had been out of circulation for a while and I had wondered where he was. Apparently he had been staying in a monastery, and undoubtedly something had happened to him.

"I've been converted," he explained, "and I'm going to go straight. Will you help me?"

I was mightily impressed by the obvious change in the wild, and latterly very violent Bobby, and rejoiced that where I had failed, some brothers in the Roman Catholic Church had succeeded. Despite my vow to do no more for the family, I felt I must have one last try with Bobby.

"Bobby! I'm delighted to see the change in you and I'll try to help, on one condition, that you keep away from the family or you're sunk!"

"I know, Mr. Cameron, I feel the same myself. They've made a mess of their lives" (so had he!), "but I'm different now from them." (A wee bit uppish, I thought, but said nothing.)

"Well, you can have a bed here for a night or two till you get fixed up somewhere else and try for a job. But every day will be a struggle for you now that you're back home."

We managed to get him fixed up in a caravan that was advertised to let, paid a week's rent, gave him basic food to take away with him, bought him a new pair of boots and some more clothes. With amazing rapidity, mother and the rest of the family converged on the Manse. Somehow they had heard Bobby was home, but we refused to tell them where he was staying. He did, in fact, to my complete amazement get a job, and he would come to the Manse each evening, often dodging in the back way to escape his searching family, and have his dinner with us. Janet and our lads, though like me thoroughly fed up with the whole McKie clan, were wonderful in their forbearance. In addition to his dinner, it seemed Bobby nightly needed a top up of his faith. But alas, the great reform lasted about 10 days, the family found him and off he went with them. Bobby's new found faith and resolution speedily crumbled before the onslaught of mother and the rest, and in no time he was in the hands of the law again.

Eventually, after many years, the authorities housed them in a cottage away out in the country where there were no neighbours to disturb, and Aldermouth, including the Manse, breathed again. The last I heard of them before leaving Aldermouth for my present Charge was that they had somehow succeeded in setting fire to their country cottage. Well, not quite the last, for after my first book *Vet in the Vestry* was published, I had a very warm-hearted letter from one of the girls, telling me that another of the boys and two of the girls had been killed in accidents, thanking me for what I had done, informing me that their mother was settled in her old age in Elgin, and wishing I was back in Aldermouth again! I was grateful for that letter, because, looking back, it has always seemed to me a story of unmitigated tragedy, a waste of lives, and massive failure on my part. I could only console myself with the thought that we, my whole family and a series of Assistant Ministers, Ben, Peter, Richard, Campbell and Donald, had tried very hard for twelve long years, and even the great "Physician Himself" sometimes could do no mighty works because of people's unbelief, and unwillingness to follow His way in life, and was comforted a little by His promise, He who loves all mankind,

"Inasmuch as you did it unto one of the least of these my brothers, you did it unto me."

"It's Chronic"

NINE

I would be about twenty-four when I discovered there was something abnormal about me. Whether it was a hereditary condition and some oddity was locked up in my genes, an undiscovered virus or possibly, as one consultant suggested, I was a carrier of Bacterium automobilis, could not be determined. Again a homespun philosopher was quite adamant that the whole thing was a series of coincidences, though this, of course, was impossible to establish. Whatever the reason, it is indisputable that over the years my presence in the vicinity of any form of internal combustion engine has sooner or later produced alarming symptoms in the creatures. Autocycles refused to budge when I was around; lawn mowers, be they two-stroke or four-stroke, the latter formerly considered an immune species, splutter and give up the ghost, and cars of any age, size, colour or make invariably show signs of distress. I myself am inclined to think it is an allergy, not that I am allergic to cars, but they most certainly are to me, for in time, any who have had contact with me just give up and refuse to budge. It is not that I ill treat them, nor have I actually caused grievous bodily harm to any of the species. They are regularly supplied with food and water, but inevitably they contract this automobilitis from me and turn ill, usually on some deserted stretch of road with no auto-hospital for miles.

Another frequent manifestation is specifically in the morning when they are quite unable even to leave the stable. I have never understood what exactly it is about me, and the experts are baffled, but the disease or disability is now so long established as clearly to be chronic.

The symptoms vary considerably. At times there is necrosis and subsequent amputation of exhaust pipes, a catarrhal, wheezy condition of the air passages, due sometimes to over much oxygen (O_2) or Carbon Monoxide (CO), then sundry groans from all parts of the external anatomy suggestive of rheumatoid arthritis, severed tendons in the CV joints affecting the limbs, an arteriol sclerosis of the main arteries causing clotting or other interference to the flow of life-giving fluid. Perhaps, commonest of all, is a stroke or other cerebral incident leading to complete paralysis.

The first indication that all was not well was on a cold, wet, November night, when, with my girl friend beside me, I was returning from my weekly evening off from the Mochrum Practice where I started my career, in the ancient but trusty Standard. We had, as always, spent the evening at an Ice-Hockey match, when half way home, the car just gave a quiet little moan and stopped. I suspected some form of disc or perhaps nerve trouble, for though I pressed the accelerator vigorously, and my foot would go right to the floor, no response came from the Standard. A telephone call to my brother Fergus brought him hurrying to the scene. Though not qualified medically, he had a working knowledge of first aid, and speedily, and extremely cleverly, I thought, discovered that a severed ligament was the trouble, the said ligament linking the accelerator or foot to the throttle or leg. A piece of wire provided a temporary artificial ligament, till some minor surgery next day put things right.

On the second onset of my condition, the symptoms were dramatic. The boss at Mochrum having taken delivery of a brand new Land Rover, I fell heir to his Ford Prefect. As was customary, I assumed that I could use it for pleasure, as well as business purposes, and was somewhat surprised when Mr. Buchan hesitated, said a guarded "yes," then added, "but I wouldn't go too far." It may be that he intended to retain the Ford in reasonable health and appearance for his own use periodically, since a Land Rover is hardly suitable for social occasions. On the other hand, I think, looking back, that he already realised all was not well with me. At any rate on my next monthly weekend off, Janet and I departed on the Saturday for Glentrool, some fifty miles away, there to enjoy a pleasant day in that renowned beauty spot. All went well, till we decided it was time to head for home, when to my utter astonishment and dismay, the gear box loudly protested, uttering the most frightful groans whenever I tried to coax it into action. I at first suspected cartilage trouble, but later decided it was some kind of brain disorder, for the poor Ford could not go forward, but readily would go backward. So we reversed over many a mile of rough, twisting road to the nearest phone box. I hesitated. Should I phone a garage or the boss? Recalling the latter's injunction, I tried all the garages around, but being Saturday evening, all were closed. So the boss it was, who, Mrs. Buchan informed me, was out on a case, and not expected back for some time. She would tell him of the Ford's serious condition when he returned, and she was sure he would speed to the rescue. We should just sit tight, and bring what consolation we could to the sufferer. I spoke to it in soothing tones, hoping it would enter into the spirit of the thing, and gallop off, but no, so I kicked it, told it this was ridiculous, and to get up off its hind legs, but this proved equally ineffective. Backwards it would go, and no other. The daylight faded, the evening shadows gathered about the stricken creature, and as a night mist descended Janet and I were forced to huddle together for warmth, which I found helped my morale considerably! Eventually the Land Rover ambulance arrived, carrying the boss, and bringing welcome sustenance to us in the form of a flask of tea and food. The sick car was taken in tow, and supported by the strong shouldered Land Rover proceeded up hill and down dale the long way back to Mochrum, with me at the wheel, thinking dark thoughts and feeling pretty desolate, for my best girl had deserted me for the warmth of the Land Rover, and I was pretty sure that Mr. Buchan, though he had been perfectly civil in the presence of a lady, might be rather less so on Monday morning when I reported for duty. I was quite correct in my assumption, and the boss made it absolutely clear that anyone with my record should never be allowed to take any vehicle, any distance, since he considered the risk of contamination was considerable. After some time in dock, the invalid eventually recovered, though I never fully understood the final diagnosis, something about bearings or big ends, whatever they may be!

Since both these incidents had occurred when Janet was present, I thought it just possible she was the source of the trouble, and this would have eased things somewhat for me, for to deliver a girl to her home at some unearthly hour and say "the car broke down" was so familiar a tale to parents as to be unbelievable. But since the next happening occurred when I, and I alone was involved, it was clear where the fault lay. This time it was our Devon Morris, COD 330, which suffered at my hands virtually from the first. It was a very ancient creature, my first car at Bristacombe, so I suppose it was understandable that regularly in the mornings it was too stiff to move, until assisted by Kenneth's Triumph. Perpetually the little van groaned and wheezed on its daily toil. Then something went wrong with the autonomic nervous system controlling the petrol gauge. The bug-allergy-virus-coincidence or whatever had struck again! It was dashed awkward, for I never knew whether I had a full or empty tank, so had to resort to rocking the car, and ascertain by its bowel sounds whether anything was present or not. Normally I carried a spare can for emergencies. But one day early in my stay in Bristacombe, I

was returning for a late lunch after a full morning of
work dehorning some thirty to forty Friesian cows for
Alf Spicer. Dehorning, particularly in dairy cattle, had
become very popular. It was safe, and apart from a head-
ache for a few days in each hornless beast, was not normally too painful, and it had been shown that the herd
milk yield increased since the timorous members of the
herd had no longer anything to fear from the bullies, and
so, thus liberated, were able to realise their full potential.
There is nothing complicated about the operation, being
rather like pulling thirty to forty sets of human teeth in
one morning! Nerve blocks with some form of cocaine
knocked out all feeling in the horns, usually, then a saw,
horn shears or embryotomy wire applied vigorously did
the rest. The choice of weapons largely depended on the
thickness of horn and the state of the operater's muscles.
As the hours pass, the rate of progress tends to slow
up as the biceps seize up. The common feature of all
dehornings is that there is a fair bit of blood flying about,
and the surgeon tends to cop it in the eye, ear, or even if
he stops to speak, the mouth, till the little horn arteries
are sealed off. It is I imagine not unlike the scene after
the Battle of Waterloo! Alf was clearly tired and ready for
his lunch, the cattle were pretty fed up at being denied
their morning ration of grass, and since I had surgery
waiting for me in early afternoon, the closing events
tended to be a bit hurried. Though wringing with sweat
under my protective clothing, I was satisfied that a quick
wash in a bucket would do me till I got home. Home
was seventeen miles away, and half way there, the disease
struck. COD 330 gave a few gurgles and expired. The
tick, tick, tick was diagnostic of an empty stomach. My
own was making much the same noise. I reached into the
back for the spare gallon, to find no can! There was
nothing for it but to walk to the nearest garage, beg for
a can, pay up, and promise to return the container. The
garage proprietor looked at me long and earnestly before
supplying my need, then came a weary trudge along the

busy highway, and through holiday crowds, who seemed to me to be acting most peculiarly. As I appeared, they would cringe away from me, and stand in little groups, pointing and chattering. I could make nothing of all this, but in the end put it down to the fact that as I was a Scot in Devon, I still had a "foreign" look which marked me out, just as the citizens of London can pick out Wembley bound Scots instantly. The old van, having been supplied with its life-giving fluid, wearily took up the struggle once more. Dropping off his can, I was again scrutinised by the garage man, who seemed to be jotting something down on a slip of paper as I departed. It was all very mysterious, till I looked in the mirror at home! My hair, face and neck were liberally spotted and streaked with blood, and clearly those beholding me were undecided whether I had tried to cut my throat, or someone else's, hence the garage man's bit of paper. COD 330 was the getaway car for number one suspect should any murder be reported in the West Country in the immediate future!

But the critical point of my allergic properties, or the zenith of my powers, depending on the way you looked at it, occurred on our honeymoon. For this Kenneth had graciously offered his brand new super Triumph, while he, for a fortnight, crammed his large frame into "Coddy" (COD 330) and developed a crick in his neck which took some time to straighten itself. On the very first day of our honeymoon, the disease, allergy or whatever, struck once more. Not even expensive new cars were safe. Proceeding in leisurely fashion, the morning after our wedding day, we had a whole lifetime ahead of us so why hurry, we were enjoying the beauties of the road to Morar, when some way past where Bonnie Prince Charlie had rallied the Highlanders to his cause, we picked up a hiker. He was not a hitch hiker, since that was still a rare breed, but a genuine hiker stepping it out with pack on back. I have always felt this was one of the most worthy acts in my life, and considering we were less than twenty-four hours married, it has seemed to me our deed almost warranted a mention in the New Year's Honours list, and was certainly not deserving of the events which followed! It may be, since we were near Cameron country, the influence was particularly powerful, or the allergy at its most potent, for shortly afterwards, great clouds of steam billowed from the Triumph's bonnet. It was a hot day, but hardly hot enough to account for this extensive sweat. Lifting his bonnet, it needed no thermometer to tell me that Triumph had a raging fever. We decided a rest might help him cool off, and this having taken place, I discovered that where there should have been water, there was none. The sufferer was completely dehydrated! We had an empty bottle, the hiker a Dixie can, so while the lady, now a Mrs. of almost twenty-four hours, took life easy, the two males trudged up hill to a Highland burn and stocked up with water, which the patient absorbed like a sponge. It took several trips to satisfy his phenomenal thirst. Clearly the fever was very acute, something like Anthrax, Malaria or Bracken poisoning, I suspected. Eventually his recovery was sufficient to let us proceed maybe ten more miles, when the whole range of symptoms was repeated, and the two men again took to the hills. So we proceeded, with many a stop, till eventually we limped into Morar, our destination, where we bade goodbye to the hiker who was glad to see the back of us! It is a moot point as to whether he would have made better time hiking along the highway, than driving, and certainly the number of hills he climbed that afternoon probably more than satisfied his hiking instincts for several days ahead.

Having deposited lady and luggage at our hotel, I hurried with anxious heart to the nearest expert on the internal organs of a car, and explained the symptoms in detail. I feared the worst, and was already reckoning that all our holiday money would have to go on a new radiator, which I understood was the car equivalent of a kidney transplant. The country car doctor had a quick examination, grunted, looked at me as if in all his years he had

never met anything so ignorant, and said, "Fan belt—
you haff no fan belt, man!" I gave a nervous little laugh,
said "Oh-ah-" and made a mental note that cars needed
a fan belt to keep their cool, or serious disease could occur
in the whole abdomen. I was learning! The fortnight
passed all too quickly, and from fields of Eden we had to
head once more for the fields of Devon. On the way, we
crammed every wedding present we could, including a
luxury armchair, into the car's rear, left a little tunnel for
a view in the mirror, and took the road south, at that time
innocent of all motorways, and infinitely more pleasing to
the eye, even allowing for the rose-coloured spectacles we
were both wearing! Some way on our trip, we encoun-
tered Kidderminster, where we decided it was tea-time,
and parked the car outside a restaurant, having carefully
observed that there was not a "No Parking" sign anywhere around. With the calories stocked up once more,
we meandered forth, to find a young PC, hands on lapels
and clearly meaning business, standing guard beside the
car. We were tempted to dart back inside the tea room,
in the hope that this new trouble would just go away,
but his eagle eye had spotted us, our anxious looks having
betrayed us. In that cool, competent voice which is the
first thing they teach budding "bobbies" at training
school, he enquired,

"Your car, sir?" Strictly speaking, it was Ken's, but I
replied,

"Er . . . yes!"

"You have been parked for almost an hour in a 'No
Parking' area!" Immediately I was all innocence, mingled
with an aura of outrage, and having glanced hurriedly
around again and failed to see any indication to the con-
trary, informed this senseless Sassenach of the fact that
there was no sign to support his accusation. He looked
at me doubtfully, and asked, "Are you a stranger here
sir?"

"Yes, never been here before, just passing through."
He paused a long time. I wondered what this latest car

trouble would lead to. It was bound to be jail, for we had not the price of a fine left between us. I wondered fleetingly if we would be allowed to share a cell, or if we would be allowed a phone call, shouting "Help" to Kenneth or the folks at home. All crime films seemed to indicate that a prisoner was allowed to make one call. The constable seemed to be pondering his next step. He took a long time at his pondering, but at last, with a voice full of regret and disappointment, and a look on his face like that of a fox hound which has just seen its fox disappear over the horizon, sighed,

"Oh, well, I suppose you wouldn't know, but 'No Parking' was painted on the road here before they re-surfaced it." Well! He was not finished yet, seemingly determined to add another "pinch" to his case book.

"Your car is very heavily loaded. Are you able to use your rear view mirror?" The car was, in fact, packed to the roof, and the cargo having slipped a bit, the view in the mirror was now about the size of a postage stamp, but I assured him we had come all the way from Scotland like that, could see behind us, and in a moment of bravado invited him to sit in the driver's seat, and see for himself. For one dreadful moment, I thought he would, but at last he nodded curtly, and said "Well, the next time you are in Kidderminster, remember you cannot park in this place."

"Oh, I don't think Kidderminster is included in our travelling plans for some time, is it dear?" I appealed to Janet. She backed me nobly.

"No, we hadn't thought of coming this way again in the near future," she replied, with the air of an experienced globe trotter. So we were allowed to proceed. I should like to have helped the poor PC, for he was clearly disappointed, and one never likes to cause hurt to a fellow human being, but then, disappointment is one of the character-forming facts of life!!

Many years have passed since these early attacks of the disease. It persisted at Moorton, and indeed very strongly at Aldermouth, and every car we have had has produced further examples of this odd syndrome. Apart from a Rolls Royce, which I would not care to risk, almost every other make of vehicle has proved my point about this being an allergy to something in me. Because of this condition, we have had to resort to binder twine, string, sellotape, chewing gum, ropes, children's school belts, coils of wire, pins, elastoplast and a host of other items essential to our first aid kit. I would strongly advise any fellow sufferer never to set out on a journey without the items I have mentioned, even if it means having to store the luggage on the roof. Thousands have been spent seeking a cure. We have sought the advice of many noted consultants, but the plague persists, so that at Aldermouth, whenever our local car GP, Chicky, heard my voice on the phone, he would merely groan and say, "Won't start again? Alright, I'll be along shortly," and he would arrive with his rescue wagon carrying about twice the normal number of spare parts. It appears that he, like me, realised that the condition was incurable. In fact, having been so long with me, I have to admit bitterly, it is chronic and as every GP in practice, human or animal, knows, such a condition is indeed the most difficult to cure!

Once Bitten-Twice Bitten

TEN

It was question time after a talk I had given to a Church Women's group on the work of a vet. I had been asked how to keep a dog from moulting, how to trim a poodle, how to stop dogs begging for scraps, how to stop a dog chasing cars, and other questions which were not really a vet's business and which I had waffled through. At last came one I could freely answer.

"Mr. Cameron! Yours is quite a dangerous job, are you often bitten by a dog?"

I smiled a superior smile, looked around my audience, straightened my tie and smugly answered,

"Never! If a vet is reasonably careful, there is no reason why he should be bitten by a dog, or for that matter a cat." Thus answers youth and inexperience, but pride, as the old adage has it, goeth before a fall, and soon I was to have to eat my words.

He looked harmless enough, indeed I was delighted to see a Scots terrier walk into my surgery in far away Devon. Not at all a common breed in that part of the world, and my heart warmed to him.

"He's a handsome fellow! What's his name?" I asked the owner who was a stranger to me.

"McTavish," came the reply, "and he's a perfect darling."

"What's his trouble?" I enquired.

"Well, we're on holiday in Bristacombe and he's dragging his rear end along the ground." The voice, unlike the breed of dog, was very clearly English, a big, florid woman, heavily made up, one of these who worships her dog, I mentally tabulated her.

"I expect it's his anal glands," I replied. "Let's have him on the table."

"My own vet usually lifts him up for me," so I proceeded to do the same, and as soon as I put my hands under him, he was round me like a flash, his teeth coming together with a sinister click as he just missed my hand. He stood on the table glancing round him solemnly, taking me in from under beetling brows, not a ghost of a smile anywhere, the caricature of a typical Scot who has just had to part with some money very much against his will.

"Has he had his glands expressed before?" I asked.

"Once, yes, by our vet in Pinner. A wonderful man! He really understands dogs."

Maybe I was over sensitive, but I felt the implication was obvious. I did not measure up to my colleague in Pinner, even though I had not done anything yet.

"It's a simple, but a little bit uncomfortable procedure, as I'm sure you know. Perhaps I better just slip a tape muzzle on him."

"Good gracious, no!" came the shocked reply. He's as quiet as a lamb and as harmless too. Mr.—never muzzles him."

"Just you steady his head, then, please, while I squeeze his glands."

The glands are situated just inside the rectum, produce an oily substance which assists lubrication, but in some dogs, often, though not always those fed on an unbalanced diet, the oil dries up, forms a brown cheezy substance, and produces discomfort in the rear. The remedy is simply to take a wad of cotton wool, and gently squeeze the anal ring, which clears the obstruction.

The lady took hold of her dog, if you could so describe

it, her hand gently resting on his head while she purred
to him,

"Mummy's darling!—a good little man—a nice boy—
who's a baa lamb then," and other terms of endearment,
while McTavish just stood there, glowering at all around
him, especially me, and muttering imprecations in his
throat. I lifted his tail, grasped the anus in the wad of
cotton wool and squeezed. The dog gave a growl, the
lady a yelp, and I a louder yelp as the stolid looking
McTavish sprang into action and his teeth, a fine set he
had, sank deeply into the back of my hand.

"Oh! You cruel man! You must have hurt him!" was
the response.

"Well—he certainly hurt me," I protested as the blood
welled up in the wound. McTavish stood as if nothing
had happened, making little noises in his throat which
sounded very like satisfaction at a job well done. It even
looked to me as if he was smiling. The owner was not
one whit concerned except for "Mummy's darling boy,
bad man hurt you, did he?" I held my hand under the
tap for a bit, dried it and clapping a bit of sticking plaster on it, turned back to my patient who was still muttering to himself between cuddles and kisses from his
owner.

"While we are here, could you look at his ears? I think
they need cleaning out."

"Right, but I'm sorry, he's got to be muzzled for that.
If he could catch me good and proper at his rear end,
he'll not miss at his head."

"Is that necessary?"

"Yes, I'm afraid so."

"Mr.—never muzzles him, but then he really understands McTavish. He's Scottish."

"So am I, and I like Scotties, but this one doesn't seem
to like me." I raised my voice "Ann!"

Our attractive and very efficient secretary/assistant
came through from her den.

"Just give me a hand with this dog, Ann, will you, and

watch yourself." Ann took him by the scruff of the neck,
I dangled a tape muzzle over his mouth and between
snaps managed to slip it over his jaws and tie it behind
his head. McTavish frothed at the mouth in frustrated
rage. Mrs. McTavish did not like it one bit either and was
more or less frothing too, but we ignored both. I peered
in his ears with my auriscope, and duly cleaned them out,
inserting a few drops of oil, while my fellow country-man
struggled and cursed continually. My love for Scotties
slipped down a peg. The job done, we removed his muzzle, and the owner immediately rushed forward to console
her "poppet," to be bitten smartly on the thumb! Her
endearments were cut off in mid flow.

"Oh, you bad, bad, bad boy, doing that to your
mummy!" I managed to restrain a smile, and while Ann
held on to the "poppet," I dressed the lady's thumb for
her. Somehow I felt the visit had not been a success.

After surgery that afternoon my first call was to an
Alsatian puppy who was described as poorly. I duly found
the house, down in the old Fishertown part of the town.
It was a poor little place, a two-room dwelling, with a
large double bed in the living room. The room was none
too clean, dirty dishes on the table, paper peeling off the
wall, and a smell of dirt and dampness. The mother of
the family and several grown up sons and daughters were
standing around, but I could see no dog. I was sorry for
the people and realised yet again how hard was life on
the dole, for Bristacombe, even then in the 1950s, had a
high unemployment rate, with virtually everyone depending on "the season" for a living. It was then the
season, but this family seemed to be still out of work and
I wondered that they had taken on the added commitment of a large dog.

After mutual greetings, I asked:

"Where's the patient?"

"He be under that bed like," responded one of the
sons.

"Just get him out, will you then," I asked.

"Us can't us 'as been tryin' all day, like, an' he just won't move. Oi think he likes the dark."

"Let's move the bed then."

So we did, but the dog kept moving with the bed, and we were no further forward.

"Look! I'm sorry, but I can't treat your dog unless you can get him out of there. Whoever knows him best get down on your knees and call under the bed." So they tried, one by one, and all together.

"Whisky! Here boy! Good lad!," but all that issued from the hiding place were growls and snarls. I did not like the sound of it at all. I grew more and more impatient for I had a long list of cases waiting to be got round. Finally, in my agitation, I broke one of the cardinal rules of vets, never tackle a sick dog when it is cornered. I should have used a dog catcher, a long pole with a noose on the end, but I had none with me, and was in a fever of haste to get on. I crawled under the bed, calling "Whisky, here boy, good lad," and reached for his collar. Even in this dim light I could see he was a nearly full grown pup, but very sick indeed, his eyes filled with pus, his rib cage heaving. Distemper for sure.

I got him out alright, his jaws clenched tightly over my wrist. The blood spurted, the pain was considerable, and I felt faint. He clung to my wrist, even when dangling in mid air. While the family looked on, none offering to help, I managed to prise open his jaws with my other hand and release my wrist. I thought I was going to be sick, and one glance at my wound showed me it was a hospital job, stop bleeding, stitches and tetanus injection, and probably an antibiotic since his mouth was also filthy with pus. Somehow I managed to pick up my case, told the silent onlookers ("after all—it be vetnary's job") someone would call next day provided they had the dog under control, and with one hand drove myself to the local hospital. I staggered in, feeling I would collapse any minute and in considerable pain from my lacerated wrist. Fortunately a doctor happened to be at our little Cottage

Hospital, and after a glance at my pale face and bloody
wrist, he made me sit down before I fell down. Then
followed the usual procedure of cleaning, disinfecting,
suturing, dressing and bandaging, a shot of anti-tetanus
serum, and instruction to go home and rest. I was surprised at how shocked I was, but mighty glad to get home
and collapse into a chair, and be coddled by my equally
shocked wife. Poor Bernard had to complete the cases for
that day, mine as well as his own, and as I lay back in my
chair, I suddenly remembered my words to the Women's
group.

"If a vet is reasonably careful, there is no reason why
he should ever be bitten."

Well, I had been bitten twice in one day, on the second
occasion through my own folly. I was never so foolish
again, but did over the years accumulate a few more
minor bites, always from small dogs, and usually ones the
owners were adamant "wouldn't hurt a fly."

I have been bitten a few times in the ministry too. As at
Moorton, in Aldermouth too, we had a regular flow of
gentlemen of the road at the Manse doors at all times of
the day till late at night. One drunk phoned me at one
o'clock in the morning and informed me he was a member
of Kirkconnel Church, a great buddy of the minister and
it was my duty as a minister to provide him with a bed
for the night. I knew all about that passage in Matthew
concerning visiting the sick, being hospitable to strangers
and lifting up the fallen, and indeed had preached on it,
but with a young family I was chary about who I had
sleeping in the Manse. Over the years I listened to the
most wonderful collection of hard up stories the mind of
man could devise, many cups of tea were dispensed,
clothes were given away, money for bus fares, and while
I gradually grew harder and knew that often, quite simply, I was being conned, frequently we helped in some
way or other.

I came home one afternoon to be met by a somewhat excited Janet.

"Darling, I've had here the most interesting man for much of the afternoon!"

"Oh?" suspiciously.

"Yes, he's one of the Murray-Fitzgeralds and has been giving me his story, and he's the most marvellous pianist you ever heard."

"Sounds as if you've had a good time. Is he still here?"

"Yes, he's been playing Beethoven, Chopin, Elgar, and oh I don't know who else."

"How does he come to be wandering the countryside?"

"Oh, he's fallen on hard times and the rest of the Murray-Fitzgeralds have kind of shut him off. Come and meet him." So I was led through to our sitting room where sat a little, shabbily dressed man.

"Ah, Padre!" he exclaimed at the sight of me, "how nice to meet you! Your lady had been listening to me play. Would you like to hear some Mozart?"

"Oh, ah well, alright."

So he sat down and played, apparently brilliantly, something that might have been Mozart or Murray-Fitzgerald. Not being up in classical music, I could not tell, but he certainly could handle the piano. After reams of music, for he just went on and on, I managed to get a word in.

"Are you on your way somewhere?"

"Yes—to Inverness. You see, I'm a scion of the Murray-Fitzgeralds but I've been cheated of my share of the estate and have fallen on somewhat difficult times. I should be much obliged if you could give me the price of a bus fare and I'll be off after the tea your lady has kindly promised me."

We talked for a bit while Janet went to get tea, and as we talked my suspicions grew. Murray-Fitzgerald he might have been, but there was something curiously off-key about his conversation. I excused myself and went in

search of Janet at the other end of our immense home,
in the kitchen preparing the meal.

"You know, lass, I'm sure all that's a load of rubbish."

"But his playing, Alec?"

"Oh sure, he can play alright and he seems harmless,
but I'm sure his stories are the fruit of his imagination."

He had his tea and talked incessantly, always with that
odd, peculiar quality to it, which unlike his handling
of the piano, was off-key. At long last he departed for
Inverness. We found out later he was an inmate of Craigdunain, the big mental hospital, and had escaped for an
afternoon, and for whom they had been searching. If only
he had said he was Winston Churchill, or Napoleon or
Gunga Din, we would have cottoned on more quickly.
Thankfully, he did not think he was Al Capone or Musso-
lini!

Our sons were long suffering, never knowing who
would be in the house when they came in from school,
nor with whom they would be sharing a meal. Actually
in the middle of lunch one summer day the front doorbell
rang and Neil, our eldest, went to answer it. He came
back and reported it was two people, a man and a lady,
quite young and wanting to see the minister. (Neil was
always polite, everyone of the female species has always
been designated a lady, a delightful trait in him, while his
younger brothers usually referred to them as "wifies"). I
duly went to the door to be met with a tale of woe. The
couple were from Bristol, I was informed, and their car
had got a puncture just outside our house. They had no
jack, and wondered if I could help. I went out and had a
look, and they certainly had a bobby dazzler of a flat tyre.
The car was no great shakes, either, looking as if it had
recently escaped from a junk yard. It was heavily loaded
with luggage and it appeared as if front and rear portions
were not on speaking terms and liable at any time to sue
for divorce. Across the back window was scrawled the
announcment "Just married," though whether this ap-

plied to the car or the couple was not at first clear. It appeared it was the latter who were young and seemed respectable enough. Remembering the car trouble we had had on our own honeymoon up north years ago, I immediately felt for them and invited them in while we got the car fit for travel again. I phoned my garage to come up and see to the tyre and ordered a new tyre, for the sufferer and the spare were completely bald.

By now anxious to help the cause of true love, I chatted to them and questioned them, for the garage had indicated it might be an hour before they could come to the sufferer's aid. It seemed the couple came from Bristol alright, had been honeymooning in the Highlands, touring, but had found troubles descend thicker and faster than usual in the state of matrimony. Somewhere in the far north the wife had gone into a ladies' room to wash, and had walked out, leaving her bag behind. Later on the journey they had realised their loss, raced back, but the bag was gone. This was disastrous for all the holiday money was in it. I thought the little husband was very trusting indeed, handing everything over to the wife this early, but it appeared he just never carried a wallet, and produced from various pockets reams of documents which confirmed his wallet-less state. He showed me his driving licence, receipt for the car and sundry other bits of paper, all in the name of Henry James.

"I wouldn't mind just so much," said the young gallant, "but my wife's ring was in the bag too." (I had noticed her ringless state and been suspicious.) "The ring was too tight, you see, and hurt her finger, so we were meaning to get it enlarged when we got back to Bristol. The police at Dornoch were marvellous," he went on, "and gave us some money for petrol. A minister helped us out too with some money, a kind man. Here's his card," and he produced it.

By now thoroughly sympathetic, I called Janet through and told her the story, and she too shared in the sympathy. She prepared a meal for them and while doing so the wife had a bath and the husband a shave with my razor, for it seemed they had slept in the car the previous night.

Eventually the car was ready for the road again, we gave them £7.00, enough then for petrol to Bristol (I had already told the garage to charge the tyre to my account), pored over maps about the best route south in those days of few motorways, and clutching two jars of Janet's bramble jelly, at last they departed, with multitudinious thanks ringing in our ears. We felt good, we had helped a genuine couple in genuine trouble, even though it had cost a pound or two.

They were picked up by the police the next evening near Aberdeen, having come a similar story to another minister who was more suspicious or less gullible than me. Aberdeen was nowhere near the road to Bristol, of course, and it turned out they were a notorious pair of con experts, working this racket as a team and already with a prison record. Well!

So over the years we saw many "patients," and no doubt were bitten many times, I found it by no means easy to pick out the genuine from the crooked, and I suppose one's consolation, if consolation it be, was that though we did get harder, more sceptical, more wordly wise, the Manse door was always open for those in need and I felt that was the way it should be. Big softie!

Night Life

ELEVEN

Brm, Brm . . . Brm, Brm, . . . Brm, Brm . . . Brm, Brm. . . .

I awoke to a ringing in my ears, and realised with a groan, it was not the angelic music of a dream, but the very opposite, the phone. The bedside clock showed 1:30 am. It was the month of March, the height of the lambing season, and this was an almost nightly occurrence.

"Hello! Bristacombe 250," I sleepily announced, hoping for that 100–1 chance it was a wrong number, faint hope at 1:30 am unless it was someone trying for a doctor or the police. At first there was just heavy breathing coming over the line.

"Great Scot!" I thought, "not one of these."

Then a voice sprang to life, a familiar voice with its splutter like the car engine sometimes on a damp morning.

"Mr. C.c.c.c.c.c. Cameron?"

"Yes, speaking."

"This is B..b..b..b..b..b..b..Bert Williamson. Sh..sh..sh..sh..Sheila's had an accident. Can you c..c..c..c..c..come please?"

I had it clearly now. Bert Williamson was a thoroughly decent man but with a very bad stammer. He was, moreover, a good client with his lovely English setter dog, Sheila.

"Right, Bert, I shan't be long," I told him, put the phone down, rolled over and swung my legs out of bed all in one go, a familiar technique I had perfected over many a night call. I always tried to be as quiet as possible and dress in the dark so as not to disturb Janet, but invariably she wakened.

"Lambing, dear?" came a sleepy enquiry from beneath the blankets.

"No, lass, an accident case, Bert Williamson's dog."

She grunted and turned over on her other side. The only time I envied my wife her life and work was when a night call came in. As I drove the mile to Bert's house, I recalled the last time I had seen him, just a few days before. He had the only English setter in town, a bitch, a beauty, and she had come in season. Very much wanting to breed from her, he had taken a taxi to kennels in Exeter, sixty miles away, and introduced Sheila to her husband to be. She was apparently not impressed, and would have nothing to do with the dog. Bert had waited all day, the taxi meter going all the time, then reluctantly returned to 'Combe. He stood beside the taxi driver counting out the considerable fare, and when he turned round, Sheila was being mated by the most scruffy old mongrel imaginable!

Bert appeared in my surgery a short time later, practically frothing at the mouth and spluttering like a machine gun. I have seldom seen a man so livid, and in his incensed state, with his stutter, it took him some time to explain what had happened. I had never heard a man with a stammer curse before, and in broad Devonshire, it was an impressive performance! I really could not refrain from laughing at the thought of him going all that way to Exeter and back, Sheila turning down a highly pedigreed show winner, and accepting a ruffian. We had given her stilboestrol, the recognised treatment for misalliance in those days of the early 1950s, and assured him all would be well, there would be no Heinz 57 puppies, but her heat period would be prolonged somewhat. Now it seemed Sheila was in more serious trouble, and I knew just how upset the likeable Bert would be for he adored his bitch.

A sobbing Mrs. Williamson answered the door to me, and mourned,

"Sheila seems bad, Mr. Cameron, and Bert's in a terrible state." Bert was, he was crying too as he knelt beside his bitch who was stretched out on the carpet before the fire. Mrs. Williamson, to my relief, acted as the speaker. She took less time and was infinitely easier to understand.

"Sheila somehow slipped out when us was sayin' 'goodnight' to some friends us'd had in, and she runned right in front of a car. Oh, the horrible screech of its brakes."

"Did the car go over her, Mrs. Williamson?"

"No-o, I don't think so, but hur seems right bad."

I turned to my patient. Her breathing was fast, her pulse fast, but the colour of her membranes was good. Gently I felt her over.

"Broken leg, Bert, but we can put that right. Let's see what else."

"Hur's b..b..b..b..-bl..bl..bl..-bleedin' at the mouth," Bert exploded into speech.

"That might not mean much, Bert. She could just have bitten her tongue, but let's have a listen at her chest."

Out came the stethoscope, no lung damage I could detect, and so far as I could ascertain, no major abdominal problems either. She had a nasty gash on the shoulder which would require stitching, but that was no difficulty.

"I think she's been lucky, Bert. We'll soon fix her up."

So the common routine was carried out. First an injection for shock, then a sedative to ease pain and make her sleepy, and I set to work with the old Gypsona plaster of paris bandages, soaking them in water and wrapping them up and down the leg like splints—nothing difficult about it, only messy, and the sole hazard being to make sure the bandage was tight enough, but not too tight. Then a scrub of the hands to get rid of excess plaster, dressing her shoulder wound, and while the gentle bitch lay there unmoving and the plaster on the leg hardened, stitching up the cut shoulder.

Meantime Mrs. Williamson had been clattering about with cups and plates, and as soon as I was finished, the tea was on the table.

"Us be right grateful to ee, Mr. Cameron," said the little woman, "comin' out of youm bed an' all, but if owt serious like happened to our Sheila, I don't know what us ad do."

Bert nodded in agreement. They were a childless couple and the dog was their family, their pride and joy.

"Don't worry, Mrs. Williamson, Bert," I assured them. "That kind of clean break heals well. She shouldn't have a limp at all, and the hair will soon hide the scar on her shoulder. She won't breed this time round, but she's young enough to wait a bit. I'll look in tomorrow, or rather later today and see how she is," I yawned prodigiously and apologised.

"Sorry, folks! I had a long day today, or yesterday and it's time for me to be off."

So I left these kindly, humble folks and headed back for bed. It took me a few minutes to drop off, and I had scarcely fallen asleep, it seemed, when the phone went again, 3:30 am this time.

"Hello, Mr. Cameron," said a bright, perky voice. "Arthur Hazlett here. Got a ewe bad to lamb. Will you come out?"

"Yes, Arthur, of course," I grunted, as I groaned quietly to myself and yawned at the same time.

"She's in the top field. Leave your car on the main road and walk across two fields. That will be your quickest way. You'll see my lantern waving. I'll be up there by the time you get out."

So with the old corduroys, a thick jersey this time, and out into the darkness once more. A drive of just five miles through the night mist, a walk across the two fields, sheep scurrying before me like wraiths in the mist, my objective, the waving lantern just visible in the distance. The patient was in the shelter of a typical high Devon hedge-cum-wall, and Arthur there waiting with a tattie bag for me to kneel on, a bucket of water which had been hot when he left the house, but was now barely lukewarm, soap and a towel. I poured some disinfectant into the water, rolled up my sleeve, soaped an arm, knelt down and felt inside the ewe. What kind of trouble would it be this time? Why type of presentation? Almost at once I realised with relief that this was one of the easier ones, indeed my favourite lambing problem.

"Twins, Arthur, locked and intertwined, but the ewe has plenty of room. This shouldn't take long."

Nor did it, for basically all you do, in case, dear reader, you ever have to deliver twins is say to one,

"Just you wait there a minute, my dear" and to the other "up you come."

Putting it in more technical terms, you sort out the tangle of legs, then repel one lamb and advance the other, and in ten minutes the job is done. As I dried my arm I grinned at Arthur. This was the good bit, the job done, a healthy ewe already on her feet licking her offspring and giving that lovely, throaty chuckle which you get only from a sheep after lambing. It was a cold, damp night, but we waited to see the lambs stagger to their feet, heading for the milk bar for that first, all important drink of mother's milk, finding their way with unerring, inborn instinct. This was the little miracle that made the toughest lambing worthwhile and that never palled on me or grew commonplace.

"Would you mind very much, Mr. Cameron, coming down to the farm when you're here anyway and seeing a lamb with joint ill?"

Somewhat wearily I said,

"Alright, Arthur, lead on with the lamp."

We reached the farm to be welcomed by Arthur's wife, Kathleen who was equally as bright as her husband, and I marvelled at the stamina of these farmers and their wives which would keep them going day and night for six weeks in the lambing season.

"You'll have tea, Mr. Cameron, won't you. The kettle just has to boil." The table was already laid, as it nearly always was in our Devon farms, where the hospitality was quite tremendous. I had a look at Arthur's lamb, a big one, which had joint ill right enough, all its joints being swollen and stiff, and a discharge coming from the navel.

"That's where the infection gets in, Arthur."

"I know. I must not have dressed this one right." I gave the lamb a hefty injection of penicillin and left Arthur the bottle to give a shot for several days, for joint ill can often be tough to shift. Then we drew our chairs into the table, which was laden with food, as if it was a normal tea-time instead of half past four in the morning.

"We had an interesting man at our Bible Study tonight, well, last night," said Arthur, "a missionary from the Congo. What stories he had to tell! I admire these men who go off to wild places like that. They must have great courage."

"And faith, Arthur, that's the main thing," said his wife. Not to be outdone, I chipped in and said, "and love. Did Paul not say somewhere that was the greatest thing?"

"1 Corinthians 13," immediately retorted Kathleen. She knew her Bible from cover to cover. They were members of the Plymouth Brethren, but unlike some of the Brethren, not at all narrow or hidebound and as they talked, I sat back and marvelled. The Hazletts were a delightful couple, their farm was too small to enable them to pay a man, but no matter how busy they were, they seldom missed the Sunday worship or the week night Bible Study. It was an education to listen to their talk. Their faith just shone out of them. It was as if they had found the secret of life and were totally content. I had seen this in a number of farmers and friends in Devon, and though I did not know it then and had not the slightest thought of becoming a minister, it was, I realised later, when I did feel drawn to the ministry, people like the Hazletts who had turned my thoughts to life's basic and lasting values, and made me in the end want to share with others this faith in their Lord.

But the night was going on. I looked at my watch, 5:30 AM. We had talked for an hour and as always, with people who are the salt of the earth, kindly, sincere, genuine, just plain good, the time had flown. I trudged back to my car, somehow lightened and cheered, even though soon in that raw night air I was chilled right through my thick jersey. Then home, and that delicious moment when I would snuggle into my wife's warm back. She never complained even though I often came in like an icy blast straight from the North Pole. In my contented frame of mind, a good dog repaired, lambs delivered, a sick lamb helped, and a kind of inner peace through just having spent an hour with Arthur and Kathleen. This time I was asleep in an instant.

As with all vets, the phone call at night was a regular disturber of the peace, but on one occasion the peace was well and truly shattered, and the phone had not given the merest little peep. The occasion, which came more into the category of things that go bump in the night, was one night when our friends Mike and Audrey Hutchison were staying with us in our little, jerry-built house grandly called Chade Lodge, which we rented along with the buildings behind from the local council. The whole thing had once been the town's abattoir and the buildings were ideal for kennels and for keeping poultry in deep litter. Mike had been at Vet College with me, and he and Audrey, now in Ulster, have been lifelong friends. Our adventures at the kennels have been recounted elsewhere, but this night call was in the house alone. Chade Lodge still had gas lighting, which was the crux of the problem that night.

What happened was that I was awakened by a stealthy creak on the stairs as someone surreptitiously ascended. It was about two o'clock in the morning, pitch dark, and as I heard this sinister creak, my flesh crept and my hair

stood on end. Clearly we had an intruder of some kind.
I put my hand over my sleeping partner's mouth to prevent her screaming, and whispered in her ear.

"There's somebody coming up the stairs."

She too was instantly awake, listening to this slow
creak, creak which gradually seemed to be getting nearer.
We lay where we were, the terror of night and the unknown gripping us. We were a petrified pair! Slowly and
quietly I slipped out of bed and fumbled my way over to
the gas light which had a pilot jet on it which burned all
the time, so that when one pulled a little chain the light
popped on, but the pilot jet had gone out, a bad habit it
had in our room. Often a box of matches was kept on
the mantel shelf for just such an emergency, but no
matches could be found. Here was a fix. We were about
to be attacked in our bedroom, it seemed, by a burglar,
and we could not see a thing. By now the "footsteps"
seemed to have stopped just outside our door, so Janet
leapt out of bed and stood by the window, ready to jump
out of our upstairs room if somebody entered. I was
no braver and thought I would call for help. So quietly
opening the window, I stuck my head out and in a voice
that was no more than a croak called across the few yards.
"Mike, Mike," to their window, "put your light on." I
knew their pilot jet never went out. As is by now obvious,
I am not particularly brave, and in the dark, having been
rudely wakened from sleep, I was frankly terrified of the
unknown. I called and called but Mike and Audrey were
apparently sleeping the sleep of the just, or had already
been murdered in their beds, and they never stirred. We
could only wait, it seemed, till our door handle turned
and our visitor was in our room.

Then I remembered the box of matches that was always
kept on the ledge on the landing, outside the three bedroom doors which were all adjacent in our pokey wee
house. So, having to show my manly courage before my
young wife, I suddenly opened the door, dashed out a
pace to the ledge, grabbed a box of matches, and slam-

ming the door behind me, rushed for our gas light, and
with trembling fingers, lit the wretched thing. Now we
were more brave. At least we would be able to see our
assailant, but no one came in. So I quietly again opened
the door and peeped out, nobody, nothing. While Janet
remained at her window, I searched the house, but all
seemed in order. There appeared to be no unauthorised
inhabitants. Finally we went back to bed, and put the
light out. However, the creaking sounds began again on
the stairs. We lay and trembled. We had not heard that
Chade Lodge had a resident ghost, but maybe there was
one, perhaps the shade of some long-gone cattle slaugh-
terman who had met a sticky end on the horns of a bull,
or shot himself by mistake with his humane killer.

So the out of bed, light the gas, search the house procedure was repeated. All was still. Every time the light went
on, the creaks stopped. Once more back to bed, creak,
creak, and as we shivered under the clothes, it seemed to
me the sounds were not on the stairs, but actually in our
room. This, if anything made matters worse. It could
only be a supernatural visitant. By now we were angry
at this person or thing playing tricks on us, and anger
overcomes fear. I opened cupboard doors, pulled out
drawers, and as I opened our wardrobe door, I saw him.
It was a mouse nibbling at the wood! I leapt back, the
mouse leapt out into the room, and Janet leapt on the
bed. A mouse scurrying about our bedroom in the middle
of the night was less frightening than a burglar or a
headless shade, but we clearly would get no sleep till we
had dealt with our little four footed frightener. So in
traditional fashion, I grabbed a poker and chased that
mouse round the room, poking under the bed, round and
round we went until the little animal was in a corner. It
would be more terrified than we had been, but it had to
go, and a poker was a quick death. I got a shovel, removed
the body, and then giggling with pent up nervous tension, and somewhat ashamed, we finally got back to bed.
Our little family and Mike and Audrey had never heard

a sound and slept through it all, and there was hilarious laughter at breakfast time at our reaction to this thing that went, if not bump, but creak in the night.

Of course, working hours for a minister are rather different from that of a vet, and night calls in our first Charge of Moorton were practically unknown. At Aldermouth the phone would often go late at night when we were preparing for bed or just into it for people knew, in that extremely busy Church, that practically the only time they could guarantee to get the minister himself was late, when he had finished his round of evening visits, or come in from some meeting. Frequently colleagues in the ministry would phone up about something, for they worked similar hours. But calls through the night were almost unknown. It had to be someone very ill, a death, or a person stranded for the night and wanting a bed, to disturb our sleep. I have sometimes explained to people, to their obvious disbelief, that I often worked a longer week as a minister than a vet, but one could usually guarantee a peaceful night and undisturbed sleep, which was a great boon.

One night, however, about two o'clock in the morning, Janet and I were roused with a loud peal on the front door bell, followed by hammering and thumps at the door. Somebody seemed also to be calling out or moaning. I jumped out of bed, threw on a dressing gown and had a peep out of the turret window of our bedroom from which we could see the front door, but in the dark all I could make out was a shadowy figure with its finger fixed firmly on the door bell. I went to the door, and before opening it, suspecting a drunk, called out "Who's there?" There were various mutterings from the other side of the door and constant cries of "Help me!" I cautiously opened the door and peered out and immediately a man rushed in, fell at my feet, grasped me round the knees and cried, "Oh Father, Father, you've got to help me. My father's come back. He's a ghost now!" I managed to free my imprisoned legs, got the man to his feet, and he more or less fell into our large hallway. He was in sheer terror, but I could make nothing of his explanations, so took him into the study, switched on the electric fire, sat him down in a chair and tried to unravel the mystery. He said his name was Dawson, so I knew him to be a cousin of the notorious McKies, but I had never seen him before. He was a tall, round shouldered, lean individual with a pale face, though whether naturally pale or from his fright, I didn't know.

"Tell me what the trouble is, slowly," I commanded.

"Oh, Father," he kept pleading. "I need help. Something terrible has happened. I want you to help me and pray for me for I've done terrible wrong."

"I'll help you if I can, and I'll certainly pray for you, but if you want a Father, you've come to the wrong house. The priest stays just round the corner. I'm a minister."

"No, it's you I want, Mr. Cameron," he pleaded.

He really was a pathetic figure, cringing, whining, in terrible distress. Clearly something extraordinary had nearly unhinged his brain. At last I got him calmed down a bit and his story came out in spurts, between cries for help and confessions that he had been a bad son.

"My father came through the wall of my bedroom tonight," he said with a shudder.

"Your father, *through* the wall?"

"Aye, that's right."

"But your father's dead."

"I ken, but he came back the nicht. Oh, it wis him a' richt an' he came into the room and just stood lookin' at me and pointing."

"Now calm down, Mr. Dawson. It couldn't have been your father and why would he point at you."

"Well, you see, I promised him I wouldn't drink and I've been drinking tonight. I've been a bad son, and he just stood looking at me." He sobbed with his face in his hands, then again fell at my feet, grabbed me and begged me for help. Now, while my business, in a sense could be said to be supernatural, I had had no experience of ghosts or other-worldly apparitions, had never been asked to exorcise a house, and I felt baffled. He clearly had drink in him, and I suppose in retrospect he was having a bad attack of the DTs, but though, of course I had seen the typical DT before, after a drinking bout, this was something new. That man was utterly and completely convinced his father had returned to rebuke him, and sheer terror looked out of his eyes.

"Coffee," I thought, "get him some coffee and calm him down. Play it naturally and coolly."

But he did not want coffee. He screamed at the suggestion of my leaving him to go to the kitchen. Just then, Janet's startled face appeared round the door, clearly wondering what in all the world was going on, with screams and other odd noises not usually heard in the Manse.

"It's alright, lass," I said. "Go back to bed. This is Mr. Dawson come to talk about a problem."

Janet shared completely in my life and work. Indeed without her I doubt if I could have given myself to others as a minister has to do, and I had often wondered how bachelor ministers or priests could do their work in full.

So it went on that night. I am not at my brightest or most patient in the middle of the night, but I had to listen to his story which I did several times over. Finally I said,

"Now, I'm sure it will be alright. Your father will have gone by now. We'll have a prayer together . . . ," he interrupted me

"You'll pray for me?"

"Alright, I'll pray for you."

So I did, and whether it was the prayer, or something I had said that was the healing medicine he needed at that moment, I know not, but he calmed down and asked me for a book to help him to be a better son. No doubt a psychiatrist could explain the whole business in a minute! I got up.

"Come, Mr. Dawson, I'll run you home," which I did, to be rewarded with voluminous thanks.

Janet was awake when I got back.

"What was all that about, dear?" she asked.

"A kind of lambing, lass. At least I've been at a delivery."

The Weekly Trial

TWELVE

Perhaps the most effective sermon I have ever preached was not preached by me at all! Perhaps I had better start at the beginning to satisfy the questing mind!

It began when we returned from our holidays to be met by John Duggie, our Church Officer, with a distinctly worried look on his face, not at all his usual cheerful self was John as he announced to us while we were parking the caravan, "Granny's disappeared!"

Here was not merely mystery but calamity of a high order. We had gone off, confidently leaving John in charge of the Manse, including Bruce the dog who was greatly attached to him. Granny was not accompanying us on holiday, but we were not worried about her, for she was an independent old lady, and John had promised to look over each day and make sure all was well, but on the very morning of our return, there was no sign of her anywhere about the place.

We all sat down with a cup of tea to revive us, and trying to console ourselves with the thought that she was sure to turn up. But she did not, so we searched everywhere. Night came, but still Granny did not appear. Here was crisis indeed! The next day a full scale search was instituted, but she remained missing. Days passed, then relief, she had been found, and in a most unusual place. In the field beside the Manse were dozens of bags of sticks waiting for me to deliver to our old folks. Covering them was a tarpaulin, and there, sitting beneath it, quite unconcerned and totally unharmed, was the old lady herself. The weight fell from our shoulders, the world took on a brighter hue, life returned to normal! Granny was safe beneath the tarpaulin and safe beneath Granny were ten brown eggs. Our venerable bantam had decided to become a mother again!

In due course the chicks arrived, pecking their way into the big wide world, and you never saw such a mixture. They outheinzed Heinz! Some were black, some white, some speckled, for Granny's ancestry was a bit doubtful and her husband was grey and white. It seemed a heaven-sent opportunity for a lesson to the children in Church the following Sunday, so, ignoring the glances of my predecessors whose portraits hung on the vestry walls, and whom I felt might not have approved, I took Granny and two of her offspring into the pulpit with me, the birds well concealed in a box. They kept very quiet during the opening hymn and prayer, and then I began my talk to the large crowd of children. We thought of how we were all different on the outside, some black, some white, some brown, different kinds of noses, different eyes, hair and so on but we were all the same inside, "for boys and girls, 'man looks on the outside, but God looks into the heart'."

Then I showed them Granny, to gasps and laughter from the very big summer congregation, and like the superb actress she was, she looked around the vast throng and clucked straight into the microphone, playing her part to perfection. I am certain it was the first time a hen had addressed an audience in Aldermouth. Briefly her story was told, then the two chicks were shown. I did not dare risk any more lest they escaped and had 600 people scrambling about to catch them. One chicken was white, one black, but both were equally dear to their little mother, "just as precious to her, boys and girls, as everybody is to God our great father. Different colours, but the same parent, you see." Her duty done, the old girl and her two bairns were restored to their box, and removed by one of the Cameron boys back to her field, and the remainder of her loudly cheeping family. I did not dare keep poultry in the pulpit for the rest of the Service lest they got out or kicked up a shindy in the middle of the sermon. For I had once seen a sermon ruined by an animal. It was at Maryshall in the little village Church we attended, situated about a mile from my home. The Service was held in the afternoon, it was a hot summer day and the Church doors had been left open for air, when plumb in the middle of the minister's discourse in trotted my Collie dog, Glen, which I had been given for passing my Highers, purchased for the large sum of £1.00. Glen trotted right up to the choir area and stood there smiling, panting, and wagging his tail, as he looked up at all the Cameron males in the choir. The audience was convulsed, the minister tried gamely to carry on, finally in a far from pleased voice saying, "Take no notice of it. The Devil has sent this creature to divert us from the Word of God." I was not in agreement with the clergyman that *my* dog could be an agent of "auld Nick," but I saw his point and removed my dog from the Church.

This business of Granny, a gimmick, I can hear many say, but I prefer to call it an audio-visual aid, went down well. Come to think of it, the Master Teacher used plenty of these too, you will find them in the four gospels and they were well received by His congregation too! Certainly for weeks folks stopped me in the street to comment on the mother hen and her chicks. My sermon to the adults was soon forgotten but Granny had put over a message that gripped every one of her hearers, poultry in the pulpit had achieved more than the minister!

Unfortunately such an act is hard to follow. Some preachers are very fond of the gimmick, which is valid, if it really has a worthwhile point to make. Even in a bygone age it seems some used a visual aid like the old minister on Temperance Sunday who was preaching on the evils of drink. Into the pulpit he took two jelly jars one with water, and in the other, gin. At the appropriate point of the sermon he produced them and from a tin took two earthworms. He dropped one into the water and it wriggled about quite happily but the one in the gin had a quick demise.

"Now," thundered the preacher, "what lesson does this teach us?" From the body of the Kirk a voice called out, "If you've got worms, drink gin!" There was one lesson that had gone awry!

I suppose only another preacher realises the difficulty of sermon preparation and delivery, particularly in these days when people are attuned, not to listen, but to watch scenes on "the box." I remember Andrew Eastham telling me he found preaching got, not easier, but more difficult as he got older. Certainly the weekly trial by public exposure as it has been described is totally different from any other form of address. For a start, one is conscious of one's own failings, and sometimes I feel we have no right to preach to others. There is the awareness that there will be criticism, and many families have roast preacher for Sunday lunch! Difficult too, weekly to have something worthwhile to say, and to hold a congregation's attention without their going to sleep.

The story is told of a certain Church where the senior elder, who sat right in the front seat, always had a snooze during the sermon. One day a student was taking the Service, and in the vestry he found some notes from the regular minister who was away on holiday. Among them was a PS.

"If an elderly gentleman drops off during your sermon, don't worry or take offence. He does it every week."

But the fiery young student was determined nobody should sleep during his discourse. Sure enough, during the sermon, the old boy dropped off, so the preacher, in the middle of his address, in a quiet voice, said,

"Stand up, all those who want to go to Heaven."

The whole congregation stood except the old man who

had not heard the words. Consternation in the Kirk! The senior elder did not want to go to heaven. The preacher carried on for a bit, then said, "All those who don't want to go to heaven, stand up," bellowing the last two words. The old elder got to his feet and looked around him, then looked at the man in the pulpit and said "I dinna ken whit we're votin' aboot, meenister, but you and I are in the minority."

Then there is the tension, the stress, of standing up before a group of people, be it twenty or a thousand (and it is easier to preach to the latter for the atmosphere lifts one), and most ministers are afflicted with pre-pulpit nerves on a Sunday. I think most of us find it easier to give an after dinner speech, or a wedding toast than to preach, for preaching is totally different from other forms of public address. I recall speaking to my New Testament lecturer, the famous Dr. Barclay who was the best communicator of the gospel and teacher I have known, making it viable, reliable, relevant, understandable, real, to the most ordinary mind, and doing this in the pulpit, on the radio and in his many TV series, which had the whole of Scotland watching. I asked him when he lost his pulpit nerves for he always seemed so calm and unruffled, never stuck or lost in his discourse. Like a flash he answered me, "Alec, I haven't lost these butterflies before I go into the pulpit, and I hope you never will, either, for the day you do, it has just become a job to do and you're no further use to the Lord." I am sure Willie Barclay was right. I personally, and I think most other ministers too, like to be alone and quiet for a few minutes before entering the pulpit, a quietness my Beadle John saw that I got every Sunday at Aldermouth before he would come, in his understanding way, and ask, "Alright, Mr. Cameron?" I often felt like the late, great Tom Allan who had a Beadle like John. One day as he was going out the vestry door for the Church, Tom hesitated, and his Beadle, anxious, asked, "Alright, Mr. Allan?" Tom Allan smiled

and said, "Yes, Bob, I'm just marvelling that the Lord
trusts someone like me with His message."

Willie Barclay, however, in contrast to most of us,
always preferred to have someone to talk to right up to
the moment he entered the Church.

But, of course, pulpit nerves can be excessive and embarrassing. I know of one young man who had to give
up the ministry for a time because he was actively sick
before facing his congregation, not that he had a congregation that made him sick, let me emphasise, just an acute
case of nerves.

Then there was another young fellow about to preach
his first sermon. The Beadle, and the Scottish Beadle is
often a real character, advised him, "If you stick at any
point, just put your arm up and say 'Lo, I come.' It
doesn't mean anything but looks good and gives you time
to think."

Sure enough, when it came to the sermon, the young
minister's notes were a blur, the congregation seemed a
sea of hostile faces and he wanted to run away. But he
tried the Beadle's recipe. Up went the right hand and he
intoned "Lo! I come." Still nothing happened. He was
stuck. So he tried the left arm with the same negative
result. Finally he thrust both arms heavenwards and bellowed "Lo! I come" and as he did so he stepped back and
tumbled down the pulpit stairs, landing in front of a lady
sitting in her pew and minding her own business. He got
up covered in confusion and full of apologies to the lady,
who tried to comfort him with the words, "Think nothin'
o' it, son. You tellt me three times you were comin'. I
should have been ready for you!"

But *the* great difficulty is the content of the sermon.
What am I to preach about this Sunday, morning and
evening? Of course there are books of sermons by the
dozen, but I have always felt it dishonest to use another
man's work, though many a good illustration has been
"borrowed" from another. The great events of the Chris-

tian year, Christmas, Easter, Whitsunday are a help in
their seasons, but, like Andrew Eastham, I too have found
preaching gets no easier as one gets older and I still have
the butterflies. Many a time I have sat with a blank sheet
of paper in front of me in my study, and after an hour it
is still blank. I have, however, had two guiding principles
over the years. "Preach the gospel, the great certainties of
our faith, for maybe there will be someone there hearing it
for the first time, and someone hearing it for the last."
The other guide has been, "remember at least one person
in your congregation has been going through a hard, or
anxious time, so try to strike the note of comfort."

I recall one of my Assistants at Aldermouth phoning
me one Thursday in a panic. He was due to preach one
of the Sunday's sermons. "I'm stuck!" he wailed, "I've
known for a month I had to preach this Sunday, and I've
spent days on it, but I'm not getting anywhere." I went
round to see him, had him preach what he had to me,
made a few suggestions on his theme, then tried to comfort him with the words an old divine had given me.

"The manna falls when it is needed."

"I wish it would," said the lad plaintively, "when I
came here I had only two sermons and I've preached both
of them. How in all the world can you do this twice a
Sunday year after year?"

I doubt if one in a hundred of the average congregation
appreciates the travail and anguish that goes into making
a sermon. The old adage about a sermon being ten per
cent inspiration and ninety per cent perspiration is not
far off the mark. It is a notable week when the sermon
just falls into place, but now and again it does happen. I
recall in my vet days, when I was doing a bit of lay
preaching, getting an idea as I drove down a farm road
with about six gates on it to open and shut, an odd place
to get inspiration, but somehow as I bumped along an
idea just flashed into my mind complete with three points,
and I stopped briefly at the last gate and jotted down the
headings before the idea, as quickly, flashed out again.

But that is the exception. Over the years I estimate that each sermon has taken up to ten hours preparation, and with two of these to prepare, plus perhaps a Bible Class talk and most weeks school talks or addresses to Guilds, Rurals, Women's Institutes, Rotaries, Men's Fellowships and so on, this hidden work of the ministry is something of which few in the pew are aware. But somehow, week by week, the manna does fall. Sometimes a sermon is well prepared, well illustrated, as perfect as an imperfect pastor can make it. On another occasion, in a busy week, something has to be put together in a hurry, and sometimes that is the one that clicks. The late A J Gossip, one of the great names in the Kirk forty or fifty years ago, a master preacher and teacher, used to tell how one week he had been simply over the head with work, so his sermon was hastily put together at the last minute. As he turned the bend in the stairs of St Matthew's in Glasgow, Jesus met him and asked "Is that the best you could do for me today?" Thinking back to the kind of week he had had, Gossip said, "Yes, Lord," and that day, that hastily slapped together address was a word of tremendous power, enthralling his hearers. A strange experience, yes, but those who heard Gossip tell that story could not doubt the reality of his experience.

But there are the special occasions when one simply *has* to be well prepared in advance, like a Broadcast Service. I remember well my first experience of this in my Moorton days. In these years of the early 1960s, Services went out live, not pre-recorded. There had never been a radio Service from Moorton before and the whole community was buzzing, but faced with a problem. They did not know whether they preferred to go to the Kirk and take part or stay at home and listen to *their* Church on the radio! I remember on the morning of the Service walking in the quiet of the garden to calm me before going over to the Church and one of our young elders, Maxwell Watson, came strolling along. When he saw me he stopped suddenly, hummed and hawed a bit, then said,

"Is it no' time you should be in the Kirk?"

"Och, Maxwell," I replied, "I thought I would just stay at home and listen to myself on the radio."

I can still see Maxwell's puzzled face as he worked that one out!

Much work had gone into the preparation of the whole Service, readings being practised by the readers, hymns rehearsed and everything down to the Lord's prayer and Benediction timed to seconds to make sure the whole Service would be included and time given at the beginning for the Church bell and at the end for the organ, played by a young teenager called John Bell who went on to become a minister, Rector of Glasgow University, a noted hymn writer, expert with young people, and one of the leaders of the Iona Community. On our broadcast day, most of the community finally came, sat like mice for the last few minutes before we went on the air, their eyes and mine fixed on the red light to tell us it was zero hour. Many of them also bought a record prepared by a company, which went round all the Churches having a Broadcast Service. Little Moorton was put on the map.

Quite early in my stay at Aldermouth we had two radio Services, one in August for Radio Scotland, and the other in October for the World Service. By now Services were being recorded in advance and one was not quite so terrified at making a mistake. I recall the engineers having great difficulty with a buzz they could not trace. They tested all their equipment and the microphones for some considerable time before discovering the mysterious noise was coming from an elderly gent's hearing aid! Again everything had to be timed almost to the split second, one's prayers and sermon submitted in advance for approval, and again the Record company had a bonanza in sales. I was told afterwards that a quarter of a million people had heard the first Service, and I felt a tremendous sense of privilege and responsibility in having such an audience. Apparently the overseas broadcast went all over the world and I had letters from Canada, New Zealand, South Africa and the West Indies.

But none of the radio Services, tense though I was, compared to the first time I had to do "Late Call" on Scottish Television. I had submitted my notes in advance along with a number of slides of hills, valleys, rivers, sheep and shepherds to weave into the talks for I was speaking on the Shepherd Psalm—Psalm 23. I was assured all I had to do was read my words off the autocue. The studio was the size of a barn and in one corner sat technicians playing cards or reading the paper, while in another was the camera, autocue and me—trembling like a leaf. Half way through the first talk the autocue broke down and I was left stuttering like a machine gun and finally gaping like a stranded goldfish. The producer came galloping down from his lofty abode above my head from where he surveyed proceedings, and looked at me with pleading, "Mr. Cameron, for goodness sake try to look a bit more pleasant and happy. Remember it's the Good News you are supposed to be putting over."

I found it far from easy to look pleasant, let alone joyful, with the card playing technicians who between "takes" shuffled reluctantly over to the camera to do whatever technicians do, looking bored. The cameraman and the autocue girl looked equally bored, but after three hours of rehearsals and recordings I staggered out in a daze. It so happened that my week's series went out particularly late that week for there was a bye-election on somewhere, but the good folks of Moorton sat up to see their man on the box, and five minutes after I said "goodnight," every light in the village was doused. I imagine they had all been sitting in pyjamas and dressing gowns, but bless them, they *did* wait up.

Of course the more one is in the public eye, or ear, the more criticism one can expect, but I was fortunate, for most of those who wrote to me were at least civil, some congratulating, some seeking help, but always I had one from some bigot condemning me for not using my opportunity to berate the Roman Catholic Church as of the Devil and the Pope, the anti-Christ himself.

On the whole, though, I escaped lightly, not like my New Testament lecturer, Dr. Barclay, whom I have quoted several times already and who influenced generations of students from home and overseas. In the Spring of 1961 he was doing a Radio series for Lent, and outstanding I thought it was. One day I was standing studying the Notice Board in the students' Common Room at Trinity, looking at the football team to play New College, Edinburgh, our deadly rivals, and also reading the draw for the Table Tennis competition, with both of which sporting activities I was involved. Suddenly I was aware of a voice hailing me.

WB had come quietly into the Common Room, unnoticed by me, and I realised he was addressing me.

"Can you spare a minute, Alec?" he asked.

"Certainly, sir," I replied, wondering what was coming.

"You know this radio series I'm doing leading up to Easter, Alec?"

"And very good it is too," I replied sincerely.

Dr. Barclay gave a wry smile. "I'm glad you think so, for apparently quite a number do not. I've had a lot of stick since my last broadcast, been condemned as a heretic by a Wee Free minister, oh, and a lot more besides." The Doctor was plainly hurt and my heart went out to this, the kindest of men, but I wondered why he was telling me about it.

"This week I'm taking the following line," and he proceeded to give me the bones of the address.

"Now! What do *you* think of that, Alec?"

"Great stuff! I don't know how you keep doing it."

"But is it scripturally sound?" he asked.

I gasped and goggled somewhat. "You, the greatest New Testament scholar in Britain today are asking me, a very ordinary student what I think?"

"Yes, Alec. I don't willingly hurt anyone or wish to

cause dissent and I know you are pretty evangelical, so I thought if you approved, that would give me the green light to go ahead."

I gasped still more! "Dr. Barclay, in my opinion, for what it's worth, your message is superb, is certainly sound, and I wouldn't lose a minute's sleep over any of your narrow-minded critics, Wee Free or otherwise!"

"Thanks, Alec, you've been a great help," and Willie toddled off, leaving me gazing after him in astonishment. Here surely was the mark of true greatness that a man of his stature, experience and knowledge should seek the opinion of a humble student.

And then I remembered! Jesus had done something the same, seeking the views of his fishermen friends.

"Whom do men say that I am?" The million dollar question for every man and woman, and the answer that opens doors to a land we have only dreamed of before.

"You are the Christ, the Son of the living God."

And Not to Yield

THIRTEEN

The match was well through and we were down 1–0 at home. Playing centre forward, I had just missed a "sitter," putting the ball over the bar and the crowd was not slow to express its feelings:

"You'm 'opeless, Cameron!"

"Go back to Scotland!"

"Oi could have put that in with me eyes shut!"

I cringed and tried to shut my ears to the raucous voices. After all, I thought, I'm doing my best, and I'm doing it for fun. I get no pay as I'm not a professional. But football crowds are only interested in one thing and that is seeing their team win.

My football career with Bristacombe Town in the Western League (one of the so-called non-league clubs of England), had begun some years back. When I first came to Bristacombe, having played Junior football in Scotland and loving the game, I had joined "the Ammies," the local amateur team. A few good performances and write-ups in the press had brought me to the notice of the professional team, made up in the main of old has-beens from English or Scottish League Clubs, and young hopefuls who played in the chance of the long shot that would bring them to the notice of a bigger league club.

Harry Bartholomew, the player-manager and some of the committee had visited me, persuaded me to put pen to paper, and I had signed for "the Town." However, since I could not, as a busy vet guarantee every Saturday off; I had decided to remain an amateur. Every second Saturday I was free, and tried to plan for the away games while on the others, at home, Bernard, with typical generosity covered for me for the duration of the match. I worked like mad on Saturday mornings, and since Saturday afternoons were usually quiet, cover was needed only for the odd urgent case.

I enjoyed my football, and being reasonably fit in those days, fast off the mark, and with a shot in either foot, I had been moderately successful and in fact for several seasons was the team's leading goal-scorer, though much of this was due to the excellent service I received from the inside men, now dubbed the midfield, crafty players like little Billy Spalding who had played for Aberdeen at one time, and the tall, deceptively lazy Horace Pickard. I was sorry I had not been with the team my first year at 'Combe, for they had enjoyed a run in the FA Cup, losing finally away to Llanelli, whose centre half was the famous Jock Stein, to whom I would have been directly opposed.

In the game of our story, with five minutes to go, I managed to put the ball in the net and the jeers turned to cheers, 1–1.

"Good ole Alex!" (As I was always referred to in Devon).

"He be a right good 'un, that Scotchman!"

"Well done, my dear!"

No further goals were scored, and as we trooped off the field, the Club Secretary said, "You've to phone your wife right away."

My spirits sank, a case, when what I needed after a hard game was a bath, my tea, and maybe forty winks. Janet's voice came over the line.

"You've to go to East Challacombe right away. Bernard has been at a calving for nearly two hours and is having trouble."

I tore off my football boots, put on my shoes, threw

on my jacket on top of my football strip, and gathering my clothes into a bundle, flung them into the car and headed for the farm in question. My arrival created a bit of a sensation, a vet arrayed in football shorts and blue shirt was, to say the least, unusual.

"Good life! What have we here?" said Charlie Coles, the son-in-law. "You'm like summat from a circus!"

"?? .. !! .. zz .. vrooh .. ar .. !? .. chooch," said father-in-law Lerwill, the owner, whose broad Devon accent I could never decipher, even after several years, the more so since he wore no teeth. He was a perky little gnome of a man, no longer young, but tough and wiry. Another mouthful followed the first, and I gathered he was describing the calf's position. I looked in mystification at Bernard who was himself looking pretty weary, and he explained.

"It's a big calf, head way back, and just no room in there at all. I've got the chains on the forelegs, but just can't get one round the head. Maybe your longer arm will reach it."

I stripped off my football shirt, soaped my arms, and looking even more peculiar, a vet in shorts and welling-tons, lay down in the gutter, for the cow was down and too exhausted to rise. Immediately my shorts were soaked, the contents of the dung channel oozing their way up the legs of my voluminous football pants. Ugh! I groaned even more when I reached away far in and was just able to touch the pool or head of the calf. Heaving about in the gutter, I gained a few more inches and ran my hand down into the mouth. "Ouch!"—I yelped, as sharp little teeth bit my fingers. The calf was still alive anyway, and if I could only gain just a fraction more, I could maybe slide a calving chain into the mouth and round the neck. So I scrabbled and heaved and grunted, having to change arms every few minutes, for there was just no room in that womb at all and in no time an arm would cramp. It was a big calf and a very deep cow, and I must have splattered about for an hour. We pumped soapy water into the uterus, for all was by now very dry, and Bernard had another go, while I leaned wearily against a stall partition, feeling my bruises from the game. No joy! We were beaten. Three hours between us and we had not gained an inch.

"Look, Mr. Lerwill," I said, "I'm afraid the only hope is a caesarian, though I don't like doing one when the mother is so exhausted." I said it with some hesitation, for caesarian section in cows was still something of a rarity, and with two tired vets, both extremely muddy, and with an exhausted cow, an operation was not a cheerful prospect.

The old man looked at me with the perkiness of a robin, head on one side, muttered, "zz ..!!. . . uur . . . oh . . . xx . . . No." I got the last word clearly enough. One of the old school, farmer Lerwill was not on for these new fangled ideas at all. I tried to persuade him, but in vain. The idea of taking a knife to his cow was absolute anathema to him. He looked at Bernard and I, both draped over a partition, filthy, limp, exhausted, muttered a screed of indecipherable Devonshire, soaped his arms in the bucket, and got down behind his cow. He pushed, heaved, grunted, sweated, while I looked on in amazement and with some shame. He had not a hope of calving her, but here was this little old man refusing to admit defeat when two much younger men, both professionals, and his strapping son-in-law were ready to throw in the sponge.

After a few minutes of watching, I was shamed into action. If that old man could go on, surely his vets whom he trusted and who were being paid to get that calf out could not yield. So Bernard and I got busy again. Taking a great gulp of air, I lay down, buried my face in the cow's back, reached as far in as I could with a rubber tube, while Bernard pumped in a fresh supply of soapy water. That would give us a few minutes, but only a few before everything became dry again. I have often found as I lay behind a cow at a calving that all sorts of thoughts

would go through my mind. I found myself thinking of
my missed goal at today's game, and near despair, then a
few minutes later my goal from a far more difficult position. I simply *had* to get that calf's head round, and in
that moist, well lubricated womb, wonder of wonders, I
felt my hand reach over the calf's poll with the chain, and
down into the mouth. In imagination I could hear the
crowd roar as the ball had hit the net. We had not won,
but it was now a draw. It seemed the same situation with
the calving. It was a case now of repelling the forelegs
and shoulder of the calf as far as possible, and while I
guided it, Bernard pulled on the head chain and to my
immense relief, slowly the head came round. We were
nearly there. Now it was time for pulling, and with big
Charlie Coles on the head chain, Bernard and little Mr.
Lerwill on a leg chain each, and my hand inside directing,
bit by bit we eased the calf towards the big wide world
outside. The poor cow bellowed as the pain gripped her,
but as if sensing that things had taken a turn for the
better, she gave a great heave which was worth far more
than all our pulling. With a plop the calf arrived, while
the men on the chains collapsed together on the seats of
their pants in the dung channel. Seldom have so many
men become so wet and dirty in one instant! But in a
moment it was all forgotten as the calf gave a splutter, a
sneeze, and started breathing.

Old man Lerwill was instantly busy rubbing it with a
wisp of straw, seeming as fresh as when the whole operation had begun, and in the midst of a flood of toothless
Devonshire giving us to understand it was a heifer too.
Bernard, bless his heart, who need not have been there
at all, was streaked in blood and filth, while I, still in my
football shorts which were practically hanging off me,
was an even more gory mess. I would have to drive home
like that, and hoped fervently I would not get a puncture
on the way, for I am sure the police would have lifted me
instantly for being indecently attired. The car would also
probably smell for days, but what matter all these things,

we had won. Inspired by an old man who had refused to yield, we had well and truly won!

That was over thirty years ago, but oddly enough the scene came back to me as I left our little Cottage Hospital at Aldermouth one afternoon, where I had been doing my weekly rounds as Chaplain. I had, like the crowd at the football match, my critics there too. There were two patients, who reckoned I had neglected them, even though I saw them at least once a week, in addition to our many folks in the hospitals of Inverness. I had gone up to one new patient in the corner bed, an elderly woman.

"How are you?" I enquired.

"No too bad. Who are you?" came the response.

"I'm the chaplain."

"Aye, but who are you. Whit's your name?"

"Cameron, and I'm the minister of the Old Parish Church."

At this she gasped, then snorted, and fixing me with a beady eye pronounced.

"The auld Kirk! The worst thing that hapened to the Kirks was the union in 1929!"

Whereupon she turned her face to the wall, and refused to speak to me further. For all these years she had carried bitterness in her heart, and would not forget or forgive.

Then I had come to the bed of Mrs. Wilson where all was smiles, and that was astonishing, for Mrs. Wilson was nearing the end of a long battle with an incurable condition, a battle she had fought with immense courage. She had faced surgery several times, had undergone all sorts of treatment, and with never a complaint had endured it all. Only in her forties, with a husband and family who loved her and depended on her, she had refused to yield to this disease, even though she knew the end was not far off.

That day she had astonished me, as I stood, feeling tongue tied and helpless beside her bed, by describing the holiday she had planned for herself and her family in a month's time, a camping holiday of all things. When I saw her she was so weak she could scarcely raise a hand, could not get out of bed, could not stand. She knew well her time was short, but with great determination and a total refusal to yield, and with thoughts only of husband and family, she was planning a camping holiday! I was amazed, and humbled, but I should have known by now. I had seen Mrs. Wilson over many months fighting her own private battles with dogged determination and courage, a courage born of her sure faith that knew her life was in God's hands, a faith which in turn had given her a wonderful serenity and calm even when all seemed hopeless. I had watched her stage by stage and been constantly amazed and humbled at what her mighty spirit had achieved when her body was weak, weary, and sometimes in pain. But as I left the hospital, I felt that not even Mrs. Wilson could achieve her final goal of her last holiday with those she loved and for whom she had fought her battles. A camping holiday in four weeks, impossible! I should have known better.

Mrs. Wilson had her holiday a month later, as she had planned from her sick bed, a holiday where her fun and gaiety had lifted her anxious family. Then, a few days later, she slipped quietly away to that place where all the hard things of this life are understood and made clear. She had not yielded. She had won. She had well and truly won!

Collar Off

FOURTEEN

"Come away in, boys, Alec, John, Gordon, Ben, good you could all come," said David. "I thought we would have a discussion on Bonhoeffer today."

We made our way into David's sitting room where several others of the brethren were already assembled, the first-comers getting the deepest armchairs. The occasion was the monthly meeting of our area ministers' fraternal when we met in one another's homes for a couple of hours of chat, fellowship and relaxation. Sometimes we had a topic for discussion, at other times we just shared experiences and incidents, cheerful or sorrowful. David, the host today, an enthusiastic scholar and a fine pastor, despite his disability and poor health, had obviously prepared a paper on Dietrich Bonhoeffer, the German theologian who was executed for his opposition to Hitler. All the denominations were represented except, sadly, the Wee Free minister who would not join us. What we never did at these fraternals was what two women, seeing a clutch of clergymen entering a Manse, thought they were about.

"Where are a' the meenisters goin' the day?" queried one.

"Och, they're away to a thing ca'd a fraternal," replied the other.

"Whit's a fraternal?"

"Oh, it's when they a' meet an' swap sermons wi' yin

anither." The first woman thought for a bit and then lugubriously announced,

"My! Oor man's been awfu' unlucky lately!"

David's wife brought in the coffee and cakes and we rose to greet her. While we were passing things around, Dan the priest announced.

"I heard a good story the other day. Three men were at an ecumenical conference in Paris, all of them from the same country town. One of them was of the true faith," Dan, the friendly Father, twinkled round at us all, "one was a Piscy, one a Church of Scotland minister."

"In Paris, did you say?" asked Gordon. "Unusual place for an ecumenical conference."

"Don't say they went to the Follies bergères," said Donald.

"Look! Don't interrupt," Dan commanded, "or I'll forget the story. It seems the conference ran from Wednesday to Wednesday and they had the weekend off."

"Even the Sabbath?" asked Hamish.

"Look! It's my story, let me tell it. Well, on the Friday night the priest said to the other two 'I've a confession to make. I'm fond of a dram and I'm going to sample quite a selection of these French wines.' "

"Always knew you boys liked the bottle," laughed Donald. Dan pushed on with his story.

"The Episcopal rector said, 'I've a confession to make too. I like a flutter on the horses and the pools, and I'm going to have a dabble at the Casino.' "

"Must have had more money than I get," muttered Joe, the representative of the Scottish Episcopal Church.

"The Church of Scotland minister said, 'I've a confession to make too. . . .' "

"Neffer!" said Hamish in his delightful highland voice, "No minister would be haffing anything to do with a confession!"

"This one did," said Dan, now red in the face. "He said 'I've a confession to make . . .' "

"That makes two confessions he had," quipped the other Alec who was a Congregationalist, and his denomination not involved in the story.

Dan bellowed, "I have a confession to make and I can't wait to get home. I'm the biggest gossip in Scotland."

Dan sat back with a sigh, his story at last completed, and there were chuckles round the room.

"I know one about three ministers too," said John, "a Baptist, a Piscy and a C of S," John was retired, a father figure, and was shown more respect than Dan had been in his story. Besides, everyone was well into coffee and cakes by now, tucking in happily. John went on.

"They were close friends and keen fishers and were out on a loch one day."

"If it's a fishing story, I'm off," said Joe, the irrepressible. John ignored him.

"After a time the Baptist said 'I need more bait,' stepped over the side of the boat, walked across the water to the bank and returned, to the astonishment of the other two. Bye and bye the Piscy said, 'I'm hungry. I'll just get my sandwiches from the bank,' and he did the same. Now the poor Kirk man thought 'I must keep the flag flying,' so he said 'It's getting cold. I'll just go and get my coat,' stepped out of the boat and disappeared. When he was coming up for the third time, the Piscy said to the Baptist, "do you think we should tell him about the stepping stones?""

"Aye, good John," said Donald, "that's an old one but I'd forgotten it."

So the talked ebbed and flowed, until the coffee was consumed, then old Hamish leaned forward and said.

"You young ministers are a disgrace to the cloth!"

"No doubt, Hamish," acknowledged Donald, "but in what particular way?"

"Look at you, you and your check shirts, hardly one of you hass the collar on. A man of Got should always be properly dressed!"

"Oh, but Hamish," I was moved to protest, "we're off duty. Surely we don't need to wear the collar this morning?"

"A minister or priest is neffer off duty," pronounced Hamish.

"Oh, come come!" "Nonsense!" "That's a bit much!" came various exclamations. "Christ didn't have a special uniform, did He?"

"Look you," went on Hamish, "a soltier iss not ashamed of hiss uniform and you are soltiers of the Lord."

There was instant and vociferous protest, except from Joe, who supported Hamish and reported "I only take my collar off when on holiday."

Hamish persisted, "If effer a preacher of the Word is to be seen in public, he should be in uniform."

"What about in the garden?" queried Gordon.

"Yes, in the garden too. I always wear mine in the garten. I tell you, you are ashamed of your calling."

"I heard about a minister who was seen bringing in the morning milk in pyjamas and dog collar," said the other Alec.

"And I know a young minister who went his honeymoon in his," said Ben, my assistant.

My mind boggled at the thought. "The idiot," I exclaimed.

That statement of Hamish's got us going and the talk ranged far and wide on Bishop's gaiters, cassocks, surplices and all the paraphernalia of the preacher.

"Bonhoeffer was a wonderful man," came in David hesitantly.

"Aye, and I don't think he wore a dog collar," said Donald.

"Look at that now," said Hamish, "maype iff he had, Hitler woult have hat more respect for him."

We finally agreed to differ, though I'm afraid I shocked dear old Hamish, a real saint, despite his views on the collar, by saying,

"I still feel more at home in a calving coat than a collar."

"Och, now, but you are the queer one, yes indeed," said Hamish, and eventually the subject died down.

"Eh, about Bonhoeffer," David tried again.

"Before we come to Bonhoeffer we've got a few things to arrange," said John. "Whose turn is it to take the Service at the War Memorial this year?"

"Not mine," said Gordon, "I did it last year."

"And I the year before," said Joe.

"Must be yours, then, Alec," concluded John, and in this easy fashion the duty was arranged.

Dan piped up again.

"Oh, Alec, about that mixed marriage you've asked me to share. The Bishop hasn't given his permission yet, and I can't do anything till he does. Sorry!"

This led to a discussion on the desirability of Bishops which brought Joe bounding out of his seat in defence of his denomination.

"Judging from the arguments you boys seem to have in your Presbytery, we're better off with Bishops."

"Nonsense, Joe," said Donald, "we're at least democratic and where did you hear of a democracy without arguments?"

"But the Bishops are in the Apostolic Succession," said Dan, to which Joe added a "Hear, hear."

"Now, you've both got Bishops in your Churches who claim to be in the Apostolic Succession. How can they both be?" pointed out Donald.

"Bishops! Bishops!" expostulated old Hamish, "look at the palaces they live in. That can't be right, and how can someone appointed by maybe a Jewish or atheist Prime Minister haf the cheek to say the Holy Spirit appointed them?"

So the talk switched to which form of Church government was most agreeable to the Bible. We were thoroughly enjoying ourselves, and as always, though we often differed, it was good natured and not in any way divisive.

"Why do you fellows insist on couples at a wedding both being baptised?" queried Ben.

This brought a long, complicated explanation from Joe, while poor David looked sadly at his notes on Bonhoeffer. As so often happened, we found plenty of topics for discussion and in one another's company felt our own particular problems lessen or even disappear. The two hours sped past and we did not get round to David's prepared paper. I felt sorry for him for I knew he would have spent considerable time preparing it, and having had to do an essay on the German theologian at college, I was interested to hear what the refreshing David would have to say. We apologised for not having Bonhoeffer, discussed where the next fraternal would be, promised without fail to hear David's paper next time, and thanking David's wife for the refreshments, departed to our several parishes, instructed, relaxed and brought closer in real fellowship.

On the way home I thought of our talk that morning, and particularly old Hamish's remarks about the collar. Of course it has its uses, if, for example, you want a railway compartment to yourself! It is a relatively new garment, but useful on occasion, as an entry to hospitals at any time without explanations, and of course, on formal duties, I feel a must. I recalled an instance where it had a salutory effect, back in my Moorton days.

My friend Bob was minister of Ibrox Church and Chaplain to Rangers FC, and one week invited me up to a game. Rangers were playing Hearts and with me were our two eldest, Neil and Ian, beside themselves with excitement for they had never been to a big match. We were given a seat in the stand and sat with the élite, and for some reason that day we were both wearing our clerical collars. Behind us were two very vocal supporters, true blue fans. Even their adjectives were the same colour as the team's jerseys, and they became bluer, in direct proportion to the amount, (which was astonishing), of whisky they consumed. Finally, by the second half, it was just beyond bearing, my sons' eyes were getting bigger and bigger as they listened to words they had never heard before, and suddenly, at exactly the same moment, quite unrehearsed, Bob and I turned round to protest. The two somewhat inebriated gentlemen were confronted by two wrathful dog collars. There was a moment of speechlessness, followed by abject apologies,

"Sorry, Father, so sorry, if we had only kenned, Father, who you were . . ." I do not know whether they thought we had wandered into the wrong match, or were Celtic spies viewing the opposition, but at any rate their style was severely cramped for the rest of the game and the air was a bit cleaner.

But there were many other occasions when I had the collar off. I cannot think of anything more uncomfortable, despite Hamish's assertion, when digging the garden. When the boys and I were having a game on our little nine-hole putting green on the Manse lawns, off would come the collar. After all I was known by most people in Aldermouth. I often visited in an ordinary shirt, flannels and sports jacket. The truth was, and is, that having come late to the ministry, and as a vet, being a casual dresser, I simply cannot see the importance of the black and white ensemble that others feel a must. My friend, Alec, the Congregational minister never on any occasion wore a clerical collar, even in the pulpit or at funerals.

Once a fortnight it was certainly discarded. This was when we had our ministers' foursome at golf. Early in my days at Aldermouth, Dr. John, our much loved GP had laid it on the line that in a Church of our size and with the multifarious demands of the many organisations (over twenty I counted once, organisations or departments), with the sorrow of two funerals weekly, the anxiety of over twenty in hospital weekly, and the stress of trying to help people with their personal problems, not to mention the long hours of sermon preparation, Dr. John had said, "You *must* learn to take time off. You *must* make time or you'll crack up."

He was a wise and good man, and the years have shown, too late, that I should have listened to him. However, discovering that Gordon, Alec and John had all played golf at one time, I routed them out and once a fortnight, usually a Monday, we disported ourselves on Aldermouth's famous championship links. We sometimes talked "shop" on the first fairway, but after that it was strictly serious business as John and Gordon challenged the two Alecs. The golf varied between bad and terrible, but we enjoyed ourselves immensely, and there was a deal of leg pulling. Most important, we relaxed, which was more than the greenkeepers did for when they saw us coming, they immediately fled for cover as if we were an approaching cloud of locusts, getting themselves behind a hut or "coorying doon" below their tractor. We played summer and winter, sometimes on a cold day being the only folks on the course, and the professional was heard to say one day to a visitor enquiring if the course was busy, "There's nobody out there but four mad ministers!"

Golf in winter could be difficult with three jerseys on, scarves, bonnets, gloves, but we would stop after the ninth hole, Alec would produce a flask of coffee or bovril and some biscuits, and in the lee of whin bushes we heated ourselves up and prepared for the homeward battle. Never on a golf course was assembled at one time such a motley collection of hooks, slices, duffs, fresh air shots pulls and for a time that dreadful disease which no golfer will mention . . . shank, which sorely afflicted me. Weather conditions varied, like the golf. On one occasion it was so misty that we could not see where the ball had gone, but we drove on regardless, and John played the game of his life. The mist lifted and his game went to pieces! He got into a bunker and had eight hacks at the ball his face becoming redder and redder, but not a comment was made. Eventually ball and club came hurtling out of the trap, John picked both up without a word, then collapsed hilariously. I was reminded of the Bishop on a similar occasion who, playing with some of his flock, and having similar bunker trouble, requested, "Would one of you laymen say the appropriate words!"

We were all keen, if very indifferent golfers, the "Clerical Clowns" as John's wife, Nan dubbed us, but the fun and fellowship were immense. I particularly admired John, for though well into his seventies, he was as keen as mustard, so much so, that one day when his ball was on the downward slope leading to a ditch, despite our pleas to lift and drop, he refused, tried to play it, fell and broke his arm.

Eventually Alec and Gordon moved away and John felt he could no longer play, so I had to look for other partners. In time a new foursome of Willie Edwards, a retired minister who had gone to the same school at Mochrum as me, and two of my elders and very good friends, Arthur Menzies and Bob Anderson teamed up. Usually Willie and I played together, saints versus sinners, though which was which was never specified. Two other friends, Henry and Peter, were members of the other course, and from time to time would treat me to a round there. Of the whole bunch, Willie was the finest golfer, having played all his life. He seldom veered from the straight and narrow, never visited a bunker and could putt like Gary Player. He had a degree in English, loved poetry, and would always crown a particularly good shot with an apt quotation, sometimes in Latin to me, and I had left my Latin thirty years behind me! Occasionally, as I was lining up a putt, out would come a screed of poetry in a dolorous voice, meant to encourage but having the effect of making me want to brain him with a brassie!

These were happy days, days of real undiluted joy and friendship, when we would return home tired, but also relaxed, and sometimes on a round with a shot to savour for an hour or two.

I was such a dreadful bunker player that I once

preached a sermon in Golf Week on "the bunkers of life," and I recalled an experience of the late Tom Allan, who influenced a whole generation, including me, with his powerful preaching, deep pastoral concern and practical Christianity. He was a keen golfer and one day things were not going well for him. He kept visiting the sand traps and his caddie said to him, "Ah doot the Lord's no' wi' ye the day, Mr. Allan."

Tom merely smiled and played on, but at the next tee he said to his caddie.

"You know, Bill, you were wrong back there. The Lord doesn't promise to save us from life's bunkers, but He's right beside us when we're in them, and helps us play the right shot."

Tom Allan was right. He knew life. He knew plenty about life's bunkers, and he knew his Lord.

Ah me, enough of this dreaming. An hour till Barbara's wedding. Collar on!

Seeing Now

FIFTEEN

One day an elderly couple came into the surgery with their Labrador dog, which was also elderly.

"It's his eyes," they said, something that was at once obvious for they looked terrible. I lifted the old dog on to the table and had a look at them. Both eyes were filled with pus, they were half closed, and the dog kept blinking and pawing at them.

"How long has he been like this?" I asked.

"Oh, he's been bothered with them for a long time, and we've had him to a vet several times before. He gave us ointment to put in them, but we've just retired to Bristacombe and they seem to have gone worse."

"Did your other vet tell you what the trouble was?"

"He just said it was inflammation, conjugal, or conjunction or some name like that," they explained.

"Well, his eyes are certainly inflamed, but I'm afraid no ointment will put them right. You see, it's more than conjunctivitis, he's got a condition called entropion where the eyelashes grow inwards and irritate the eyes, then germs get in, and cause all this matter. It's a very painful condition, like having something in your eye all the time, only worse."

"Oh dear! Can anything be done?" asked the wife.

"Certainly! There's a quite simple little operation which

can turn the eyelashes outwards and take away the irritation."

"An operation!" they both gasped in unison.

"Oh, it's quite a little one, and it would make all the
difference to him. What's his name, by the way?"

"Terence!" said the wife, and at the sound of his name,
the old dog's tail beat a tattoo on the table.

"Couldn't you just give us ointment like the other vet?"
asked the husband. "You see, he's old to have an operation."

"Yes, I could give you ointment, but it would not cure
the condition, only soothe his eyes a little for a time. I
strongly advise you to let me do the operation. It would
take away all the pain, make his eyes clear again, let him
see properly, for he's really a handsome old fellow, and
it's a pity to see him like that."

"Would it be safe?"

"Yes! It means an anaesthetic, of course, and there's
always a very slight risk with an anaesthetic, but it's maybe
1 in 1000. I'll just sound his heart," which I did, and got
a fine, strong, regular beat.

"Sound as a bell, Mr. and Mrs. . . . . eh?"

"Murgatroyd," said the man.

"Er . . . how much would such an operation cost?" he
asked.

"Oh . . . about three guineas."

"Oh . . . is that all," said the old chap. "What do you
think, Celia?"

"I don't know, Cyril, but if he was going to be operated
on, I'd want to be there. I think we should both be there."

"Oh, I wouldn't advise that," I hastily exclaimed. "Most
people get upset to see their animals being operated on.
There's bound to be a little blood, you know."

So they talked to and fro, finally decided on surgery,
but only on condition that they could stay with their
"dear old fellow." I did not like the idea one bit, but
for the dog's sake, agreed. Our operation day, apart
from emergencies, was Wednesday, so Terence Murga-

troyd was duly fixed up for 11:00 am, the next week. I decided I had better take some precautions, so Mrs. Drury, our original Secretary/Receptionist/Assistant/Book-keeper, who was with us in my early years with Kenneth as partner, was despatched to lay in a bottle of brandy for the surgery, and two chairs were placed in position, a bit from the table, on the morning of the operation. The dog was lifted onto the table, and I cleaned up his eyes, then explained to Cyril and Celia the procedure to be adopted with Terence.

"First I give him an injection of anaesthetic into a vein, and he will just go quietly to sleep. Then I cut out carefully a little elliptical piece of skin above and below each eye. This has the same effect at tightening up a piece of elastic, and pulls the eyelids outwards, so that the lashes no longer rub against the eye. Perhaps you would find it more comfortable to sit down to watch."

But they did not, Mrs. M in particular, a stout woman, wanted a close up, and her small husband, not to be outdone also hovered nearby, so four heads were bent over the now recumbent Terence. The operation is not difficult, but requires care and concentration, and I was wrapped up in what I was doing, as was Mrs. Drury, constantly swabbing the area, when after a short time, I heard a faint voice saying, "It's awful warm today!" and engrossed as I was, it took a moment to sink in. When it did, I turned quickly to say "sit on the chair," but I was too late. There was a mighty crash and I was just in time to see large Mrs. Murgatroyd sit down on the floor, right on top of her little husband who had tried to catch her, both of them missing the chairs. The little man peered out from underneath and murmured, "My wife appears to have fainted!"

I had seen many people faint at surgery, even big husky farmers watching a Caesarean in their sheep, but never quite a situation like this. There was nothing for it but to suspend operations, and while Mrs. Drury and I eased the wife up, for her husband's ribs would be in dire peril, the little man crawled out from underneath, like a tortoise coming out of its shell. Between us we carted the unconscious lady into the Waiting Room, and not without difficulty, deposited her on the couch. Mrs. Drury produced the brandy, and since poor little Cyril looked as if he was about to faint too, gave him a little, then left him sitting beside his wife, lying in a heap on the couch, her hat askew.

"Best just to leave her as she is," I said (I didn't really know!) "and when she comes round, perhaps a little sip of brandy." Poor Cyril nodded, and Mrs. Drury and I left him patting his wife's hands as we trooped back to our patient.

In due course the operation was finished, just in time, for with the interruption, the effects of my short-acting anaesthetic were wearing off. I dressed the wounds, and squeezed some chloromycetin ointment into the dog's eyes, for the long standing irritation had produced a great deal of inflammation and keratitis, but fortunately no ulceration of the cornea that I could detect. We lifted the old dog down, laid him on a blanket, then hurried through to see the other patient. She was a little bit ahead of Terence, being able to sit up, though pale, and with the hat even more askew, her eyes a bit glazed, and a glass of brandy in her hand, she would hardly have qualified at that moment for a temperance advert! Cyril, I noticed, was also at the brandy again, and I thought the profit from the operation had already been drunk! We were able to cheer Mrs. M up a bit by telling her Terence had come through his surgery well, and when they were ready, we would carry him out to the car and they could take him home.

They returned in ten days to have the stitches removed, and this time they both stayed in the Waiting Room. I was agreeably surprised at the improvement already in the old dog's eyes, the chloromycetin twice daily allied to the removal of the irritation having worked wonders. They came back a fortnight later, and it was lovely to behold. Terence was frisking along like a young dog, looking about him everywhere. I imagine it was a long time since he had seen the world properly, but he was seeing now alright, and had a lot of catching up to do. His eyes were clean and bright as a puppy, a complete transformation.

I have seen this transformation in the ministry too on numbers of occasions. Alec Mullen grew up in a large housing scheme in Glasgow in a street where every single house had somebody with a prison record, including Alec's home, although he, the eldest of a large family, was a steady sort of lad. He had a younger brother who was a real tearaway, but Alec was very fond of his wild brother.

One day the younger lad, a fellow in his early twenties by then, took seriously ill. The doctor was called, and visited daily, but as time passed the doctor became more grave, and informed the family that things could go either way. Why the boy was not removed to hospital, I know not, and as he saw his brother lying helpless in bed, Alec too felt very helpless. Surely something could be done, but what? Alec thought of prayer, but he knew no prayer, had never prayed, and never been near a Church in his life. But that night, Alec did the only thing he could think of. He said Psalm 23 . . . "The Lord's my Shepherd," which he had learned at school. The sick lad, in time recovered. This set Alec thinking. Maybe it was just luck, coincidence, chance. Maybe he would have recovered anyway, but maybe, just maybe, there was something in this prayer business after all.

Some time later, Alec himself was ill, and advised to get a job in the country air away from the then, smoky city. Thus he came into my parish at Moorton, where he worked on a farm as a general handyman. In time he became a shepherd to the kindly Dalgliesh family. Old Mr. Dalgliesh was one of my senior elders, a kind, gentle, good man, and they encouraged Alec to come to Church. He attended every week, and eventually, though much older than most of the others, came to a Young Communicants' class for prospective Church members. After the course, I had a long chat with Alec, and my delight was like that when seeing the old dog's eyes clear again after surgery. The great surgeon had clearly been at work in the young man's life, and now he not only knew the shepherd psalm, he knew the Shepherd. He was seeing, now, things he had been blind to before, and the world was a wonderful place. It was like all successful surgery, no spur of the moment thing. The cure was permanent.

One evening in Aldermouth, years later, my phone rang.

"Is that Mr. Cameron? My name is George Gray and I'd like to join the Church. Could I have a chat with you sometime?"

Now every minister is delighted to get that kind of request, and since I had already to visit in that particular street that very night, I called on Mr. Gray, who, with his wife and family, was a comparative newcomer to the town. He was a man in his thirties, and welcomed me warmly, if somewhat shyly. We talked of this and that, and then he told me his story.

He had been brought up in the Shetland Islands by his grandmother, a real godly, severe warrior of the old school. The young George had been sent or taken to three Services every Sunday, Church of Scotland in the morning, Methodist in the afternoon, and Plymouth Brethren at night. He grew up with a considerable knowledge of the Bible, but a hearty dislike of the whole business. At the age of sixteen he went off, like so many of the islanders, to sea. As he left, his granny gave him a Bible which he put in his kit bag, and there it remained, unopened, for years.

He prospered at sea, rapidly climbed the promotion ladder, for he was a clever, highly intelligent man, and when he met me that night, was First Officer on one of the huge supertankers, shortly afterwards indeed becoming Captain. In the course of the years he had married, the daughter of a Methodist minister, and in time they had two children. Though his wife and family would go off to Church, not George. He had had enough religion to last him a lifetime, he reckoned.

"And what has made you change your mind?" I queried.

"Difficult to explain clearly, Mr. Cameron. It's been a gradual thing, but over a period of time, often when I've been on watch on the bridge away in the Persian Gulf or some such ocean, with the vastness of the sea all around me and the even more vast starry sky above me, I've felt very small, and also somehow as if I was part of some great master plan. So many of the things I learned long ago in the Bible, and thought I had rejected for good, have come back to me, and the interesting thing is that now they make sense. It's been like a giant jigsaw puzzle falling into place, and all I can say is that I'm seeing now, and want to be part of God's Church, for I like what I see."

So one could go on, instance after instance of people who had found a faith. In Alec's case he started from scratch; in George's case, there was a background of knowledge and a Christian wife. But the end result was the same.

The operation had been successful, and dim eyes were now seeing God's wonderful world, and His plan for His world, in all its splendour.

Of course such "surgery" has been going on from the beginning of the Christian era. Most famous was the man Saul, an upright man who kept to the letter of God's laws for His people, the Jews, but a man with a deep and bitter hatred for these upstart Christians. On a mission of destruction of these pestilential Jesus people, he was met by the Master surgeon Himself, was actually, literally blinded for a time by the brightness of the Shekinah glory of the risen Christ, and when he recovered his sight, he was no longer Saul the persecuter, but Paul the apostle, and the baiter of Christians had become one himself,

a complete about turn, or to use the word beloved by
evangelists, a Conversion.

Over the long centuries of Christendom, many have
experienced this spur of the moment encounter and
change, like laser beam surgery, a change evidenced by
a completely different outlook, different set of values,
different code of behaviour and most of all a deep com-
passion and caring for all mankind. In my ministry I have
seen this apparently instant about-turn on a number of
occasions. I have also to admit to some cases where the
surgery was only successful for a time, and eyes were
clouded again so far as commitment to Christ was concerned.

Much more frequently, though, has been the gradual
change, as if bit by bit scales fell from the eyes, till people
saw differently. Jack Miller was like that. I knew Jack first
when in my summer holidays as a vet student, I worked
in, of all places, an Income Tax office. My first summer
holidays I worked on a farm and there was no prouder
teenager in Scotland than me as I carted hay ricks into
the stack-yard on the old hay bogeys with my very own
mare for the summer, Pearl. These were happy, halcyon,
carefree days, but unfortunately they did not pay very
much, and in the closing years of the war and immediately
after, there were few student grants. True, I supple-
mented what little my parents could afford by playing the
organ in Crosshills Church, and got £1.00 a week for
playing football for Maybole Juniors. But much more
was required, so, finding that His Majesty's Inspector of
Taxes employed students and paid about twice that of the
farmer, reluctantly, on several occasions I worked at this,
to me, hateful job. Jack was on the permanent staff at the
Ayr office, a happy-go-lucky, devil-may-care, extremely
likeable man, nothing bad about him, a man typical of
millions who lived his life without thought of God or
Church and saw no need for either.

Every night after work, he would head for the pub
before going home, and on Sundays, while his wife and

two daughters went off to Church, Jack usually headed for the Golf Course and after his round spent the rest of the day at the nineteenth hole, until one day some words spoken with the innocence of a child changed things. He was pottering in the garden that Sunday morning and as his wife and little girls went out the gate for Church, Jack overheard one ask, "Mummy? Does Daddy go to a different Church from us?"

Just that! A child's question, but somehow it stung Jack and set him thinking. Hell-raiser though he undoubtedly was, he doted on his family and he thought, "I'll go along next week to keep the children happy."

He did, feeling very strange going in a Church door, and hoping none of his nineteenth hole pals saw him. He had the uncomfortable feeling that everybody in the place, big building though it was, had their eyes on him alone. But as he came out he thought, "That wasn't so bad. Folk seemed really friendly, as if they were glad to see me, and that fellow in the pulpit talked some sense, even raised a laugh, didn't think folk ever laughed in a Church. The kids were pleased too. I'll give it a month's trial." The month passed, and another, and another, and Jack, to his utter amazement, found he was enjoying himself, actually *enjoying* himself in that bright Church where there were many young couples and a superb minister.

I met Jack many years later when I was myself a minister and had been preaching in his Church. He was the same cheerful chap, the same friend of all, but yet there was a difference too. He seemed to be seeing things differently, he had a verve, a sense of purpose, a joy about him that seemed to go deep down. He told me he was leader of the Youth Club, was Session Clerk and involved with old folks in the area.

"Alec," he said, "I know now why you became a minister. I'm seeing now in a way I never did before!"

Another operation by the celestial Surgeon had proved a complete success, and the great Consultant's still at it.

Patch up Job

SIXTEEN

"Hello, Alex," came the voice over the air of Charlie Trevelyan our local zoo keeper. "It's ham."

"Beg pardon?"

"It's ham!"

"Eh?" I was completely puzzled.

"I want you to come up and look at ham."

I really could make nothing of this at all.

"Charlie, have you got a wrong number or something? Should you not be phoning a grocer or a butcher?"

"Eh? What's that, Alex?"

"Well, why do you want me to look at ham?"

"Because it's off colour." The mystery deepened. I looked at the phone in perplexity. "Charlie, ham comes from pigs, I know, but it's usually live ones I see."

"Oh! Ah! Ha, ha, ha. Oh, that's a good one," Charlie roared with laughter. Eventually he composed himself and said,

"I mean Ham, the lion cub. You know, Shem Ham and Japheth, Butch and Mary's cubs."

"Ohhhhhh . . . now I understand. I didn't know you had gone back to the Ark for names. I'll certainly have a look at that kind of Ham, though I'd rather it was something safe like your goats. What seems to be wrong with it?"

"I'm not certain, Alex. He's going about with his head all to one side and he's off his food."

"These cubs must be a fair size by now, Charlie. How are we to get near him?"

"Oh, don't worry, we'll net him."

"Well, make sure Butch and Mary are well out of the way or they'll make ham of us."

"Don't worry, Alex, and while you're up, I'd like you to see a young llama I've bought."

"A llama! That's more in my line. I'll be up shortly."

So I headed for the zoo, not exactly looking forward to the visit, for in these days of the early 1950s we had no knock out darts. To treat an animal, you had to get in beside it while it was still in full possession of its faculties and restrain it as best you could. True, you could sometimes slip nembutal or some other anaesthetic or sedative into its food and hope it would not notice it, but since wild animals seldom showed symptoms of disease until they were really ill and by then off their food, most often this ploy was not on. I tried to remember on the way up the steep hill to the zoo perched right on the top just how old these lion cubs would be by now and concluded they must be very well grown. My spirits sagged somewhat!

Charlie was waiting for me at the gate and hurried me through his large zoo at his usual break neck pace, past the sea lion enclosure, the many pavilions of tropical birds, the pets' corner, the ostrich pen, many cages of monkeys, the black bears and finally the lion's corner. There were Butch and Mary in their cage, Mary looking a bit thin and careworn, so, since the lion and lioness were together again, clearly the cubs were weaned. My spirits sagged even more!

"Mary's got the European record," Charlie proudly informed me, "she's had forty-three cubs."

"She's beginning to look it too, Charlie. Do you not think she should stop now?"

Charlie hesitated. "Her cubs sell well. Maybe she'll manage one more litter, Alex."

In a cage next to father and mother were two well-grown cubs.

"That's Shem and Japheth. We've got Ham separated in the next cage," Charlie explained.

I stopped abruptly at the next cage, gazed, gulped, swallowed a jagged lump that seemed to have suddenly sprouted in my throat and murmured.

"He's big, Charlie, a lot bigger than the other two. Do you think we can hold him in a net?"

I found I was sweating somewhat, especially as Ham at that moment gave a roar which sounded pretty grown up to me. In fact, I am sure he was past adolescence and his voice had broken!

Charlie gave me a slap on the back.

"Don't worry, Alex! Never had a vet eaten yet! We'll hold him."

"Let's just watch him a minute, Charlie, and see if we can get some idea of his trouble." You can learn much by just observing an animal's behaviour and it was also postponing the dreaded moment when I had to go into that cage. Our vet course at College had said not a word about lions. I could control a horse weighing a ton, had little fear of a bull weighing fifteen hundred weight, but a much smaller lion had not been mentioned. I kept telling myself "it's just a big cat" but somehow myself was not convinced. I watched the cub for a time. He was prowling around continuously, growling to himself all the time, his head tilted noticeably to one side. Clearly he was in considerable pain. "Ear or tooth," I thought. Just then he lay down, groaned loudly and pawed at his right ear.

"It's obviously that ear, Charlie. Where's your net? We'll need to have a closer look."

"Irene, Michael and Tom are bringing it."

"Irene? Will she go in there?"

"Oh, Irene would tackle Butch single handed. She's

got no fear, that girl." That made me feel a bit ashamed of myself and a bit braver. If that slip of a lassie could go in there, surely a six foot vet could too. Just then the trio arrived with a large net, Charlie opened the cage door, and in we went, brave me last, but then I had my cases to carry! Ham retreated before us into a corner, Charlie shouted, "1-2-3-now," and the net was flung over the young lion and quickly pulled up tight. It was slickly done, except that somehow Tom got caught up in the net, and I doubt if either he or Ham appreciated the skill. Tom was out in ten seconds flat, looking a bit pale about the gills. Ham roared ferociously, which started off Butch, Mary and the other cubs, and outside the black bears joined in the row. The whole line of cages vibrated with animals pounding about and leaping at the bars, the whole din not calculated to calm one's nerves.

"Sure these connecting doors are well fastened, Charlie?" I yelled.

"Certain sure."

There was no way that Ham was going to lie absolutely still, but enmeshed in the net as he was, his movements were limited and I was able to get a fair look at his ear and inside it. I would have appreciated a drug like Immobilon to knock him out, but it was not around then either.

"It's an abscess, Charlie," and as if to confirm my diagnosis, at that very moment there was a gush of pus from the lion's ear. The struggle with the net had probably caused a "ripe" abscess to burst, to my and Ham's great relief. I did not like lancing in ears, even in anaesthetised, still animals, let alone a struggling, fighting fury. I got out some cotton wool and through the mesh of the net, with a pair of forceps, cleaned out the ear as best I could, then, when the pus was down to a trickle, squeezed in a whole tube of chloromysetin ointment. Then back to the black case, a syringe and a dose of long acting penicillin which I jabbed into a rear leg.

"That'll keep him covered for three days and hopefully

will be enough, but at best it's a bit of a patch up job in a lion this size."

"He must have suffered some with that ear," said Charlie.

That was typical of this man whose first thought was not what money he could make from the various attractions at his zoo, but the well-being of his animals.

"He certainly did, Charlie," and I marvelled again at the stoic courage of creatures of the wild. "Never show weakness" was the law, for "the weakest goes to the wall." I remembered as I closed my case the agony my father had suffered with a similar condition in his ear, almost climbing the walls with the intensity of the pain.

"Right, Alex, out you go, and the rest of you. I'll get the net," and typically Charlie was last out of the cage. The young lion was still crouched in his corner, but already his head was less tilted. The pressure in the ear had gone, and much of the pain. In a domestic animal there would have been daily dressings, but that was not very practicable with a young lion, but I had hopes that my patch up job might suffice, and so indeed it proved. Ham was reunited with his brothers, next day was back on his food, and shortly afterwards was sold and grew to full manhood, or lionhood, in another zoo.

I went into the house to have a good scrub up before I touched another animal for my hands were well splashed with germ laden puss. I had a cup of tea, listened to our zoo keeper's enthusiastic talk of his various charges, proposed extensions and future plans and thought as he rattled on that if ever there was a man happy in his work, it was Charlie Trevelyan.

"How about this llama, Charlie? You haven't had one of them before."

"No, Alex, it were goin' cheap, like. It ben't full grown yet . . . came from a Pets' Corner kind of place."

"Right! Let's have a look at him."

"It's a she," he corrected me.

We made our way round to an open air enclosure and

as I saw the llama, I stopped so suddenly, Charlie coming behind, bumped into me. I stared, amazed, a bowly legged llama!

"You know, the last time I saw anything like that was in the streets of Glasgow during and after the war when you would see wee men and women with legs like that, caused by lack of a proper diet."

"Be that the cause then?"

"Yes! It's rickets, of course and it's a deficiency of vitamin D, and also calcium or phosphorus. I don't know what your Pets' Corner place fed this poor beast on. No wonder you got it cheap!"

"Oh, I'm sure you'll be able to put it right, Alex." Charlie was always good for my ego. He thought I could do anything and after I left for the ministry, he had even more confidence in Bernard, my partner, who although very quiet, unassuming, and perhaps giving the impression in the early days of lacking in confidence became an outstanding vet and absolutely superb surgeon, as he still is.

"Charlie, rickets is irreversible. The damage has been done. The bones have grown and are setting in that curved way. I don't know whether a first class orthopaedic surgeon would break these legs and try to straighten them, but I doubt it." I had said the wrong thing! "Right, Alex. Have a go at that!"

"No, no, no, Charlie! You don't understand me. First, I don't know whether its ever been done, second, I'm sure it has never been done in animals, and third, I'm not going to risk laming this poor beast for life by trying. You can always put a football jersey on her and bill her as the only football playing llama in captivity. Lots of the best football players are bowly legged!"

"Surely something can be done? Come on, Alex, I've never known you stuck before."

That was not true, but our ebullient zoo keeper was the most generous and enthusiastic of men. I gazed at this creature from South America, now resident with animals from all over the world in North Devon. I, obviously, just to keep Charlie quiet, would have to try something.

"Well, she's not fully grown and her legs could get even worse as she grows. First, we'll get her on to a course of minerals, calcium, phosphorus, vitamin D. Keep her outside. The sunlight helps. Feed her well, be good to her, and to stop the legs bending further, I'll put them in a light plaster for a few weeks. It won't straighten them, but might, hopefully, keep them from getting worse as she grows, but at best it's a patch up job."

"Right, Alex! I knowed you wouldn't be beat."

Charlie was quite content; something was being tried, and if any of the public complained, and he was very sensitive to, and hurt by complaints, I knew he would say he had a top class vet treat them! Yes, Charlie was good for the ego!

I had to nip back down to the surgery for a large supply of gypsona, the plaster of paris bandages. We got the team of keepers assembled again, caught and cast the gentle creature, and after soaking each bandage, swathed her legs in gleaming white plaster. The llama looked distinctly odd with four dazzling white legs, and when it walked it seemed as if it was on stilts, and went clump, clump, clump round its pen. For two months it was one of the principal attractions of the zoo and daily there was a crowd highly amused by this high stepping, gentle-eyed, friendly beast which soon realised it was a star. She would come up to the fence hopefully and be given all sorts of tit-bits. If it had been starved and neglected at its previous home, it made up for it at Bristacombe. I do not, to this day, know whether I did the right thing or helped at all, and there were no llama experts in Britain to consult. All I know is that the legs became no worse as the animal grew to its full size, and I am sure it was sorry to lose its plaster legs, for it then also lost its daily crowd of spectators. It was, like many treatments in animals, especially creatures of the wild, or immigrants from other countries, a bit of a patch up job.

Some days later a Mr. and Mrs. Fordyce came into the surgery with their fine Golden Retriever dog, called simply Goldie, though having come from a long line of champions, he had a much more impressive kennel name. The couple, who were strangers to me, seemed pleasant folk, and clearly very attached to their handsome dog.

"We're new to the district, Mr. Cameron," they informed me, "and have just come to live at Birleton. We've always had animals and you and your partner were recommended to us for our vets by our farming neighbour, Mr. Huxley. In fact he said you were the best vets in Devon."

"Good for Len!" I laughed, "but I think he's exaggerating more than a little. Now, how can I help you today?"

"Goldie is limping and we think it's his paw. He's a bit sorry for himself too." They lifted the dog on to the table. He really was a lovely creature, soulful brown eyes, proud carriage of the head, straight back and that glorious sweep of golden, wavy hair which is a feature of the Retriever. He was obviously as good-natured as he was handsome and a long tongue came out and washed my face while his tail swept across the table continuously from side to side. His trouble was not hard to find, nor very serious.

"He's got an interdigital cyst, see here, between these two toes. It's all swollen and inflamed, a very common condition. We don't really know what causes it but we have an injection which should put it right." I reached for the bottle, measured out a dose, and like all well mannered dogs, Goldie never moved as I slipped the needle in.

"That should clear it up in a few days, but if you like you could soak his foot in warm water and epsom salts morning and night which will hurry things up and soothe the foot."

They paid cash, observing that their vet in a London suburb would have charged three times as much, and threw open an invitation to call and have a coffee with them any time I was at Birleton. Clearly they wanted to make friends and I thanked them and promised I would call one day.

I happened to be at Len Huxley's farm of High Yeoford only a week later to treat a cow with Red Water and Len spoke highly of his new neighbours.

"They be proper gentlemen, both of 'em," he told me earnestly. "They're from away, o' course, but I dare say they can't help that." I smiled at the friendly Len's verdict on his new neighbours and thought there was quite a contrast between the well groomed Fordyces and Len in his braces and ancient bonnet, but clearly they were already well acquainted. Len was a rough diamond, swarthy of complexion, but with a heart of gold.

"Thanks for the testimonial, by the way, Len."

"How do ee mean, Mr. C?" he always called me Mr. C.

"Telling them we were the best vets in Devon."

"Taint naught but the truth."

It was a fact that I had never had a failure on Len's farm, and true to form, the Red Water soon cleared up in his cow. Len Huxley was a first class farmer despite appearances and I was glad he was on our side for his word carried considerable weight over a wide area. Like all vets, I had found there were farms where everything always seemed to go right, and others where, despite similar conditions and similar treatments, things went wrong. Success meant a lot to us as we continued to build our young Practice, and expand it steadily year by year.

I had time on my hands so decided to call on the Fordyces in their lovely old manor house, walking up a path through lawns dotted with flowering shrubs of various kinds, and admiring a glorious pink and white Clematis montana growing up the wall of their home right to the upper windows. I was warmly welcomed by the couple, Goldie and two Siamese cats, regaled with coffee and given a brief synopsis of their background. Mr. F was a company director in London, but now, in his fifties, had decided to fulfil his yearning to escape to the country, and although he had periodic trips to the capital, much of his business was conducted from his home. They had a family of six, all away from home, except the youngest, at present studying law at Cambridge. After coffee they said, "Now come and meet the other members of the family."

They conducted me around, Goldie bouncing along in front of us, and asked me to inspect two lovely Toggenburg goats and three hunter horses in a field behind their home. Ducks, hens, geese, guinea fowl and turkeys wandered around at will, a real pastoral scene. Referring to the horses, they said,

"We don't hunt, but ride a bit," then asked,

"Well, what do you think of our little estate?"

"Lovely!" I enthused. "What a delightful place to live and work."

"It's heavenly," breathed Mrs. Fordyce, "we've dreamt of doing this for years, but we're pretty ignorant, real townies and we'll be calling on you for advice frequently."

"Any time," I assured them, "don't hesitate."

"*Do* call whenever you are passing, Mr. Cameron," and they obviously meant it.

That was the beginning of a growing acquaintanceship with the couple. I did call several times in the next few months for our farms at little Birleton had a spell when they seemed to be in regular need of a vet, and over the summer I met most of the Fordyce family on visits to their parents. They were really grand folk whom it was a joy to know. To see people so blissfully happy with their lot was a delight to behold.

Summer passed, and autumn was just beginning to give way to the first cold touch of winter's hand. The prevailing south westerlies had all but stripped the trees of leaves, and I was glad on night calls that the modern cars, unlike my first, had small heaters in them. One night late the phone rang. It was Mrs. Fordyce, clearly very upset.

"Oh, Mr. Cameron! I'm so sorry to call you so late but I'd appreciate it if you could come out. Leonard's away and Goldie is very ill."

"Sorry to hear that, Mrs. Fordyce. I'll be out right away, but what exactly seems to be Goldie's trouble?"

"Oh, several things . . ." She started to sob. "It's horrible. Please hurry."

I drove to Birleton Manor wondering what calamity could have overtaken the dog sufficient to cause such distress in a sensible person like Mrs. Fordyce. One of her daughters, evidently home for a few days, opened the door to me and conducted me to the kitchen where the never-out Raeburn gave a cosy glow on that cold night. As at the zoo, once again I stopped, as if smitten, and stared in concern at my patient. He was certainly not the Goldie I had come to know. The big dog lay on a carpet in front of the stove, his neck stretched out, his rib cage heaving rapidly, his coat dirty and dishevelled, but what really transfixed my eyes was his near hind leg. It was grossly swollen and on the end of it was a foot that was no longer a foot but a huge, club like appendage, just barely attached to the leg. It was black in colour, about four times the normal size, the toes swollen and distended like huge sausages. A great deep groove above the foot went right down to the bone, over which skin and muscle had disappeared, revealing the naked bone. I did not need the voice of Len Huxley to say at that moment,

"Gin-trap, Mr. C. Ought to be a law against it!"

I had not noticed Len till now, and glanced round the comfortable, well appointed kitchen. Mrs. Fordyce was sitting in a chair, twisting her handkerchief in her hands, sobbing quietly to herself, and the daughter's eyes were also swollen from weeping. Mrs. Fordyce looked up and said,

"Thank you for c-coming so quickly. Leonard's been in America in business for ten days. What a homecoming for him! Goldie went missing the day he left and only came back tonight. We've been searching everywhere for him every day, reported his disappearance to the police, and I was just g-going up to bed tonight when I heard him crying at the back door. He was lying there with that dreadful thing on his leg. Oh, . . . it was horrible." She broke down and cried again at the recollection. "There was just Fiona and me and we couldn't open that awful trap. We phoned Len and he came over and got it off, bless him. He'd been in bed too."

Len looked a bit embarrassed, took off his bonnet, twisted it between his hands and muttered, "Taint nuthin! What be neighbours for?"

I examined the dog's foot carefully and gently. It was clear at a glance that nothing could save that paw and the bottom part of the leg. Blood vessels, tendons, nerves had all been severed and the bone was roughened and gouged out with the iron jaws of the trap as Goldie had tugged and twisted to free himself from this terrible object that was cutting deep into his leg and causing indescribable agony. It was an all too common picture in these post-war years when gin traps were still widely used. I wondered what, if anything, the person who had set that trap would feel as he looked at this end product of his handiwork. Possibly nothing for "taint agin the law be it?" The dog had presumably been caught ten days ago as he wandered off to search for his master. He had had nothing to eat or drink as was obvious by his lean frame, and when he had finally uprooted the trap he had clearly dragged himself a long way. Obviously, the trap setter had not checked this trap for at least ten days, which was criminal, and this . . . this obscenity was the result. It would mean an amputation, but Goldie was also far through, with a temperature of 106°F, the lungs under my stethoscope giving the ominous sounds of a raging pneumonia, the stress of the terrible, constant pain, total exhaustion, hypothermia, starvation and toxaemia from that wholly gangrenous paw. The whole thing added up to a very sick animal indeed.

"Will it mean him losing the leg?" asked Fiona.

"I'm afraid so, though dogs can manage fine on three legs, but first we've got to save him. He's very ill tonight."

"Do you really think you can cure him, Mr. Cameron?"

asked the lady of the house. "I'd rather you told us straight."

"Mrs. Fordyce, I can only try. The leg looks horrible, but more serious tonight is this bad pneumonia, the poison that's swirling through his body, and the shock of it all to the system. I know that you'll give him the best possible nursing and if we can get over the next few days, there's a fair chance. We'll ignore the leg tonight, for I doubt he could stand an anaesthetic right now, but first thing in the morning when Ann my assistant comes in, we'll consider surgery. We'll leave him with you in front of the fire for he's warmer than he would be in our kennels, treat the shock and general condition, give him something for the pain which will also make him sleep, and perhaps in the morning you can bring him down to the surgery. I'm sure Len will help."

"O' course, anything at all. Now don't 'ee worry, Mistress. Us's had three cats lose legs in gins an' they all got over it, caught mice again too."

So I gave the big Retriever a shot of morphine which would take him away from pain for the night, a hefty dose of mixed antibiotic, and an injection for shock. I stayed till I saw him drop into a deep sleep, we covered him with a blanket, and left him.

"Try to get some sleep, ladies," I said, but I knew that mother and daughter would probably sit up all night.

"Thank goodness Leonard will be back tomorrow," Mrs. F murmured, then recollecting her duties as a hostess, exclaimed, "Oh, I'm sorry, I haven't offered you or Len any tea. I can soon get it."

"Nay, missus, don't ee bother," said Len. "Oi be off 'ome to bed an' don't ee worry. It'll be alright, you'll see. Mr. C saved our cats," and the kind hearted but far from genteel farmer awkwardly patted the lady's hand. "Same with you, miss," he said to the daughter, "these traps be works o' the devil, but animals can stand a lot. Your dog will be running around in no time."

Len's prediction proved partly true. It was a risk with

such a sick dog, but next morning, with Ann assisting expertly and watching the anaesthetic with great care, we amputated Goldie's leg high enough up to give us non-gangrenous tissue which would heal properly, and enough healthy muscle and skin to stitch and give a good pad for the stump. It took a bit longer than Len's "no time" for Goldie to be running around, but eventually he was. Bernard and I were responsible for the fact that quite a number of dogs, and even more cats in the area were going through life on three legs, and coping wonderfully, but it was the kind of surgery that gave me no satisfaction, always, I felt, a patch up job.

The Fordyces were very grateful and said so, Goldie gradually adapted to life without one leg, and as I stroked his head at Birleton Manor a few weeks later I thought, "Better a patch up than no job at all."

There were many occasions in my ministry at Aldermouth when I was called to try to "patch up" some problem too. When first I arrived, I discovered there were no Social Workers or Marriage Guidance Counsellors in the town. Our Kirk Session wrote to the authorities, pointed out this lack, two post-graduate students used our premises as headquarters for a whole winter's survey, and to our astonishment the town was flooded with, initially, six experts. Previously all the problems labelled under Social Work had been devolved to the ministers and doctors. Ministers were, of course, not really trained for this par-ticular kind of thing, but after the initial rush to the Social Workers, I found a curious thing happened. Many with problems seemed to prefer the minister to the profes-sional Social Worker. I am not sure why. Perhaps it was because I was by then well known; perhaps the minister was preferred to the professional because they did not become cases on files, no notes were kept, and no details repeated to anyone and maybe, just maybe, in some cases, excellent though the work of the Social Workers was some felt, wrongly I'm sure, there was a more sympathetic, listening ear with the minister. Whatever the reason, the crowd kept coming. I remember in one week, after the oil boom hit Aldermouth, three young wives came separately to me to ask if I could help in their marriage problems, three girls who had not the slightest connection with any Church, but were at their wits' end. This sort of thing went on all the time.

Typical were Billy and Sylvia, whom I had married in my early days. Billy was a wild loon, had come from a broken home in a nearby town, and not without some misgiving, I had married him to Sylvia, who was from a good, steady home, but, like Billy, had not the slightest interest in Church except as a "nice" place to be married. Billy was one of the boys, a hard drinker, rough and ready, by no means unintelligent, but evidently felt that life, whether as a bachelor or a husband, was for living, for him alone, and proceeded to do so in his own swaggering manner. From early on there was trouble and several times Sylvia or her mother came to see me to talk over problems that had arisen. Mind you, the faults were not all on one side. They seldom are. Eventually, I would speak with Billy and things would be patched up for a time.

Then a baby arrived. Billy was delighted with his wee bairn, and all was serene for a time. But only for a time, alas. Periodically I would visit them and try to talk some sense into the situation, and in particular make Billy realise his responsibilities. I was constantly patching up. Then Sylvia's father died, a good man, quiet, unassuming, a mediating influence. Now Billy became the man of the family, now he would decide everything. Regularly he would break out into an orgy of wild living . . . and yet there was a likeable bit about him despite his rough ways and mode of life. To my great delight, he got involved with one of the youth organisations of the Church, became a junior leader, and the responsibility seemed to steady him. It was marvellous to see him in Church weekly and I hoped we had turned the corner. So indeed it seemed for a time. The baby grew, the couple got a new house, and in due course a second child was well on the way. But gradually Billy drifted away again, and Sylvia came to me one evening in an appalling state. She had clearly been misused, told me, what was obvious, that Billy was beating her and the night before, though over eight months' pregnant, had knocked her down. I had patched and patched at that marriage and now I saw red.

I went straight out to their home and confronted Billy. He was brash, cocky, wild, "what's it to you" in his attitude. By now I knew them so well I felt I could talk like a Dutch uncle, and gave him a piece of my mind in far from gentle, distinctly non-ministerial language. I pointed out it took a really brave man to knock down his pregnant wife, as he had done. He rose from his chair blood in his eyes, mouthing curses as he came towards me, and I really thought he was going to strike me, and rather hoped he would! I was much more a wild vet confronted by a bull at that moment than a gentle minister. I am afraid in that situation I would have found it difficult to turn the other cheek, but then the Bible also tells us to defend the weak, and speaks of righteous indignation.

"Go on, then, Billy, have a go at someone your own size. Have a go at me."

I really do not know what I would have done if he had, but I am afraid I would have flattened him. He glared for a time, mouthed more insults, and then threw himself in a chair. Once more I tried, calm again, to mediate and patch up what had become an almost hopeless situation. On the way home I thought with some shame, of my reaction, then remembered Dr. Barclay's words.

"Anger for oneself is nearly always wrong for a Christian. Anger for others might very well be right."

There was no more wife battering, but a fortnight later when Sylvia was in hospital having their baby, Billy nipped off to live and sleep with someone else. That, alas, was the end of things. Separation and divorce followed.

The trouble with patches, I felt sadly, is that they do not always hold and if the garment they are patched to is rotten, they tear away, which, after all, is what the Master Teacher said about it.

Many were the patch-up jobs I tried. Some, praise the Lord, succeeded, like the middle aged wife who came to me in great distress to say that her man was out drinking till one o'clock every morning, and then going out next day and working an enormous crane at the yard, high up on the platform, and putting lives at risk. That patch seemed to stick, but sadly, as I look back, though I did a lot of stitching, hour after hour, days and days of reasoning, counselling, advising, pleading, praying, many, like Goldie, finally resulted in an amputation. But I felt I had to try, spending much time and nervous energy, often with people with no Church connection, like the woman who came to me with a black eye and announced,

"My man gied me this last nicht. I didna ken whether to come to you or go to the polis but I thought I'd try you first!"

It was wearing, wearying, often disappointing work, but I felt that where there was any hope at all, I must try, and after all, there is no disgrace in a patch, as my mother used to say, provided it holds.

I sometimes felt guilty in my later years at Aldermouth that I was in danger of spending more time with non-Church members than with my own flock as my life would be taken up with social or personal problems, but then I would remember the words of the great healer.

"They that be whole need not a physician, but they that are sick," and from time to time, as I saw a couple sitting together in Church or walking as a family in the High Street, a patch up job, like Ham, the llama and Goldie, this kind of surgery, seemed quite a worthwhile thing after all.

The Constant Question

SEVENTEEN

Like, I suppose, most people, my favourite months of the year are May and June. The winter is past, the days have grown longer and warmer, trees are bursting into new life, fields have greened with their covering of that marvellous crop, grass, roadsides and banks are aglow with a multitude of wild flowers, providing homes and nurture for a myriad of tiny creatures. In Devon the lanes would be spangled with bright yellow primroses, making them a delight to drive along, and on the road to the little village of Lee, just outside Bristacombe, by June, fuchsia was growing wild along the hedgerows. The annual miracle of nature had occurred once more and the earth was touched with a fresh beauty, like a young girl prepared and adorned for her first party.

In our veterinary world, the noises of the lambing pens had died away, spring calving cows had produced their offspring, end of winter conditions like acetonaemia in cattle and twin-lamb disease in ewes were over for another year, and in the Practice, we would have time to draw breath once more. It was a period of rejoicing and relaxation for Bernard and I, and for Ann and Janet, on the end of the phone. In fact it was marred for me by only one thing. When May and June came along, farmers thought it was time to have their yearling, or sometimes two year old colts castrated. I dreaded this annual event

as on castration days I was tensed up in the morning as
I contemplated the day ahead. The reason for this tension
was that I was not really a horseman. Oh yes, I could
treat horses and in my ten years in practice and my years
as a student treated many hundreds, for all sorts of conditions, and for the most part with success. I knew as well
as the next man the symptoms of the various equine
diseases and disorders, and how to cope with them. But
I early came to the conclusion that a real horseman was
born, not made, one who seemed instinctively to understand and empathise with a horse, and was absolutely at
home and at ease around a stable. For myself, although
I could admire the beauty of a handsome young colt or
filly, I was more at home with other animals so far as
understanding them and treating them were concerned.
In our vet course, oddly enough, the horse was still king,
classed as number one, and everything else a poor second.

In many areas of the land there would be someone who
had the reputation of being a horse expert and he would
travel the countryside for weeks cutting the colts, rigs and
even sometimes full grown stallions that had not made
the grade at stud. This was particularly so in the true horse
breeding districts of Britain, and in places like Newmarket
where there were dozens of thoroughbred stables. But
North Devon was off the beaten track for these experts,
and for the most part our horses consisted of ponies
or hunters, which were on every farm, the occasional
thoroughbred and the surviving working horses, the
great majestic heavy breeds like Shire, Clydesdale or Suf-
folk Punch. So the farmers were quite content to use their
own vets. They did the job perfectly well and cost a
lot less than the horse consultants in their Bentleys and
Jaguars.

For years the traditional method of castrating a horse
was to cast it with ropes, chloroform it, truss up its legs
to expose the site, and then operate, but surgery in the
standing position had become popular with many owners. It was less trouble provided the horse was quiet and

behaved itself; it required fewer men to assist, and being carried out under local anaesthetic, it avoided the slight risk attached to chloroform. However, I hated it, it was a dangerous business for the operator and I was convinced it was also a less efficient surgical procedure. Normally Kenneth or I, or after Kenneth left, Bernard and I would go out together to do the job, and I can still hear the rattling of our instruments in their dishes in the back of the car on our way to castrations. It sounded to me like the knell of doom. Occasionally, if the horse was being done in the standing position, I would go by myself to do the job.

That was the case one May morning at Park farm where Dr. Fulton had a fine herd of Ayrshires, a flock of North Country Cheviot sheep, which he had brought south from Sutherland, and a few horses. Dr. Fulton was a nationwide figure, having been Principal of an Agricultural College in Scotland for years, then agricultural adviser to a large Arab country, until he finally settled in a very fertile area on the edge of our practice. I held him somewhat in awe at first, for he was a clever, knowledgeable man, well versed in all the ways of animals, and while he always treated me with courtesy, I was conscious, senior partner though I was, of my relative youth and inexperience compared to him. He was probably our biggest and most lucrative client, and in the early days when he came to us, I was always apprehensive lest something go wrong. But I had done quite a bit with his sheep, treated many of his pedigree Ayrshires for all kinds of ailments, and also his horses, with complete success, until the week before I set out to castrate his colt which he specified be done in the standing position.

I had been treating a cow with a bad Staphylococcal mastitis, a very serious condition, even with the advent of the wonder antibiotics. Mastitis is, of course, inflammation of the udder and most cases responded to treatment since most were caused by the Streptococcal organism, which penicillin soon cleared up. But a Staphylococcal mastitis was a different kettle of fish. The udder would become as hard as a board, the discharge be foul smelling and teeming with organisms, and very frequently and very quickly, the infection would spread throughout the whole body until the cow was suffering from septicae- mia, or blood poisoning. One of Dr. Fulton's best cows had developed this as soon as it calved, and despite daily visits, massive doses of serum, antibiotics and other drugs, had grown rapidly worse, and when I had seen it the day before, it was just clinging to life and no more.

I arrived at Park farm to be given the news the cow had died that morning, which did not put me in the best of spirits for my surgery. However, work has to go on. The colt, a beautiful bay, was brought out of the stable by Dr. Fulton's son, and positioned with one side against a wall. I laid my instruments in their steriliser and enamel dishes on a bale of straw, and scrubbed up to begin. A twitch (a stick with a loop of rope on the end) was applied to the pony's upper lip by the son, and twisted till it was really tight. This was an age old method of restraint and the idea was that the horse would be so taken up with the wretched thing on his nose, he would not pay too much attention to what was happening elsewhere. I cleaned the scrotum and inguinal area thoroughly with antiseptic, gingerly injected local anaesthetic into testicles and spermatic cord, all safe so far, scrubbed my hands again, then reaching for a scalpel made my incision. Just then, though feeling no pain, the horse realised what was being done to it, and proceeded to rear, kick and plunge about.

"Screw up that twitch," I shouted to the son, who had the twitch in one hand, a halter in the other. Still the animal pranced about, at the worst possible time, with the incision made, bleeding, and liable with its kicking to get dirt into the wound. Dr. Fulton whistled up a couple of men and they leaned against the little horse's side, pressing it hard to the wall. Then I used the emasculator to crush the cord, artery forceps to stop the bleeding, and the testicles were removed. I again cleaned the whole area with antiseptic solution, puffed sulphanilamide powder into the wound, gave a shot of penicillin and an anti-tetanus jab, checked that the haemorrhage had more or less stopped, and proceeded to gather up my instruments with a sigh of relief.

"A bit tricky, Mr. Cameron, but a nice clean job," said the Doc. "I'm very fond of that little fellow, you know, and glad things have worked out so well."

"Oh, he should do alright. I'd turn him into a nice clean paddock where you can keep an eye on him today, or if you prefer it, keep him in a loose box, but they usually do better outside. Let me know if he bleeds or if you have any trouble."

I was taken into the house where Mrs. Fulton had a welcome cup of coffee ready, and being both Ayrshire men in a "foreign" country, we talked of home and discovered mutual acquaintances. Then for the road home and a couple more straightforward cases on the way, the instruments this time, I felt, playing a merry tune in their dishes.

Three days later I had a phone call to say the pony was very swollen and stiff, and scarcely grazing at all. I called, not worrying over much for post-operative swelling and stiffness were not unusual, but a temperature of 105°F had me worried. I examined the wound, with difficulty, for he was very tender there. I did not like the look of it; there had been a little bleeding which was collected in a sac of the scrotum, so, using the twitch again, I enlarged the wound and drained it. I did not like either the colour or the odour of the discharge and so really hit him with a massive dose of antibiotic, bathed the wound, and left instructions to bathe it twice more that day, and I would call again. Next morning he was worse, the swelling was spreading down his rear legs, the whole inguinal area a dirty colour, and the poor little fellow a thoroughly miserable animal. I syringed out the whole of the scrotum with a powerful antiseptic solution, then dusted the wound again with sulphanilamide, and again giving a large injection of antibiotic, departed, a worried man. So it went on.

I could not sleep for thinking about my patient, nor could I understand it. I had never had this trouble with any castration before, went over the whole procedure in my mind again, and concluded that somehow, in his prancing about during the op, or perhaps from the soil of the paddock, he had got that same Staph bug which had killed the cow.

On the seventh day when I called, I was met by a somewhat frigid Dr. Fulton.

"He's just died, I'm afraid," then he went on, "You haven't had much success here lately, have you, but some people are like that. Maybe you've just been unlucky." I fully understood the implied criticism in his remark, but in my gloomy state I felt just a little hurt by it when I considered all the previous successes I had had at his farm, and that I had tried to save his colt. All I could say was, "I'm sorry; very sorry. It's no consolation, I know, but I've never lost a colt before." Nor did I again.

No coffee appeared that day, and I felt sure I had lost our biggest client, but I imagine as he thought things through, for he was a fair man, he must have decided I could not entirely be held responsible. Despite disappointments, life has to go on, and I had plenty to occupy me for the rest of the day to keep me busy.

Getting back in the early evening from my afternoon round, I found a large dog tied to our operating table with a piece of string. There was a note on the desk to say he was to be put down, having more or less gone berserk at Martincombe where he lived, bitten several people, and terrified the whole terrace. Now I knew that dog. I had visited him once at his house for some minor complaint, and even with a tape muzzle securely fastened and the owner, a big, husky fellow, holding him as firmly as he could, he had struggled, fought and snarled in a pretty terrifying fashion. Apart from a St Bernard and Newfoundland I had treated, he was the biggest dog I had ever seen, an alsatian crossed with, I suspected, a tiger, and here I was, alone with him in the surgery, and somehow I had to get near him and give him an injection. Why not shoot him, I can hear you ask? Well, I did not possess a gun, and even if I had, shooting in a surgery with a dwelling house above is somewhat frowned upon. Even my humane killer was no better, for that still required holding the dog and putting the instrument to his head.

He was uttering the most fearsome snarls which confirmed my suspicion of his tiger ancestry, showing his teeth, ears laid back, lashing about on his restraining bit of thick string. I filled my syringe with Euthatal, and paused to consider how I could get near him, when lo, I did not need not wonder any more, for suddenly he was near me, his cord having parted like thread. He leapt for my throat and I leapt back in considerable alarm, and before I knew it, he was chasing me round the surgery, and somehow I did not think he wanted to lick my face!

I kept on the move, being careful to have the operating table between us, and praying fervently I would not slip or trip, for without question he would have torn me to shreds. I realised I had only one hope, being all alone in our premises, and that was to somehow get a dog catcher and restrain him with that. We possessed several of these, long hollow metal tubes with a rope running through them, ending in a loop which you tried to drop over a dog's head and pull tight. Unfortunately, though, the dog catchers were all kept hanging on a hook in the passage outside the surgery and I wondered how I could reach the door in one piece, and at all costs I must not let this mad creature out of the door and possibly on to the street. So I went on the offensive, roared and snarled at the dog, pushed the table on its wheels in his direction and leapt for the door. Collecting the strongest catcher I could find, I cautiously re-opened the door. He was waiting for me just inside, and sprang at me. I fought him off with the metal rod, then the positions were reversed, as

I started stalking him around the room, trying to drop the noose over his head.

I don't know how long it all went on, but it seemed forever. Eventually the dog stopped, clearly puzzled about what to do next, and I had him. The noose went round his neck and I pulled it up as tight as I could until he was half throttled. It was far from scientific, in fact it was downright brutal, a horrible way to treat an animal, but this animal was prepared to kill, and it was him or me. He struggled with immense strength and ferocity, and I kept on pulling the cord, cutting off his air supply. Eventually, in his struggles to free himself, he fell on his side, and immediately I threw myself on top of him, reached up for my loaded syringe, and injected the Euthatal into his peritoneum. This was a slower way to destroy a dog, but it was quite painless, and I had no hope in our wrestling match of hitting a vein to produce instant death. Gradually he relaxed as the drug took effect, and I was able to slacken the rope. He passed into a sleep, and when unconscious, I gave him another dose into a vein and in seconds he was gone. At least his end had been painless, which was more than mine would have been, I was sure, if he had succeeded in catching me.

It took me some time to stop trembling, but eventually I drove home, had a late tea, recounted the day's work to Janet, who was horrified at my encounter with that wild dog, and shared with me in my disappointment at losing the colt. As always, when talking to her, and reliving the fight to save the horse, things looked better, and seemed less like the end of the world. That has always been one of the wonderful things about my wife. She would share to the full with me in the happenings of my work, but always have the ability to point out certain basic things, make me see events in a different light and lift me up. Life with her has always been a total partnership.

Although my whole life as a vet was concerned with disease, sickness and death, I cannot recall ever philosophising much about the whole question of suffering. Only occasionally was I moved to wonder, or indeed to anger. Perhaps when trying to save a sea bird burned through and through with oil because of man's heedlessness or carelessness in its vast world of the ocean, and suffering with the silence of its kind, occasionally the whole moral dilemma came home to me. Again, when having to put down a perfectly healthy dog which was just unwanted or as when watching Dr. Fulton's colt suffer, and go down fighting, just on such occasions I would ponder and question. But although the constant question of *why* suffering was there in the animal kingdom, it was only as a minister it came home to me, and became, indeed *the* constant question. Why all this suffering?

Of course there were the many glad occasions in the ministry like weddings, baptisms, work with children, seeing young people grow up straight and true, and the constant joy of preaching the glad news of the gospel. Yet was the gospel not also about one who had suffered and died? In addition, hardly a week went past without some family knowing illness, pain, anxiety and death. In Aldermouth we had a hundred funerals a year in our Church, two a week on average, and this became *the* constant question of my ministry, the thing I have been asked times without number. "Why? Why suffering? Why sorrow?"

Sometimes one could give a ready answer. I recall at Moorton one day heading for the hospital for my weekly visits, and being overtaken at speed on a corner by a Mini. It was a wet day, the road was slippery with a sort of skin on top of it, and care was required. Just around another bend, about a mile on, I came on the Mini right across the road, lying on its side, its wheels still spinning. I stopped my car as did several others, and we helped the occupants of the stricken car to safety. Fortunately no one was really hurt, but all were shaken, and out of that little car came five adults, three children and a dog. The car's tyres were bald as a coot, obvious in its upside down position. I was wearing my clerical collar, and at the sight of this, a middle aged woman from the tilted car rounded on me in anger and demanded, "Why did your God do this to us?" An overloaded car, going too fast on a wet road and a bend, with bald tyres, and it was God's fault that they had crashed! I thought, as we pushed their car upright again, they should have been on their knees thanking God they were still alive despite their folly.

There are instances in life when we can see the cause of suffering very clearly. If a man gets behind the wheel of a car with drink in him and kills a child, the source of blame is clear. If I smoke, despite the government warnings, I must be prepared for the consequences. If a person is promiscuous, can he or she really wonder if they get *Aids*, and so on. In many instances we bring suffering or eventual death on ourselves. But there are the many others. As I have noted, sorrow came to some Aldermouth family virtually every week, and many times I have stood at the graveside with a question in my heart, and visiting the bereaved family later, seeking to bring the consolations of the gospel, feeling very helpless in the face of their questions when the heart is broken. Studdart Kennedy, "Woodbine Willie," the famous Chaplain of the Great War, once said, "the person who is not moved by suffering and grief is either hard in the heart or soft in the head," for every death brought heartache to somebody.

I suppose, after doctors, ministers see more of death than anyone else, and many people feel we get used to it, even get hardened, and after all it is our job. I have never "got used" to the fact of death, and on innumerable occasions have stood beside the bed of one of my folks who over the years had become a friend, and would willingly have given my right arm to relieve them. Especially I found the death of a young person hard, and we had a spell in Aldermouth when it seemed as if every day was bringing bad news.

Three bright young men, at about the same time, contracted leukaemia and one looked on in wonder at their courage as they fought this thing whose very name produced a pall of fear. They battled, and were at times amazingly cheerful, but all were taken, and terrible indeed to behold was the parents' grief. I had only to look at my own young sons of the same age range to know how the parents felt. Then there was John, a brilliant young man in his early thirties who developed a particularly virulent form of cancer, and had the whole range of treatment. After some months he came to my Vestry Hour one week with a young lady, and announced they had decided, despite the circumstances, to go ahead and be married. I concurred in their decision to have some happiness together, however long or short, for both knew the situation to the full. It was a particularly poignant wedding, and was, understandably, totally desolate; folks spoke of the foolishness of their marriage, but I was glad that they, like so many couples in the war, had even these few months together.

In rapid succession three of my younger elders died, one the local schoolmaster who was one of my closest friends, a man who had so much to give to school, Church and community. I remember the tremendous shock to staff and pupils when I had to announce his death to the whole school one morning. Fit, strong, in the prime of life, he had been golfing the evening before. Why Lord?

Eric trained the local Highland League football team, had given our own son Ian his first chance in senior football at the age of fifteen, as he had done with many other young people. Yet this man, who was infinitely gentle and kind, but would not countenance either dirty language or dirty play, no matter how great the star player, and had an immense power for good in many lives, the most respected man in northern football, was taken. Why Lord?

Donnie, a quiet, unassuming man had brought up his four daughters well, and they, with their parents, were in Church every Sunday and involved in the life of the organisations, and in addition, as the town gardener, had annually created so much beauty for locals and visitors alike to enjoy, yet was also snatched away young. Why Lord?

One evening I had a phone call informing me there had been an air crash at Sullom Voe and included in the casualties was an Aldermouth lad of nineteen. I did not really know the boy, they were a non-Church family, but I recall well that message given by the boy's aunt.

"I believe in God, Mr. Cameron, and I know death is not the end, but I don't know what my sister and her husband believe, but could you please come down and try to help, and would you be willing to take the funeral?"

I went immediately to the house, wondering, as so often, what I could possibly say. Often, I am sure, I failed, but often too it is amazing how one is given a word that will help. I met with that family in their deep grief, and among other things told them of Willie Barclay, my old New Testament lecturer and his experience. He too had lost a nineteen year old daughter in a drowning accident, his only girl. At the time he wrote a letter to a friend which included the triumphant words.

"We who believe know that while this is the end of the chapter it is not the end of the book. Barbara has many chapters still to write." There speaks the confidence of faith, and without that same belief, I would never have dared take a funeral.

It has been said that sorrow either drives us to God, or from God, and I have seen both often. In the case of the lad in the air crash, his parents were drawn to seek consolation from a Father who had Himself lost a Son, and such a seeker never seeks in vain. I took the funeral when our large Church was filled to its 1000 capacity, hundreds of those attending being young people meeting death for the first time. I have never forgotten the tremendous hush and stillness, which was later repeated at the graveside. Even the hardest of hearts could not fail to be moved and to feel that even in this stark tragedy, the Lord was truly there, for "in all their afflictions He was afflicted."

Two brothers, sons of a widow, were killed together in a car crash and as I again conducted this funeral and visited the mother regularly afterwards, she said to me one day, "I didna' think I could get through, Mr. Cameron, and I couldna' see hoo I could manage to go on and wasna' sure I wanted to go on, but He gied me the strength one day at a time," . . . a sentiment many have expressed to me over the years . . . one day, even one hour at a time . . . but why, Lord? Why the sorrow? Why so often the best people who seem to be taken? Many times I felt like weeping with the family at the funeral, but somehow one has to keep going for the sake of all the mourners present, and one does.

The death of little children; cot deaths, the death of a baby, were all particularly hard and the grief of the mother often so terrible and so private, that I felt I could not intrude, only be available.

In the face of all this weight of sorrow, what does one say, for even in the passing of someone who had lived a full life there would be a wife or husband left, or a family. It is hard and I have often felt I did no good at all, as hard though one tries, as with Dr. Fulton's pony, it is a losing battle. Many times too, recalling my fight with that big, vicious dog, I felt there was something evil, something demonic, at the heart of things.

One morning our Dr. John phoned me. He had just come from the home of Mrs. Baxter, for her husband had gone into the bathroom that morning to shave, taken a massive coronary, and died instantly. They had to break down the door to get in. The Baxters were a retired and retiring couple, closely knit and childless. Mrs. Baxter in particular, though she was a fine woman, being a shy person by nature, not outgoing, and with perhaps few close friends in this new area.

"Can you go out?" asked Dr. John, "and tell Mrs.

Baxter what you said on Sunday in your sermon. I think it might help. I couldn't recall it exactly for her."

"Oh, John," I protested, "I can't remember my sermons. They aren't worth remembering. What was it you had in mind?"

"That definition you gave of death. It's the best I've heard," said our good and godly doctor.

I remembered now. I had come across it in a book written by a young minister's widow, and she had included this description. I don't believe it was hers originally, for Joyce Grenfell quotes the same words, but I had latched on to it as both practical and beautiful.

I sat with Mrs. Baxter for a time, then she said, "The Doctor said you had some words that might help me." The Baxters were normally in Church every week and would have heard the quote, but had missed the previous Sunday. So I gave her the definition which had helped me, and I believe it helped her:

"Life is eternal" (it does not end here)

"Love is immortal" (it does not end here either. "We'll meet again")

"Death is but a horizon, and a horizon is only the limit of our sight."

That sums it up, and is true to the teaching of the only One who ever Himself conquered death and who said, "In my Father's house are many dwelling places. Why, if it were not so, would I have told you." I like that confident assertion, "if it were not so." So, in the confidence that her man was but out of sight over the horizon and that death could not destroy, only separate in the body for a time, Mrs. Baxter and many another, have laid their loved ones to rest.

"Now you're preaching, Cameron," I can hear many readers say. "Of course you ministers would say something like that." Maybe, but over the years if I had not believed in Life Eternal before, I would have been forced to by the experience of countless souls I have known in the vale of tears. But still there remains that "why suffering?," that constant question. You know, I think for us mere mortals, it will have to remain for the present.

Dr. Sangster, the great Methodist preacher, and a saintly man who himself died quite young, put it well in a little story. A boy had gone off to an organised camp with some of his friends. He was given enough pocket money to last him the week, but in two days it had all gone. So he wrote a hurried postcard home, which basically said, "Out of cash, send by return, RSVP instantly. Love Tom." But no reply came. His pals, who were also bankrupt and hoping to share in the loot said,

"He can't have got your card." Tom did not think that very likely.

"Well, your Dad's forgotten all about you." Tom knew that was not so.

"Well, it can only mean he doesn't care about you." Tom was certain that was not true. Finally they asked,

"Well, what do you think yourself? Why has he not done what you asked?" Tom thought for a bit, then said,

"I don't understand it, but I'll ask him when I get home."

I too am content to wait till Home to learn the answer to that constant question, why?

The Hand that Feeds

EIGHTEEN

"Hello!" bellowed the phone at me.

"Hello!" I subconsciously bellowed back.

"Hello!" double forte, came the roar. I held the instrument further from my ear.

"Yes, hello!" I managed to keep it quiet this time. "Bristacombe 250."

"Hello! This danged machine be'nt workin." There was a thunder in my ear. The speaker had obviously banged the receiver on something. "That's better! Ah can hear it speak now. Be that the vetnary?"

"Yes, Cameron speaking."

"What's that? Dang me, it be'nt talkin' yet! This is Bill Narracott," came a roar like a bull, which nearly burst my ear-drum.

"Hello, Mr. Narracott," I shouted, "Mr. Cameron speaking. What's your trouble?"

"Trouble? It be this blasted talkin' thing. It don't seem to speak straight!"

Despite my tingling ear-drum, I smiled to myself. Bill Narracott and brother Bert, in an old-fashioned part of the world, the West Country, where life was slower than in many other places, were even more old-fashioned than most. They were middle-aged bachelors who lived in a tumble-down farmhouse with ancient buildings. They still had horses for work and a minimum of machinery.

Their farm and stock was their sole interest in life. They dressed in the thick trousers popular years ago, had for their top an ex-army tunic or some old flapping jacket, their caps were green with age, they appeared to wash but seldom and shaved maybe once a week. I did not think they had the phone installed in their farm of Barton Mill over Mortecombe way, and consequently they generally approached the instrument with mystification. Mr. Narrocott's next words proved me right.

"Oi be speakin from Ossaboro, Vetnary," (the neighbouring farm) "Us 'as a dead bullock—struck with lightnin'. You'll 'ave to come out."

"Right, Mr. Narracott, I'll be out as soon as I can. Lightning eh? That's a surprise. I don't think we had lightning in Bristacombe last night."

"What's that, young man?" came the bellow, angry now.

"I just said I'm surprised at the lightning. We had none over here."

"No? Well . . ." came the voice. (There was no actual lightning but plenty of thunder over the air, I thought) "Us 'ad it here. Must 'ave, else how could our good bullock be dead, eh?" It was undeniable logic to Bill!

"Righto. I'll be with you shortly."

I was glad to put the receiver down. My head was singing with the assault on my ear-drums, especially first thing in the morning. We were at breakfast and our boys were clearly puzzled.

"Shout! Daddy shouting in a big voice," said young Neil.

I smiled at our eldest son, aged at the time about three, sitting at his breakfast that June morning. Little Ian, some seventeen months his junior, was propped up in his high chair and he proceeded to show he could shout too.

"Quiet, Ian!" I said, my voice inadvertently still raised.

"No need to shout, dear," said Janet.

"Och—I didn't mean to. My brain hasn't settled down yet."

"Are you worried about the case, Alec?" queried my wife.

"A bit. I hate these lightning stroke cases for they are so vague and are always liable to get you into trouble with the client."

"What a client, Daddy?" piped up Neil. He was always surprising us with his vocabulary, and as typical proud parents, we felt he was very clever for his age, almost in the genius class.

"A client's a man with a sick animal, son, usually a farmer," I explained.

"Milk comes from farmer," Neil informed us.

"That's right, drink yours up."

He obeyed, and Ian, trying to do the same, promptly spilled his. Altogether it was a bad start to the day, and with brothers Bill and Bert Narracott to come, I felt it would very likely get worse.

I set off on my visit, having gulped the rest of my breakfast, and as I drove my little Austin 8 van, I mused that lightning stroke was hardly the best way to get in the good books of farmers and the Narracotts had but recently come to us as the Practice steadily grew in size. Actually they seldom had a vet, using the old remedies peddled by the reps of the old drug firms, and only when a beast was on its last legs did they call the vet. Practically all I had done for them was their annual tuberculin test, when I had got into trouble, for they had one cow that was doubtful, and had to be isolated and re-tested. They were clearly not pleased and it was equally clear they thought I was responsible for this "blasted red tape." Fortunately the beast had passed second time round, when they announced that they had known none of their bullocks could possibly be reactors and the whole thing had been just a waste of time, "a load o' govment nonsense." Lightning stroke was sometimes impossible to diagnose for there were often just no symptoms nor post-mortem signs. The book said, "There is generally some amount of scorching, especially about the bases of the

horns and at the coronets. There may be an irregular
'lightning mark' connecting these places. On removal of
the skin, there is generally a streak of bruised subcutane-
ous tissue seen under the scorched areas, but in other
cases there may be no visible signs of the electric shock."
No visible signs, I thought. Helpful! Farmers knew about
the "irregular lightning mark" and some had been known
to try to scorch the skin with a candle or even a blow
lamp to produce this and convince the vet. If the animal
was found under a tree that was sometimes a pointer, but
all in all it was an unsatisfactory and unscientific business
to diagnose the condition. The great concern of farmers
to have lightning stroke diagnosed in every sudden death
was that their insurance covered such an emergency, and
the vet had to fill in a form for the insurance company
testifying lightning as the cause of death and putting a
value on the animal. The companies were generally very
good at paying up, but often the vet's valuation did not
come up to the farmer's expectations and this could lead
to trouble.

Bill and Bert were waiting for me outside their anti-
quated farmhouse, their pipes drawing well, traditional
hob nailed, turned up toed boots on their feet, their
ancient trousers hitched up at the knees with string, the
flapping khaki jackets and even more ancient bonnets, the
lining of Bert's sticking out so much it seemed to be
outside in. I was dressed in my usual garb of corduroy
trousers, unlike some vets of the older school who still
wore breeches, and when I pulled on my wellingtons and
donned my black waterproof coat, I was ready for the
fray.

"Right, gentlemen, where's the beast?"

"Hur be in the paddock," and they led the way. I
followed with my black case. To be exact, the animal
was in a fairly deep stream that meandered through the
paddock, the water flowing over all but the head, which
was resting on the steep-sided bank. Sadly, there was no
tree anywhere near, only an electric pylon just over the

stream. The animal was a well grown Ruby Red, as the native North Devon cattle were called, about two years old and in good condition.

"Has she been ill at all, off colour, poorly?" I queried.

"Nay—sound as the Bank."

"Had any trouble with Staggers this year?"

"Nay, but look 'ee here, that thar bullock was killed with lightnin', a'm zertain zure," said Bert, pointing with his pipe.

"It could well be, Mr. Narracott, but you see, in any sudden death we have to make sure it isn't Anthrax first of all, then look for something like Staggers or a Heart Attack, and if we can find nothing else, then it's probably lightning. I'll just take a little blood from her and test it for Anthrax."

There was nothing for it but to go down into the brook and soon the water was over the top of my wellingtons. I nicked the ear and drew a smear of blood on to a glass slide, stuffed a bit of cotton wool into the ear and scrambled back up the bank.

"I'm afraid we'll have to go back up to the car so that I can look at this blood under the microscope."

"Blasted nonsense!" exploded Bill, "a tell ee, it be lightning."

"You could be right, but you see there are no burn marks on her, and although she's not yet stiff, which points to lightning, where *rigor mortis*, that's stiffening is slow, I would be in deep trouble if I let an Anthrax case go to the knacker's yard."

"Aar," grunted Bert, "that thar govenment has just a lot o' new fangled nonsense."

I fixed and stained my smear of blood, put the microscope on the bonnet of the car, and in the already bright sunlight of a glorious June morning, had sufficient light to see by. I knew it was no use going into the house to have an electric light shine on the slide, for electricity was one of the many things the brothers did not deem necessary. My procedure was far from satisfactory, but the best I could do, and as I peered down the microscope, I was relieved to find none of the square shapes of Bacillus anthracis, one cause of death eliminated.

"No anthrax, gentlemen," I spoke up cheerfully, endeavouring to spread a little light around, for Bill and Bert were far from a sunny pair. Thunder was in the air, I felt.

"Back to the bullock now."

"Now look 'ee here, Mr. Vetnary," said Bert once more, emphasising his words by poking me on the chest, "oi be zertain our good bullock was killed by lightnin,' so why can 'ee not say so now without all this 'ere fuss. That bullock be worth a tidy bit to us, an' us means to have our due." It was quite a speech for Bert. I nodded and replied, "Don't worry, Mr. Narracott, but you see *I* have to be sure too. Did you hear any thunder or see any lightning through the night?"

"Well . . . no," reluctantly admitted Bert, "but the only thing I hear o' nights is Bill snoring."

So we trudged back to the paddock, I slithered down into the stream, and once more looked at their beast.

"Can you see any marks on her, gentlemen?" I asked.

"Hur hair be kind of standin' up just behind shoulder." I peered at their bullock and decided Bill was seeing with the eye of imagination, or hope. I looked in the beast's mouth. Sometimes animals were struck down while actually chewing grass, but sudden deaths in June were also common from Staggers, magnesium deficiency. I had no wish to deprive the brothers of their rights, but I had to be as sure as I could be. By now, they were becoming apoplectic as they awaited my decision, puffing their pipes furiously. I scrambled up the far bank, the one where the electric pylon rested, and immediately got a considerable electric shock, even through my rubber boots, which mercifully I was wearing. I gave a yell and hastily splashed back through the water and up the other bank. Why I had not had at least a mild shock in the water I know not, but I was at one and the same time more than a little startled by my narrow escape from electrocution, and relieved that I had a positive diagnosis, very positive.

"Your beast's been electrocuted!" I shouted at the brothers, seemingly quite calmly studying my antics. "It's a mercy none of you went over that stream, for with the nails in your boots, you could have been killed too. There's been a leak from that pole and the sooner we get the electricity people out here the better. You'll still get your compensation, for your Policy covers electrocution."

It was hard to tell whether Bert and Bill were more relieved at their escape from possible demise, or delighted at their prospective cheque, for they merely took their pipes from their mouths and gave forth a few "Aars and Uurs." We hastily got back to the farmhouse, and while I despatched Bill back to Ossaboro to phone the electricity Board to send men out at once, Bert and I went into the great stone flagged kitchen with its enormous open fireplace and rough hewn furniture, and after considerable rummaging about in drawers, he eventually extracted an insurance form, which I promised I would fill in that very day.

I went home for a dry pair of socks and my spare wellingtons and while Janet dispensed coffee, I decided to fill in the form and get it off. "You have to treat the client," we had frequently been reminded at College, and I thought some prompt action might make the Narracotts a little better disposed towards me. The last question on the form, however, had me worried, the estimated value of the animal. I have always felt this was an unfair question for vets. The easy way, of course, was to ask the owner, but while most would give an honest valuation, others would bump it up on the principle that insurance companies were able to afford anything. I have never kept up with the weekly market prices of livestock, so I phoned two Devon cattle owners I knew I could trust, and asked them the current price of a two year old Ruby Red. One, whose cattle were a bit of a mixture, said £50, the other with top class animals said £90, so, rightly or wrongly, I decided to take the average and put down £70.

A few days later I had Bill in my surgery, a Bill so incensed he was almost foaming at the mouth. There was certainly lightning now, I thought, and it looked as if I was in for a shock!

"Us 'as just heard from that thar insurance an' they said you said our bullock was worth £70. Now look 'ee here, Mr. Vetnary, we expect our rights, for our bullocks allus top the market and us an 'ave gotten £90 or £100 for our beast. You'm bitin' the hand that feeds you, Mr. Vetnary."

I looked at the incandescent Bill, and decided that rough and ready though he was, he was honest. I explained I was not an expert on prices and told him how I had worked out my valuation, without, of course, saying which farmers I had contacted. I then apologised and said I would contact the insurance people and have it put right. I made discreet enquiries after Bill had stumped out, somewhat mollified, but still repeating like a litany his phrase about "bitin' the hand that feeds you." He obviously thought that was a good one! My enquiries revealed that despite outward appearances, the brothers Narracott truly had just about the best North Devons in the area, so I immediately informed the Company of my error, and the farmers duly got £100. We also, as a Practice, saved a client I was in danger of losing, and I mused wistfully that one's honesty, ability as a vet, not to mention risk to one's life were all poor second bests to money.

I had a similar accusation levelled at me one never to be forgotten week, many years later, at Aldermouth, though the circumstances were different, and the subject not money.

Frequently we had visiting groups to our large and very beautiful Church, Scouts, Guides, Boys' Brigade camping in the district, Drama Groups, Bowlers' Federations, companies of golfers, visits from the Glasgow-Aldermouth or Toronto-Aldermouth Associations and many others, and almost invariably one or more of the visitors would read a lesson in a Service. Lessons were also read by Sunday School, Bible Class, Youth Fellowship members, representatives of the women's organisations and frequently by elders like Henry, Arthur, Bob, Bill, Andrew, Peter, Sandy, Dave or Alastair my quiet, gentle, wise, humble Session Clerk and others, all fine men and fine friends. The congregation, furthermore, seemed to enjoy others taking part in this way. In addition elders like Arthur, Ashley, Malcolm, Bill, David and the other Alastair also conducted whole Services, to the delight of the congregation and the relief and gratification of the minister. Never was there a word of protest till "that week," and here we must have a little political history.

When we went to Aldermouth, the MP was a Conservative, and also the Secretary of State for Scotland, a good man and a good friend who would help anybody, especially the handicapped, for whom, being disabled himself, he had a fellow feeling. He was actually a member of the little country Church of Croy, but often he and his wife, sometimes with a pew of visiting friends, would worship with us, partly because, I am sure, of our magnificent choir and the marvellous singing of a congregation of many hundreds. He told me too, that he looked on Aldermouth Old as the mother Church of the area, and on one occasion he took part in a Service. A leading member of the Conservative Cabinet had grown up in our Church, once in my time being involved in a special Service, and his mother was, in fact, still one of our members. She was a dynamic woman who did an immense amount of good in the town and country, but a formidable person who at first terrified me, for she barked at you. I eventually discovered that she only respected you if you barked back!

I recall visiting her in her delightful home in the country one day. Quite by chance, it happened to be the day the Tory party was voting for a new leader, and her son was one of the candidates. She was rumbling like a volcano that day, and suddenly erupted,

"*That* woman Thatcher. It seems nobody can see past her, she's done this and done that. What about my son and what he's done and they're making him seem a nincumpoop!" As all the world knows, *that* woman won the vote, and for twelve years afterwards had no more loyal supporter or wiser adviser than our son of Aldermouth.

Now I am a strictly non-political animal, certainly in public. I have never agreed with colleagues who use their pulpit for a party political platform and claim that the Tory or Labour manifesto is the latest edition of the Sermon on the Mount. I did not even discuss politics on visits if I could possibly avoid it for I recognised that people can be committed Christians and hold opposite political views. Sometimes, in a sermon, I would speak out on a topical moral or ethical issue which did not involve any particular party, but despite my forbearance and attempts to remain non-political, I have in my time been labelled everything but a Communist!

In the election of the early 1970s which saw the SNP win many seats, our highly respected Tory MP was one of the casualties, and a well known, redoubtable lady of the SNP became our MP. One Saturday long after the election, and with no other election pending, I was informed by two elders that our MP was to be in Church the next morning, and what about getting her to read a lesson? I could see nothing wrong with this. After all, others had done it, and she *was* our MP. It was the Sunday after Games Day, the Church was crowded, the lesson selected by me was read, in fear and trembling, the MP told me, "for this was the Word of God and not some rubbishy parliamentary speech." I had no inkling that I had trodden on toes nor of the storm immediately brewing. But the next morning, the storm, of gale force, hit the Manse. My phone started ringing early.

"Is it true," demanded the voice at the other end, "that

that woman read a lesson in Church yesterday?" The tone was, to say the least, biting.

"Yes, that's right," I answered.

"No! That's wrong!"

"Beg pardon, why is it wrong?"

"Well, she's an . . . eh . . . eh . . . she's an SNP."

"She's also our MP and the Church has room for all political opinions."

"Not *our* Church."

"I have to disagree with you, but *our* Church is very much for all."

That was just the beginning! It went on and on, the phone was red hot, some callers enquiring, some openly abusive of me, one demanding to know what lesson had been read, and finally the remark from one pompous gentleman that "I had bitten the hand that fed me." I pointed out that my stipend was paid, actually from Church headquarters, and privately thought that if I had been depending on that particular man, I would long since have pined away to nothing. Then the letters started appearing in the local press, and even in *The Scotsman*.

"On Sunday last the Church of Scotland showed its true colours. I have been a member all my life, but now that the Church has become SNP, I will never darken its door again."

Another was of the opinion that the minister of Aldermouth Old "should be hailed before the General Assembly, publicly rebuked, if not indeed unfrocked."

I was flabbergasted! All this about one single Scripture reading in a Service totally devoid of any political content, but obviously something had to be done for the town was buzzing, the elders distraught, people taking sides, and I was being treated to some strange looks when I walked down the street. I hastily convened a meeting of our Kirk Session, read them a letter for their comments, a letter I had very carefully drafted to answer the critics, I thought a very reasonable and moderate letter. The Session agreed with it, I sent it off to various newspapers, and gradually the furore died away, though I was aware that many comments were still being made behind my back. It had been thunder and lightning with a vengeance. Undoubtedly a case of electric shock like the Narracott's bullock, though without the compensation at the end!

Two things I had noticed, and one suspicion I had held had been confirmed. First all the criticism perhaps understandably seemed to come from members of the defeated party, for all anybody knew, perhaps my party, folks who were clearly sore that their much-loved former MP had lost his seat, though no criticism of me came from the man himself, thorough gentleman that he was. Second, the great mass of caustic comments were uttered, or written, by folks who were seldom, if ever in the Church, but who knew from their superior knowledge what the Church should be doing, or in this case, not doing. My confirmed suspicion? As with the Narracott brothers long before, the only thing that seemed to matter to most of my critics was "me," "my point of view," "my Party," "my interests come first," and for the non-committed or half-committed Christian, when there is a clash between faith and politics, politics wins every time.

But life goes on, and after all, I consoled myself, Christ had plenty of critics too, and when the powers that be hounded Him to death, was not it, at least in part, a question of politics?

I have never knowingly bitten any hand, whether it feeds me or not, but when self-interest is involved, who believes a "vetnary or a parson"?

If Only They Would Talk

NINETEEN

Times without number as a vet I have had it said to me,
    "Yours must be a hard job for your patients can't talk,"
to which I have usually replied,
    "Touch the sore spot and they soon let you know."
    But, of course, it *was* true that one of the difficulties of
being a vet as compared to a doctor was that the animal
could not tell you what was wrong. Oddly enough, I
found this one of the fascinations too, making every case
like a jigsaw puzzle or a crossword, taking the bits of the
puzzle, the clues, and fitting them together. Diagnosis
was all important before one could treat, and while the
owner could tell you a certain amount, you had to depend
on the signs and symptoms to reach a correct diagnosis,
and usually, eventually did, but there were cases when
one longed for the patient to tell you exactly what was
what.
    Take Fran, a lovely little Dachsund belonging to Kay
Wilcox. Kay often acted as a baby sitter for us at Chade
Lodge when our family consisted of two wee laddies,
Neil and Ian, and I knew her dog well. Both Bernard and
I had been treating Fran for fully a week for what we
thought was tonsilitis, throat inflamed, husky cough, off
her food, temperature and a total unwillingness to have
her mouth opened. She had had pencillin and then strep-
tomycin, but grew worse rather than better. We were

puzzled and at last decided we would X-ray the throat. Bernard was the X-ray expert (I'd had not a word on how to work the machine at college) and he came up with a very clear picture of a darning needle lodged across Fran's throat, just beyond where one could see, looking in her mouth. There was nothing for it but to operate which, after administering a general anaesthetic, of course, I did, to find, no needle! I looked again at the X-ray plate. It was as plain as could be. You could even see the eye of the needle, so I searched about a bit more and found, no needle! I was mystified. Where was the wretched thing? Then I had a thought, "X-ray her stomach, Bernard," which he did, and there was our needle. Clearly the relaxation of the muscles of the oesophagus under anaesthetic had allowed her to swallow the needle. We left it at that for once a needle is in the stomach, it normally finds its way out alright, and indeed this happened.

About the same time in Bristacombe, whenever I think of Fran, I recall a little eight year old boy called Graham Harris, who was playing with his meccano set one day, making a car. Now, as everyone knows, when making a meccano car, two hands are not enough and Graham had a bit held in his mouth, when suddenly he gulped, and lo and behold, swallowed it. Panic stations! Rushed to the doctor, then to hospital for X-ray, and there was the meccano, snug in his stomach. The doctor decided to try to oil it through with liquid paraffin for a few days, but that first night when saying his prayers Graham said, "Lord Jesus, please send my back axle up or down." Which way the ambulant axle took I never learned, but a further X-ray a few days later showed it had disappeared. Of course, it would probably have gone anyway, but little Graham had learned the lesson which as adults, in our wisdom, we soon forget, that there's nothing too small or unimportant to "take to the Lord in prayer."

On another occasion I recalled a Labrador dog, a big, strapping, normally full of life animal, which was brought to the surgery. As always, one depends initially on what the owner says, but all he could tell was that it was completely off its food, constipated and vomiting. Palpation of the abdomen revealed a fair sized lump; what was it, cyst, abscess, tumour or what? It was in our pre-X-ray days and when two days' treatment failed to bring about an improvement, there was only one course open, exploratory laparotomy, go in and see. The dog was duly anaesthetised, the abdomen opened up, and there was the lump in the small bowel, a medium sized hard rubber ball.

"We wondered where his ball had gone," the owner said when I showed him the evidence. The dog recovered uneventfully, but did not get his ball back, for while I am all in favour of dogs having toys, as with children, they have to be sensible, safe, danger-free articles.

Only two cases, the needle and the ball, where, if only they could talk, would have solved the problem.

But of course there is communication in other ways, body language, an animal's behavioural pattern, the pained look on the face, a complete change in character, a dog licking a sore paw, whimpers and many other means of "talking." Indeed sometimes communication is as clear or clearer than mere speech.

I think of one of the most obvious ways of communicating, a limp. Prince was a very big Clydesdale gelding and had a decided limp. The first task always is to ascertain which leg is affected, which is not always as easy as it sounds. Where in a human a footballer can say to the physiotherapist "it's my left knee," or a husband "my wife asked me to get a spider off the ceiling and I fell off the chair and hurt my back," one has to decide the affected leg by the way the horse nods as he walks. In Prince I decided it was his right foreleg, but where was the injured part, shoulder, knee, fetlock or hoof? By examination and a process of elimination I arrived at the hoof which to the touch felt warmer than the other front hoof. A gentle tap with a hammer had the big horse raising his foot from the ground where he held it trembling for a bit before putting it gingerly down again. So out with the hoof knife, pick up the foot, hold it on or between one's legs, and proceed to pare the hard horn. There was, as there usually is in such cases, a dark line running across the horn. It was along this that I pared. It was mighty hard work as Prince obviously thought this kind man had just come for him to lean his weight on, and soon the sweat was blinding my eyes as I pared away slivers of horn. But at last eureka, success as a trickle of pus came out of the hole I had made. It is all a bit like a child digging in the sand on the shore till water bubbles up. I enlarged the hole, till the pus from his septic foot, caused undoubtedly by a nail prick, was flowing freely. Then a shot of tetanus antitoxin, an injection of penicillin, and instructions to put a bread and epsom salts poultice in the corner of a sack, put the foot in it, and change it twice a day to draw out all the pus. Two more visits and shots of penicillin sufficed, and the big horse was almost sound again, all because he had communicated his woes with a limp.

A cow standing with elbows out, a pained look on her face, off her food, running a temperature, and producing a grunt when the diaphragm is poked, and she has told you in nine cases out of ten that she has a foreign body, a nail or wire in her reticulum, or the second of her four stomachs.

A dog sitting over its drinking bowl all day long or drinking from puddles, with this excessive thirst the dog is practically saying it has nephritis (inflammation of the kidneys) or diabetes.

I remember a four month old puppy I had been treating at Bristacombe. There was nothing to go on except the owner's information that it was vomiting. I had wormed it, given it our usual stomach mixtures, but the little animal grew steadily worse. It was a pathetic, thin little creature, able to keep down hardly any food. Then one day on the surgery table it vomited while I was examining it, the stomach contents coming out in an arch, like a fountain, and it had "told" me its trouble, that type of vomiting being symptomatic. It had pyloric stenosis, a narrowing of the exit of the stomach, requiring a simple but delicate operation to put right. This was duly done and in an incredibly short space of time, we had a healthy, thriving and soon quite fat little dog.

But there are other forms of communication which have proved a great boon to thousands of men and women. I remember at Bristacombe one day in Church. It was a weekday evening, the Church was crowded, for there was a very notable visiting preacher. He was certainly worth listening to, and watching, for he was an "active" preacher, using his arms to the full, pounding the board, pointing and clearly a master of the art of holding a congregation's attention. Suddenly, to my utter amazement, I heard a snore coming from further along my pew. I could not believe anyone could fall asleep with such a preacher, but clearly someone had. A few moments later the snore, a real prince among snores, was repeated, and startled, I looked along the pew and saw the culprit, a lovely wavy haired blonde fast asleep *under the seat*. I had a quiet smile to myself, for I knew that blonde well. She was called Sheila and regularly she walked into my surgery on all four feet, a beautiful, light colored golden retriever, but a very special one. Sheila was a guide dog and she had transformed the life of her young owner, who, until Sheila appeared on the scene, had been virtually housebound. I used to watch them going along the busy Bristacombe streets, the dog weaving in and out of the crowds, and communicating its instructions via its harness to its mistress. At the kerb she would halt, look right, left, then right again, and if the road was clear "tell" her mistress to cross, a wonderful empathy, oneness and trust existing between dog and girl, except for mutual agreement on the matter of sermons! It was as if the dog was saying, "I know your eyes are no good to you, but don't worry, as your Good Book says, mistress, I will guide you with my eye!," a communication every bit as good as mere talking.

So the many thousands of species can "talk," alright,

not only in a wide variety of ways to one another, but also in the animals we have domesticated, to man.

But in the ministry I confess I have often sighed, and said of my fellow Christians, and the members of my congregation, "if only they would talk." The Gospel, the good news first spread round the world in days without television, radio or newspapers because those who had found this wonderful new faith "gossiped" the gospel in their homes, in the market place, in caravanserai as they journeyed until they took it from its cradle in Palestine to the heart of the civilised world, Rome, and spread far and wide across Asia, Europe and even heathen Britain. It is still happening! In China, for instance, a Church is re-opened every day and in non-Muslim parts of Africa, many thousands become Christians daily. Yet in so-called Christian Britain, and the western world generally, numbers are on the decline. Churches are closing, the Church is like an army fighting on the retreat. Now not for one minute do I suggest that talking about Christ or His Church is the only way to influence or impress, as I shall try to show, but it *is* important, and my, we have become unco blate in Scotland about speaking of life's basic values and Christ's truth.

One of the delights I had in Aldermouth was to go off on several occasions to the nearby conference centre of Kilravock with my Elders and over a weekend of fun and fellowship discuss the affairs of the Church and what we should be about. We played together, laughed together, ate together, prayed together and talked together. I remember people like Eric Gilchrist, Dave Peterson, Jack Rodgerson, Eric Rae, Peter McIntosh, Henry Dow, Robin Kerr and many others speaking out, many of them speaking in company for the first time about "my faith and my job," "my faith and my home," "my faith and my recreation" and many other topics. It thrilled my heart to hear these good men, who previously had felt they could not talk openly about their faith do just that. As the

Church grew, newcomers came in, some who had lapsed came back to the fold and several visitations were paid to a large new housing area in our parish. As I have noted elsewhere, some of these men even took the pulpit on occasion and I recall Arthur Menzies' talk on our faith faculty, and I have in my possession still two sermons preached by Ashley Thomas and Alistair Campbell.

The revival of the Church in China today can be traced to great souls like these two intrepid spinsters Mildred Cable and Francesca French who went to the Gobi Desert, Gladys Aylward, that amazing little housemaid turned missionary, men like Eric Liddell and the spiritual giant Hudson Taylor so that a Church was built up of ordinary men and women who withstood thirty years of clamp down, persecution, imprisonment and death inflicted by the State. In Africa the story has similar beginnings, and a harvest is being reaped today of the seed sown by greats like Mary Slessor, David Livingstone and hosts of lesser known souls who had the motto "each one win one." Alas in Scotland as Lord McLeod has so vividly put it "while Jesus Christ called the disciples to be fishers of men, we in the Kirk have tended to be keepers of the aquarium." If only they would talk, the great Master story-teller must sigh. But, as with animals, there are also other ways of communication, and I saw many of them at Aldermouth.

Every Sunday morning I would sit in my vestry waiting for that dread moment when I had to climb the pulpit steps and face a congregation of hundreds, and as I sat musing and meditating on the Service ahead, I would thrill to the music of our blind organist Jim McMichael as it soared to the heavens and brought calm, healing and inspiration to me, and I am sure to many of the assembled throng. Jim was communicating alright as only he could. But even prior to the organ's melodious message, our Beadle, John, would have climbed up to the tower and for ten minutes rung the great bell there, inviting people to come and worship their God. It is not easy to ring a large bell. I tried it but could never get the dings and dongs in their proper order as John could. In my time alone at Aldermouth, his great bell "talked" to the whole town some 1200 times.

The Service would commence with a rousing Hymn or Psalm and people, hundreds of them, who would have hesitated to speak their faith, cheerfully sang it, led by our magnificent choir which contained men and women who had sung there all their lives. To hear them in the Anthem each Sunday, with perhaps a soloist like Billy Fowler singing "Seek ye the Lord" was indeed to listen to people expressing their faith. One could mention so many who had cheerfully given a lifetime to that choir and I would sit back in the pulpit and listen, to the sopranos soaring to the heights, the contraltos balancing them perfectly, the tenors with Bill Crooky and the others coming in and the solid rock of the bass section giving body to it all. One could mention all thirty who were certainly "speaking" their faith alright and I used to feel that even if my sermon was rubbish, the congregation was fed, instructed, cheered and challenged by Jim and his merry band.

Another way of communicating his faith, as I have already alluded, was that of John, the minister's man's way, a Church polished, shining, heated just right, sitting in its neatly kept grounds. A master baker, John need not have become full time Church Officer at a lesser salary, but this was his way, and his wife Elizabeth's, of witnessing and worshipping.

After the evening Service, the two "girls," Marian and Jean, both in their sixties, would wait for their minister's suggestions as to who should get the Church flowers that night, and miles they walked delivering their floral message, presented with a suitable card and a big smile of encouragement by this cheerful, faithful twosome, lifting up the spirits a little of many a lonely or weary soul. Then of course there was the beautifying of the Church week by week, done by a succession of Flower Convenors in my twelve years, the fruits of God's good earth in the hands of experts or just willing folk. This was yet another way of communicating one's love for God and His Church. When Norah Ferguson was Flower Convenor, she organised a Festival of Flowers, blooms of every conceivable colour and scent arranged all round the Church by many willing and expert hands, even the umbrella holders at each pew being filled with flower heads by young Nessie Archibald and other youngsters. As we rose that Sunday, a great throng singing "How lovely is Thy dwelling place" was undoubtably true, surpassing lovely, and again in flowers and Psalms communicating the faith of these women, like the woman in the New Testament anointing her Lord with her most precious gift.

Another means of communiction, of showing one's love, was in gifts the Church received. The Archibald family contributed a beautiful blue Pulpit Fall in memory of Nan's parents. Mr. and Mrs. Gunning, to give thanks for twenty-five years of happy marriage, gifted two exquisite Communion chairs, matching perfectly the existing ones. The craftsman who delivered the chairs from the Lord Robert's workshop for disabled ex-servicemen gazed at the glistening wood of the pulpit and gallery fronts and commented that then (in the 1970s) it would take at least £40,000 to replace the wood alone and the whole magnificent edifice had been built in 1897 for £9000! A tremendously generous gift was from Bill Heard who, after his wife's death, gave the price of a house he had sold, then offered his own large house at about half its market value as a dwelling place for a much-needed Assistant minister.

A remarkable man, Bill, for although long retired, he took a trip to India to fulfil a long cherished dream, and soon found himself helping a company of Roman Catholic brothers, who, like Mother Theresa, scoured the streets of Calcutta for the sick and dying and carried them in to their night shelter where there was comfort and real caring. Bill stayed for years working among these poor unfortunates, many, indeed most of them, dirty, diseased, destitute, and by his every action was "talking" of the One who in His day cared for such poor wrecks of society, thus showing love to the unlovely.

So one could go on. There were many other gifts, some of them in memory of a loved one, but there was also a great deal of compassionate work by individual Christians, not specifically for the Church, but most certainly motivated by the Head of the Church. I think of hospital visitors like Henry Dow, people who delivered meals on wheels, Winnie Murray who every morning would light the fires and cook the breakfasts of several old folks, all forms of "talking," of communication in the name of the One who said "Feed my sheep." Long ago Struthers, a famous minister in Greenock said "what is needed most is for Christians to do a bonny thing." I saw some bonny things done in His name in Aldermouth, and the same can be said of almost every parish in the land. Yes, many ways of "talking," of communicating one's faith and love.

I remember hearing of a funeral, particularly pathetic as there were only five mourners for the old man who had died alone. One of the five was a high ranking army officer. As the coffin was lowered into the ground, he stood to attention and saluted. Afterwards the minister asked if he was related to the deceased. The Brigadier smiled and said,

"In a way. Long ago John was my Sunday School teacher. I first saw God in him."

Yes, many ways of "talking," but still, if only more of the flock would naturally and unashamedly actually talk of their great Shepherd!

Parson's Pot-pourri

TWENTY

I was standing at the Marine Hotel overlooking the Links, a natural amphitheatre where annually the Highland Games were held, and where Aldermouth Cricket Club played their matches. It was a glorious July day of sunshine, the sea a deep blue, and across the water the Black Isle seeming but a step away. The vivid green of the Links contrasted with the soft blue of the sky, across whose benign face here and there some puffs of white cloud were meandering, as if they too felt it was a day for taking it easy.

I was really on my way to a wedding reception, having just come from the ceremony in Church, but since there is always a time lag for photos and so on, I felt I could spare a few minutes watching the cricket. I was particularly interested for Neil, our eldest at seventeen, was opening the batting against Leicestershire 2nd eleven, who were making a northern tour, and I had just seen Neil felled by a bumper which a giant of a fast bowler had hurled down, hitting Neil on the chest. It was all I could do to prevent myself running on to the pitch to make sure my son and heir was alright, or thump the bowler! The scoreboard made sombre reading for Aldermouth, four batsmen being out and a mere ten runs showing on the scoreboard. The giant bowler had evidently wrought havoc. Some smelling salts revived Neil, and to sympathetic claps from the crowd, he picked up his bat again and faced Goliath. Down whizzed another short pitched ball and to my great delight, he stood up to it and hooked it for four runs. I was getting quite excited, my chest swelling with pride, and would fain have watched longer. Just then I was joined by a man, totally unknown to me, but who apparently knew me alright, and who immediately expressed his opinion with a sneer, "Aye, you've a fine time of it, you ministers. Working one day a week and a slap up feed every Saturday."

Mind you, many times I have had this one day's work business flung at me, but on such a day, with all nature smiling, I did not feel like any explanations, managed a grin and said, "You're right, friend. The easiest job in the world! Just the one day for working, after all a wedding's not work!" He looked a bit bemused for he had evidently expected an argument, but as Neil hit another bumper for four, I was the little friend of all the world! The wedding reception proceeded like all such functions with the minister, as was nearly always the case, proposing the toast of the couple, and by eight o'clock, I was home. With one or two receptions nearly every Saturday in summer, I seldom stayed for the dance, for Saturday night in a busy Church is required to check the sermons, but as I changed into some more casual and comfortable clothes, the one day's work-a-week business came back to me. So, just for interest, I flipped over the pages of my diary for the past few months to see what I had been doing, and found an infinite variety of "cases," every bit as varied as in my vet days.

There was the day of the doctors. It had really begun the night before when about ten o'clock I answered a ring at the front door. There stood a man and a little boy.

"Can we come in, Mr. Cameron? We've nowhere to go," said the man. A Manse door is always open, so of course they were invited in. I knew the father slightly, a Mr. Spence. He was considerably downcast and explained that his wife had put him and their youngest, aged five, out of the house.

"But you've other children too, Mr. Spence, have you not?"

"Yes, two other boys but the wife has always been against young Simon here. Mind you, she's not always in control of herself. She's had several nervous breakdowns."

We talked for a bit. I promised I would visit his wife next day, and managed to get him and his pathetic little five year old fixed up for the night.

The next day started with a visit to the Clinic for a minor ailment I had. We were very blessed with our doctors in Aldermouth, all of them, but normally I saw Dr. John, or, as that day, Dr. Bryce. The latter always had a wisecrack or two, but his flippant exterior could not hide a caring heart. From there I made my way to the Spence household, rang the bell, and was very reluctantly admitted by the young wife, who was clearly in a hysterical state. I was only in the house briefly, wondering what on earth I could do to help, particularly with the memory of a sad little five year old face from the night before, when the young wife and mother started shouting and screaming at me, and ordered me out of the house. Her talk was wild and she was in a very dangerous mood, threatening to end it all by putting her head in the gas oven. It is the only time I have been put out of a house, and although I've heard psychiatrists say that those who openly threatened suicide seldom did it, I felt I could not take the risk. I drove straight to Dr. Hannah, her doctor, who had a single-man practice in the town. He was at the Spence house in minutes, and in further minutes the ambulance was at the door, the doctor clearly feeling as I did, that this was a potential suicide. I visited the young woman in Craigdunain Mental Hospital a few days later and found to my horror that she had been put in the geriatric ward, surrounded by seventy elderly women, many of them incontinent and mindless. It was a ward that always made my blood boil for the beds were so close one could hardly get between them. I wondered how in all the world Mrs. Spence could recover her sanity and calm in such surroundings. I continued to visit weekly. She was in time moved to another ward, then eventually returned home, took her husband and son back, and a sort of uneasy truce between the various members of the family was arrived at.

In the afternoon of "the doctors' day," I visited Dr. Ferguson who with his wife Norah lived in a lovely flat overlooking the heaving waters of the Moray Firth, its waves lapping the shore just at the end of their lawn. Always the welcome there was warm and sincere. The doctor had retired to Aldermouth, quite often stood in for Dr. Hannah, but was now himself unwell. I have often thought that it must be difficult for a doctor to be ill for he knows all the symptoms, and likely outcome of the condition. Dr. Ferguson was very poorly, but seemed glad of a visit and, in Norah, had a first class nurse.

Then I went to old Dr. Matheson, another retired medic. He had practised in England but never lost his lovely, lilting, Highland tongue. It was really Mrs. Matheson I had come to see for she was far from well, but the old doctor, well into his eighties, was in his usual sparkling form (In fact he lived to his nineties, still golfing three times a week). He always tried to trip me with some obscure Biblical quotation, conducting his own version of Mastermind. But that day he told me a story of his youth in Applecross. One Communion season, which lasted from Thursday to Monday, a notable Doctor of Divinity had been preaching at the Sunday morning Service. In the afternoon of a glorious Spring day he was taking a walk when he was accosted by Angus standing in his Sunday blacks outside his croft.

"Are you on an errant of mercy?" demanded Angus.

"No, just having a walk," replied the distinguished Divine.

"You shoult not be walking on the Sabbath tay," he was informed.

"But I'm enjoying the beauties of God's handiwork all around us."

"We are not meant to enchoy ourselves on the Sabbath." Angus thought deeply and came up with his judgement,

"Well, if He dit, He shoultn't have." End of conversation! Dr. Matheson chuckled at the memory, then paid me a compliment I very much appreciated from such a cynic as he had become over the years.

"You know, I'm not at all pleaset with you, no, not at all."

"What have I done?" I asked, wondering what was coming.

"I hat more or less stoppet going to Church for I've seen so much hypocrisy, but, tash it, man, you make me want to come."

We had a simple word of prayer, and I went on my way, gratified that I had at least one satisfied customer.

I flipped a page of my diary. Ah yes! That was the week I got up at 7:00 am each morning to go to Mrs. Evans' house in the Fishertown. She was a loner, a widow with one son the length of the country away. She had had a mild stroke, had shut herself off from her neighbours, so I lit her fire each morning, stocked up with coal, gave her a cup of tea and toast, asked "Meals on Wheels" to call, and the doctor arranged for a nurse to go in daily. In the early evening I looked in each day to check up on her. After a week the son came home. But that is not minister's work, you say. Away with you! Didn't Jesus wash feet? Thinking of mornings in the Fishertown brought to mind one Saturday morning. Our boys all, in turn, had the same paper round in the harbour area. One day one of them, Alan, I think, had to be away early for he was playing football some distance away, and the bus was leaving very early. I said I'd stand in for him, hoping I would not meet anyone. But I did. It was an early morning worker, and one of our members. He stopped, looked astonished, said "Mr. Cameron" and went on his way, presumably thinking times must be pretty hard in the Manse when the minister had taken a paper round.

I flipped over the diary pages to a Thursday. That was the evening I held my Vestry Hour, usually nearer two hours. I had written "Baptism—Jacqueline Clark—that makes nine for Sunday." I remembered Mrs. Clark's visit well.

"Oh, Mr. Cameron, I know you always have baptisms on the first Sunday in the month, and I'm at the last minute seeing you, but I've just had word that my mother's coming up from London this weekend and I wondered if you could do Jacqueline when my mother's here?"

I looked at her with a perfectly straight face.

"Certainly, Mrs. Clark, if you don't mind being number nine. In fact on Sunday I'm going to use a hose." She looked at me uncertainly then gasped, "A hose!," before, seeing the twinkle, she laughed somewhat doubtfully. So I went over the Baptismal Service with her, though normally I always saw husband and wife together, but since it was not their first child and time was short, I thought mother would do this time.

I always loved baptisms, as did the congregation, though all my ministry I have had a private fear that I would get names mixed up and maybe call a John, Jane. It has not happened yet, but perhaps there is still time! I did not use the method of a certain minister in Glasgow who always, on taking the baby, asked the father its name. On one occasion the odd reply came,

"Spindoner."

"Eh? Oh well, Spindoner, I baptise you—"

"Naw, naw," interrupted the agitated father,

"It's pinned on her."

Another page of the diary was turned. Ah yes, one of my monthly trips to 121 George Street, Edinburgh, Church Headquarters, for a meeting of the Union and

Readjustment, (U and R) Committee, which always met in the evening. I had written a piece after that particular meeting, "Now I know what Hell is like! It's a series of committee meetings going on *ad infinitum*."

The sample that day was two and a half hours long, during which the committee voted to close Churches, link or unite others, and give others a minister not under fifty-five. I have heard various ministers describe the work of the U and R as an evangelical exercise. You know, that puzzles me somewhat! I cannot for the life of me see how closing a Church or giving a minister four instead of two churches to supervise helps the mission of the Church in John Knox's Scotland, where he and the Reformers had the dream of a Church and school in every parish of the land, and achieved their goal. Of course, there is a twofold reason for the shrinkage, money and ministers, shortage of both, but there have been many times, in my humble opinion, when the U and R have been a bit heavy-handed. They also appear to have the same notion as the education authorities (and what Scottish education owes to the Kirk) that town is better than country, so frequently, they tag one or more country churches on to a town one, almost always to the detriment of the country church.

That meeting was a shambles. There was a Chairman, but flanked by the two full time Secretaries, he seemed like a Mini with a bus on either side, and a Mini that had even lost its toot. He scarcely opened his mouth, even when the Revd Charles in a corner behind me, got so loud in his own private conversation with his cronies that one could not hear the proper speaker. I wonder if Charles checks his children for butting in when others are speaking? Beside me was an expert on Church law and he kept me informed, "matter for the Synod" he muttered, or again "clause 14," whatever that might be! Revd Charles, having suspended operations with his pals, broke in to speak for ten minutes on something which mystified us all until he and we discovered it was not on the agenda, and really the wrong committee. Then another brother protested at length about closing a church to find it was the wrong church. I learned it was very dangerous to establish a precedent and step out of line, and other matters were valid by dint of "use and wont." The most animated discussion of the whole evening came when there was an interminable argument about whether a clause should be worded "is" or "shall be." That got everyone awake! The Church militant! Almost all the talking was done by the full time Secretaries (mind you, they have a rotten job), but after six years on the committee it seemed to me I was meant to be just a rubber stamp!

The Lord's business done for another month, I drove the 160 miles up the old, winding A9 which, since there was snow about, was practically deserted by that time of night, and more than once my headlights picked up herds of deer beside the road in the Drumochter Pass. Somehow their life seemed simple and uncomplicated compared to our tortuous committees, but who knows, maybe they had committees too! At last, the Dava moor and home on the stroke of midnight.

All my ministry I have served, like most ministers, on a variety of General Assembly Committees. Some have cheered and enlightened, many have informed, some have inflamed, but all are an attempt at democracy in the Kirk, but well, if not Hell, certainly Purgatory could not be much worse than some of them!

A flick over another diary page and I found it was a Sunday, but quite a Sunday, even if it *was* the only day I worked! Perhaps my critic at the cricket would have grudgingly admitted I had earned my corn that day.

It was one of our Communion Sundays, beginning with a meeting of the duty elders at ten. Then the Service at 11:00 am, another Table of Communion in the afternoon, following which I nipped up to the Church Eventide Home for a short Service and Communion with the elderly residents. Half past six and our evening Service of Thanksgiving was followed by a short message over their earphones to our local hospital patients.

Finally I joined Allan Ross at the sixty-strong Youth Fellowship of senior teenagers. When first I went to Aldermouth, I found I had to run this lively group all on my own, and it was the hardest work of the day, for almost all the young folk were at the rebellious stage and either hostile to the Kirk or totally apathetic, but it was the only gathering of the week in the whole town for their age group. Just to keep order was an achievement. Early on I had the help of the Police Sergeant, Sergeant Riddock for a year, then Allan, one of our younger elders and a hotelier became my assistant and eventually leader. He had a marvellous gift of getting on a wavelength of 16–19 year olds and many happy nights we had in the Hall, and later Kirkside, premises we bought for our expanding youth work. We had several weekends away with the youngsters, Janet going along as housemother, and bright, happy, fruitful occasions they were. The Youth Fellowship was a handful, but great times they were. How fruitful only eternity will show, but if you think it easy to interest and influence that number of teenagers week after week, I invite you to try. After Allan had to resign through pressure of other work, I had another excellent leader in Bill McInnes, who had tragically lost his wife at an early age, and brought up their lovely children on his own.

Ten o'clock and the working day was over, leaving me limp, played out, exhausted, but happy. To unwind I frequently took a walk down Manse Road and there with Henry and Nana Dow relaxed, drank tea and chatted over the day's happenings. Wonderful encouragers were Henry and Nana and finally at eleven, it was home and a welcome bed.

Every minister needs a bolt-hole, someone he can go to and share his problems, or be encouraged in his work, and I had several such blessed retreats close by. There were Alastair and Margaret, my Session Clerk and his wife, who was Sunday School Secretary. Though disabled from the war and often in pain, there was no more gentle and understanding man in the parish than my fine, efficient and ever willing Clerk, who was also my Bank Manager. He was a straight, upright man, goodness shining from him as kindness and sympathy shone from his wife. There were also the Archibalds, Andrew and Nan, our friends from the Moorton days, always with an open door and an encouraging word. Billy and Cath Miller lived just round the corner from the Manse. Billy, our Church Treasurer, and Cath, leader of the Playgroup. Billy succeeded the long serving George Farm, the Town Clerk, as our Treasurer. Of course I had my Beadle John, and his wife Elizabeth. I saw John virtually every day and his quiet voice and understanding words were like soothing balm when I was "up tight" about something. One house I visited often was that of Arthur and Cath Menzies. Arthur edited our Church magazine, a gifted man, a tremendously patient man, a man of God, who over many years nursed and encouraged Cath, who most of her life had very poor health. Every Wednesday evening I called at Jim McMichael's home to be greated by Jean's words "Come away in" and after talking of the praise lists for Sunday, Jim and I would weekly put the world right, for, though blind, he was right on the ball of all the happenings near and far. One could go on, writing more, much more, about each of them, and many many others, not forgetting the Minister's committee, composed of senior elders whose wise advice and constant encouragement saved me from many errors. I was a lucky, lucky, man in the number of encouragers and willing helpers I had for my one day a week job!

A short note in my diary caught my eye, "Visit Bruce and Rosemary in their new home." Bruce Bunker and his father were both elders, father Willie being a builder and stonemason and son Bruce, a remarkably successful business man. He had asked me to look in and see them and ask a blessing on their new home, a lovely request I was glad to fulfil. Bruce, at the time, had a large bookshop in Inverness, having started with a smaller one in Aldermouth, and the various ventures he turned his mind to over the years all seemed to thrive. He had the golden touch, but Church meant much to him and his charming wife, Rosemary, and it was always a delight to call on them. Bruce thought deeply about things. He was not the kind of man whose Christianity was confined to a Church building, and I remember him expressing his dilemma as a Christian business man as to whether he should be selling books on, for example, Karl Marx. A lovely visit!

On the way home I popped into Tom and Moira Hastings' home for a few minutes for they were practically next door. Tom had one of the loveliest gardens in the town, was ever present in Church, but Moira, poor lass, was one of the many sufferers from that cruel disease, Rheumatoid Arthritis, which causes such continuous pain, deformity and difficulty for the sufferer. She had shown incredible bravery through teens of operations, but despite many set-backs, Moira kept trying to be well enough to golf again. Folks like that get little publicity, and sometimes little sympathy, for it is not normally a killing disease, but my, they know what suffering is!

Another page, a Monday, and I had written in "three months since I have had a day off so golfed with Peter McIntosh, who took me on to the Dunbar Course this afternoon and slaughtered me!" Peter was, and is, one of the finest men I have known. He had worked in Glasgow all his life where he and his wife threw their home open to every youngster from Aldermouth who was working or studying in Glasgow, or to any Scout from anywhere, for Peter had been Scouting for many years. Eventually they retired to their beloved Aldermouth.

I knew Peter had been in the war and a prisoner of the Japanese but he seldom spoke of it, just like Alastair my Session Clerk who had been in a German POW camp. How often the brave keep quiet! However, that day as we walked up the sixteenth fairway, having just trounced me, he told me of a remarkable escape he had had. Imprisoned on one island, Sumatra, I think, he, with thousands of other prisoners was on a boat transferring them elsewhere. At the last minute, he was taken off the boat, for the MO of the camp, which was remaining had insisted he needed Peter as his assistant. That ship was torpedoed with total loss of life. Peter was too humble a man to say God had protected particularly him, but when one thought of the fruitful life he and his gentle, caring wife had lived for the good of others afterwards, there was no doubt in my mind that "the shade of His hand outstretched caressingly" had indeed held and saved him.

I found myself looking in my diary at one of the success stories and happiest events in our church calendar. I smiled as I thought back to that week and indeed to previous weeks. There was an air of mystery about it too, I found, and the town wondered what we were up to in the Old Presbyterian Church. Certainly the shop attendant looked at me in mystification when I asked for a hair net. She supplied me and remarked that an awful lot of men had been buying hair nets, and was clearly puzzled for all the men were of the short back and sides variety, some even bald. There was also a run on thick, black wool, it was known that John, the Church Officer had borrowed a policeman's uniform and various people were searching for white gloves, man size. Tile hats were also in demand. What was going on? Certainly the annual Church Concert was coming up. Could there be a connection? Surely not, for the previous two years it had all been by the various Sunday School children who had performed in the Church Hall. They were similar concerts to those I had organised at Moorton.

"It's in the Centre this year," the cry went round, "bit ambitious if you ask me and they've taken it for three nights! They'll never fill a Hall that size!"

So the opening night of the concert came round with the various mysteries still unresolved. Despite gloomy predictions, the big hall was packed full, parents, grandparents and hosts of non-aligned spectators, all anticipating a good night with the bairns, if the previous two years were anything to go by.

They were not disappointed. The tiny tots began with their simple choruses, though the task of teaching three and four year olds had been far from simple, remembering they could not read. They won the hearts of the audience, it merely adding to the fun that some forgot to face the front, one lad kept coming in too soon in the songs, another young gentleman had bother hitching up his velvet trousers, while yet another had to be led off to the toilet! Chaos? Not if you were a parent or grandparent with eyes for only one child to see how he/she would behave. The artlessness and simplicity of these little ones won over the audience right away, the 5–7 year olds kept up the good work, then came the main Sunday School, exquisitely dressed by enthusiastic parents as they did a selection of Songs from the Shows (they all wanted to sing the Edelweiss solo!), followed later in the programme by Songs from Ireland, the girls in green skirts and capes, and the boys with a green sash. It was all very colourful and the singing of a high standard. In between acts while scenes were being shifted behind the curtain, our youngest Alan, aged about twelve and two of his pals told a series of Irish jokes in a very fair attempt at the Irish brogue, jokes as old as the hills extracted by father from a book of jokes of various countries, like the far from new,

"I wish I knew where I was going to die, Paddy!"

"Why's that, Mick?"

"Sure and I'd never go near the place!" or again

"Did you know that the last coach was the most dangerous on a train, Mick?"

"Is that so, now. Why don't they just take it off?"

Ancient stuff, but a now thoroughly warmed up audience laughed as if hearing it for the first time, and as the
night went on, the three comedians grew in confidence.
The Bible Class, superbly directed by Lena Hammond,
Aldermouth's equivalent of Joyce Grenfell, and a life long
teacher of teenagers in that department of the Church
life. On this occasion they performed beautifully a Hans
Andersen classic. Then, the audience could not believe it,
elders of the Kirk singing "Oh you canny shove your
granny aff a bus" and other "high class" stuff, including
a biographical sketch of most of the office bearers, not
sparing the ministers, written by schoolmaster and friend
Bill Barnet. The Woman's Guild Choir sang well-loved
Sankey hymns, the BB lads leapt and somersaulted all
over the stage, and while the stage was prepared for the
next item, Alec Campbell, another cheerful elder, had the
feet tapping with his accordion, or the three comedians
popped up again with more ancient-chestnuts in what was
a non-stop performance. There were several solo songs by
youngsters, thrilled that they were singing into a microphone like Elvis, though without Elvis's wiggle! Among
them was David, dressed in rags, bringing tears to mothers' eyes, and a lump even to his father's throat as he sang
in a plaintive but very true boy soprano's voice "Nobody's
Child," repeating the part older brother Ian had done at
Moorton years before.

It was all great entertainment, but no real surprises till
the curtains parted to show the elders again, sitting round
in earnest discussion as "The Vacant Committee," choos-
ing a new minister (something every congregation should
study!). It was a skit, which in places, was not too far off
the mark. I had written it in a hurry, my first effort as a
playwright. It had taken much rehearsal, but went off
pretty well, all fifteen parts being played by men, though

Willie Birrell and Billy Miller had changed sex for the occasion, dressed in their wives' cast-offs. John was there in his policeman's uniform, there was a farmer in welly boots and with a pet lamb and dog, the Colonel in a tile hat demanding they choose a DD minister. Bruce, the bookseller and Ben, the assistant minister, both quiet men, revealing that they had the loudest laughs in the county, and Bill, Superintendent of the Eventide Home with his "bunnet" in his hand, his lines surreptitiously hidden in the cap, while Dave Peterson, his hair liberally sprinkled with powder to make him old and wise, attempted to keep order as Chairman. Eric Gilchrist managed to get his bogey line right "I've had naethin' to dae wi' doos", for in practice it had always been 'do with daes'" (doos are pigeons). It was a rip roaring farce, but the *piece de resistance* was still to come, the penultimate item on the programme.

To gasps of incredulity, hearty laughter and much pointing, when the curtains opened the audience saw the Black and White minstrels before them, all looking exactly alike, and providing a puzzle as folks tried to identify the elders. For the elders it was, all wearing white gloves and black, curly, woolly wigs. The hair net, black wool mystery was solved! As all sang and danced about the stage, the two ministers included, singing old favourites like "Lily of Laguna," "I'll be your sweetheart," "Home on the Range" and many others, I think the only positive identification was that of dear wee Bobby Sim, who took the solo parts, but something that took a sore knock was the picture so many have of ministers and elders as dour, humourless creatures.

Then came the closing scene with all on the stage (except the tiny tots who had long since departed for bed), with all the cast joining in negro spirituals, modern hymns with a swing, and "The King of Love" in whose name and for whose sake we had made our offering of fun, pathos and beauty, after all David danced before the Lord!

Such an event demanded much busy planning, rehearsing, coaxing and cajoling for many weeks, and involved many willing helpers like Stan Walker and Allan Ross as stage managers, Mrs. Paterson on make-up, Mrs. Temple and Jim at the piano and hosts of others, not least parents and wives. To see so many happy faces on and off stage made it all worthwhile and bound us all in a warm glow of real fellowship. Who said Christ or His Kirk took the spice and joy out of life? But I suppose my critic at the cricket would not have classed all the planning as work! I mean to say, it could not be as I was not wearing my working collar!

My mind had wandered far and wide that Saturday night, as I flicked over my diary pages when I should have been at my sermons but I was caught and held by the bonds of memory. One more page, I thought. I remembered the day well. A funeral from the Church at noon, a quick bite of dinner, then a funeral from the Fishertown at 2:00 pm where I had to stand at the door to try to let those inside and the vast crowd outside hear. Then, as in the old days, all the mourners walked behind the hearse to the cemetery, and in a deep hush, we laid a good man to rest. I went back to the house where the relatives were gathered and over tea, talked with most of them.

I thought I would just go and see Mrs. Gilmour on my way home, a poor soul whom I felt might well be my next funeral. She lived in the Queen's Park area of the town, and was far through with cancer. To my surprise I found her sitting up in bed, her face aglow, a strange light in her eyes. We talked for a bit, then she said, very hesitantly,

"Mr. Cameron, *please* don't laugh at me, but Jesus came into my room last night and stood just where you are standing. Really it *was* Him. I wasn't dreaming, and I'd had no pain killers."

"I'm not laughing, Mrs. Gilmour. I believe you," and I did.

Whatever any of us reading this may think in our wisdom, that woman believed she had seen the Lord, and I believed her, for in my ministry on numbers of occasions, people have described similar experiences. But if you are still sceptical, my friend who reads this, let me say that from that moment, Mrs. Gilmour, a dying woman, whom I would not have described as a particularly religious person, nor was she a neurotic, from that moment she started to get well. Doctors call it a remission. Call it what we will, the cancer abated, and Mrs. Gilmour lived for years afterwards.

So my critic from the cricket, whoever you are, ministers have been known to work on other days besides Sunday, involved in the rich tapestry of all life, every bit as varied and busy as when I was a vet.

We try, in His Name, to hold a torch aloft to reveal the young Prince of Glory, and in all our doings, the joyful and sad, the ordinary and the extraordinary, try to show that great heart of love that beats at the centre of the Universe.

Twists and Turns

TWENTY-ONE

"Hello! Mr. Cameron? Derek Hocking, High Deane, here. Us's got trouble wi' some fattenin' pigs. I wish you'd 'ave a look at 'em." It was early afternoon, and while Ann, our secretary/receptionist went home for lunch, the calls were switched through to us at Chade Lodge.

"What seems to be the matter with them, Derek?" I queried.

"Them be dowie like, right poorly, some off their grub, an' most of 'em is scourin'."

"Right, Derek, I'll be out later this afternoon. I have a call to make after surgery, so I should be with you about four."

"That's fine, Mr. Cameron. I be right worried 'bout them pigs." Young Derek was one of my favourites, a good client, a prodigious worker, with a large dairy herd and maybe two hundred pigs. Though his father still did a bit, he was one of the old school who thought you should only call the vet when all the patent medicines had failed, but Derek was more forward-looking, and I was often at High Deane.

I got there about four as planned just as they were starting the afternoon milking. I had a walk up the byre, or shippen as it was called in Devon, and found Derek, as always, flying on, looking after about six milking units at the one time.

"See you haven't taken my advice and switched to a good cow, Derek! Still sticking to these Friesians! Man, they just give white water!" I did not really think that about Friesians, knowing full well that since first introduced, the butter fat content of their milk had greatly improved, but it was a standing joke between us, his choice of breed. He laughed.

"Aar—you and you'm Ayrshires. They be just toy bullocks!"

"The pigs be at Upper Down, Mr. Cameron. I'll come up with 'ee." He called for his father and brother to take over the milking, and we set off for the adjoining little village where Derek had a small piggery in addition to his much larger one at High Deane. We got out of the car. Derek threw open the pig house door, and with my first glance at his pigs, I stopped, and felt a clutch of fear in my stomach.

"How long have they been like this, Derek?" I queried.

"Oh—some days. They be pigs I got in the market 'bout ten days ago. They was goin' cheap, like an' I thought I'd got a bargain but don't look like it now."

"It does not, Derek. I don't like the look of them at all."

"Serious, then, you think?"

"Could be. Have you given them anything?"

"Aye—I wormed 'em. They was scourin' a bit an' I thought could be worms, but they's gone worse since then."

There were twenty in two pens, most of them lying half-buried in the straw, but those that were walking about were really sick looking, shivering now and then, and with a foul smelling diarrhoea oozing from them. A description came back to me from my pig diseases textbook, for some parts are stamped into the memory. "Young pigs affected with this disease have a high temperature, refuse to feed, lie hidden or half-hidden in the litter, and when forced to move do so reluctantly, giving little annoyed squeals. Their backs are arched, their tails uncurled, the brownish diarrhoea is of a foul odour and the whole appearance suggests acute misery and sickness. The breathing is frequently distressed, the sufferer being attacked with a fit of harsh, dry coughing."

I had hoped I would never see it, but here before my eyes was a classic example of the book's description. I turned to Derek who was watching me intently, for clearly my anxiety had shown in my face.

"What's the cause o' the scour if it be'nt worms?"

"Oh, there's different causes of scour, Derek, wrong feeding and a whole host of germs called Bcoli, Salmonella and a few others."

"I've heard o' that thar semolina, but be that not wot comes in food poisoning, get it from chickens?"

"Let's catch one or two, Derek, and take their temperatures." So we did, they were easily caught, temperatures were raised several degrees. I examined the skins carefully, was there a reddening like the book described or was it my imagination? Suddenly Derek shouted.

"Dang me! There be a dead 'un here in the straw!"

"And the way they look, there'll be a few more soon, I'm very much afraid."

Derek was by now very solemn.

"What do 'ee think it be then?"

"Well, Derek, unless I'm very much mistaken, they've got Swine Fever. I'll do a post mortem on that dead pig and maybe will be more sure then."

So I did a PM. There were suggestive signs, enlarged lymph glands, pinpoint haemorrhages in liver and kidneys, but they could be caused by other things besides Swine Fever, and thoroughly though I searched, I could find none of the button ulcers in the bowel which are the main diagnostic feature. I straightened up, looked at the pathetic pigs, then looked at the young farmer.

"The position, Derek, is this. I'm not the one to diagnose SF, only the Department of Agriculture can do that, but I'm ninety per cent certain that's what you've got."

"Be there no cure for it, 'en?"

"No, but there's a preventive, called Crystal Violet Vaccine which we could use on your pigs at the farm. This thing spreads like wildfire. You could carry it on your boots or clothes, mice, even lice, can carry it. It's believed to be caused by a virus, and I'm very sorry, but it's the worst possible disease you could get in your pigs. Here's what we must do. First we have to disinfect our boots, and as best we can, our clothes. When you get home, take off what you're wearing before you go near another pig. Don't let anybody else up to these pens here. When you come next, leave your wellingtons and overalls behind you, for it if gets into your main lot of pigs, you're in big trouble, and when I get home, I'll phone the Ministry vet for advice and have him out here tomorrow."

Derek was by now very pale, twenty pigs condemned, I was sure, and maybe 200 more, though just in case I was wrong, and for the sake of doing something for the miserable sufferers, I gave him a bowel active sulphonamide. I knew it was hopeless, for in my heart I was sure we had this disease all pig breeders dread, but I felt I had to try something for the pathetic creatures. I went to the car, got out a bottle of disinfectant, and we scrubbed our boots, the wheels of the car and my outer black waterproof, and departed to deposit the anxious young farmer at his home. I went home, scrubbed myself all over again, changed clothes which were laid aside for the washing machine, and phoned the Ministry vet.

"Why didn't you post the bowel of the dead pig to the Lab?" he demanded.

"Because by the time they got it at the Department, there would be several more dead. Besides, there were no button ulcers to be seen."

"That's not for you to decide, Cameron."

"I know, I know, but just the same I think you should see these pigs tomorrow."

"I take my orders from higher up, young man, you should know!" I kept my temper with difficulty, and went on.

"I know that fine. It's also true I've never seen Swine Fever before, but I'd still be grateful if you could get permission to come out tomorrow." He hummed and hawed, muttered "highly improper," but finally agreed to come. My wife had been listening to all this conversation with dismay, and then said sympathetically, "I'm afraid you've got more trouble, another case, dear. Ann phoned about half an hour, a cow down in the yard at Higher Chade, they don't know what's wrong with it, and Bernard's away at another case."

I groaned, for I had started the day with a calving at John Atkin's farm at 5:00 am, and had been at it non-stop, and my first brush with suspected Swine Fever had taken a bit out of me. Bernard had also had a full day. I gulped a cup of tea while I dressed in fresh clothes, then skimmed off in my little Standard 8, the best car I had been able to afford so far. It was still a small and cheap car, but to me as precious as a Rolls Royce.

Higher Chade was only a mile away, and when I entered the yard, there was my patient lying flat out on the concrete with Ivor Huxtable, the owner, standing looking at it moodily. He was a good natured character, young like Derek Hocking, and likewise a keeper of Friesians, famed for his quaint sense of humour and peculiarities. You never knew what he would say or do next but equally one could say anything to him. What he said to me was predictable.

"Did 'ee 'ave a good tea then? I phoned so long ago it must have been nigh yesterday!"

I grinned at him, slapped him on the shoulder, and enlightened him, "I was at an urgent case, Ivor."

"Aar! What was that, 'en?"

"A budgerigar."

"Oh well, that be different 'en, them budgerigars be mighty valuable like."

He poked his recumbent cow with his toe, his hands thrust deep into his pockets.

"Can't make this thar bullock out. He be due to calve

an' some waters come away, but nothin's showin', an' when I finished my milkers an' come out to turn the dry 'uns back to the field along with 'em, there he be—flat out."

I had by this time got used to the Devon habit of describing every bovine as a bullock, but it still startled me to hear some farmers call a she, a he. The preliminary diagnosis was easy, but coming from Ayrshire where every farmer recognised the condition, and some, even in the 1950s, were injecting their own cattle, I was constantly surprised that so many in Devon had never seen Milk Fever. I got out my calcium bottles and flutter valve and injected directly into the mammary vein, Ivor holding the bottle up for me for the gravity feed, one hand still in his pocket.

"Now, Ivor, if you can bear to take your hands out of your pockets, would you bring me a bucket of warm water, soap and a towel, and we'll see what's happening in here."

Ivor slouched off and eventually came back with my requirements. I had no alternative but to lie down on the hard, filthy, concrete yard to examine her, for the cow was still down on her side. My hand went just into the entrance of the womb, and then it was all I could do to poke two fingers inside. I groaned, one of these, a twist, a torsion of the womb, a tricky business.

"We've got a problem, Ivor my lad, and it's more than you and I can handle."

"Ur! What be that 'en?"

"This cow has a twist in her womb. The waters have broken, so she's at her time, but there's no way we can get the calf out till we straighten out that twist."

"How do 'ee do that 'en?"

"We have to roll this cow over and over while I keep my arm inside her, and hope that we can unwind the twist, for it's a bit like a corkscrew in there just now."

"Do 'ee tell me that? Will it work?"

"Well, say a prayer it will, or we're in real trouble. Can you get a couple of men to help us?"

"Reckon so," murmured the unperturbed Ivor, departed, and returned quite quickly with two men from the neighbouring farm, practically next door. By now the calcium was taking effect, and the cow was sitting up on its brisket, but not yet trying to stand. I needed a fit cow for the calving, but I did not want her on her feet just yet.

"Now boys," I explained, "you have to tuck in her legs and roll her on to her side, then right over on her back and so on to the other side. But remember my arm will be inside her all the time and I've got kind of attached to that arm, so if I say 'stop,' stop at once."

"Right, boss," murmured Ivor, "us'll 'ave a go."

So I soaped my arm, put it in as far as I could and said "Now . . . roll!, which they did, and immediately a tremendous pressure came on the arm and I had an awful feeling I would never get it out again.

"Stop!" I yelled in agony, "we're going the wrong way. Get her back as she was, quick!"

They worked well, and rolled her back to where we had been at the start, as I scrabbled about on the hard, wet, mucky concrete.

"Now try the other way!" which they did. "Keep going, right over with her, and over she went, and oh the relief, for it was like coming out of a dark passage into the light, ascending a spiral staircase and reaching the top. The womb was opened up now and already a live calf was moving towards the exit. As if realising that things had taken a turn, or several turns, for the better, the cow struggled to her feet. Now it was time for the calving chains, and the pull of four husky men, for the calf was big, and the cow not yet able to help 100 per cent. Even with four of us, it was a tough pull, but eventually out dropped the calf, hitting me on the chest as I tried to catch this slippery bundle of new life, so that I sat down in the yard, the calf on top of me. I got up, and stood grinning at the calf as the young farmer rubbed it down with a wisp of straw. He glanced up at me, covered from head to toe in filth, and streaked with blood, and in his droll way said, "You best get back to you'm budgerigar. I reckon it would take one look at 'ee and shout for the police, but I be mighty grateful to 'ee just the same. I never see'd owt like that afore," then as an afterthought he grinned and said, "Come in an' have a wash. Maybe you can straighten missus out too. She be mighty twisted times, specially when I snore of nights."

So it was home for yet another change of clothing, after a soak in a strongly disinfected and scented bath. The phone stayed quiet, but I could not put Derek and his pig problem out of my mind. I mused on the unlucky twist of fortune he had had to turn a bargain into a nightmare, so I took a run out to High Deane to see him and chat over his next steps. I explained the whole position to him if our worst fears were confirmed, and advised him, since all the affected pigs were in one place and had not been in contact with the others, to have all the rest, boar, sows, weaners, bacon pigs, the lot, vaccinated. We worked out costs of vaccine, cutting this as low as I could, for Derek's losses would already be considerable. I was desperately anxious to prevent this scourge, which had been known to wipe out ten per cent of the pigs in Britain, from spreading.

The Ministry vet came out next morning, when three more pigs had died. He was more pleasant than he had been the night before on the phone, and as he looked at the sufferers, just shook his head in silence. He did a PM on the dead pigs, but again none of the famous button ulcers could be found. He wrapped up the intestines of one to send to the lab boys, who alone were authorised to make a positive diagnosis. I wondered what they did at the lab, remembering the old gag that they threw the guts at the wall, and if they stuck, it was SF, if they fell off, it was not. The Ministry imposed a stand still order preventing movement of pigs over a wide area. The farm was isolated, the police informed and the original source of the pigs checked out. There was a feeling of near panic in the area. We trembled, and waited.

So it went on for several more days. More of Derek's twenty died, more samples were taken, and eventually after a week, a positive diagnosis was given. The survivors of the original twenty were slaughtered and the carcases disposed of in the fashion laid down, buried in quick-lime.

Meantime I had injected all Derek's other pigs with Crystal Violet Vaccine, and about half of all the other pigs in the district. Injection was behind the ear, one of the few areas of thin skin on a pig, and a messy business it was, for sometimes at the crucial moment a pig would struggle free and some of the brightly coloured vaccine be deposited on pig handler or Bernard and I doing the job. For weeks afterwards we were a highly coloured pair of vets. I kept worrying in case I had inadvertently spread the killer disease on my clothes or by car, but no further outbreaks occurred. In time the restrictions were lifted, and the pall of fear in the pig community melted away.

Over the years in the ministry, I have had many tortuous, twisted "cases" to deal with too, and at times in Aldermouth, especially after the oil boom came to the area, as I have already indicated, I felt I was more of a social worker or marriage guidance counsellor than a preacher of the gospel.

There was, for example, Frank, with whom I had dealings all my twelve years in the town. Frank was an alcoholic, had been "dried out" innumerable times in Craigdunain, the big mental hospital in Inverness, but invariably he broke out again, sometimes hitting the bottle by way of celebration the very day he was discharged, a celebration that would last for weeks. He was essentially a decent fellow, never violent and when sober a good worker, but what a life he gave his wife! He visited us at

the Manse often. More than once, watching a late TV
programme, about the only time I saw television, the
back door would quietly open, and while everybody's
hair stood on end (especially if we were watching a horror
film), and our eyes moved to the inside door as it slowly
opened, Frank would come staggering in. The children
of ministers are frequently thought to have led sheltered
lives, but that was certainly not true of our four. They
never knew who would be admitted to the Manse, or
would admit themselves unbidden. We had trouble the
last two years at the Christmas Eve Service at midnight,
with a very small number of teenage drunks coming in,
being sick in the Church or otherwise disrupting this
most beautiful of all occasions of worship. To counteract
this, we had to start the Service before the pubs closed,
shut the great front door of the Church, and have elders
stationed at all points of entry, but still somehow Frank
came staggering in late, having found a side door unat-
tended.

He never came for money, not once. It was not a touch
or a con, it was a cry for help in his twisted, tortuous
soul. Often he would be in tears at night, bemoaning the
mess he had made of his life, but I soon learned that these
words of penitence were no more than crocodile tears
and vanished with the dawn. He had two sons who lived
furth of Scotland and who were the apple of his eye,
and if ever one of them was coming home, he made a
Herculean effort to stay sober.

Sometimes he would come in such a state that he would
plead to be taken to hospital, and I would run him in and
see him settled in his familiar ward. At other times I
would drive him home and even put him to bed. He was
made redundant from his job (he was about sixty) and
for many months he was at the Manse every day, just
sitting there and talking, a place to go other than the pub.
Janet was marvellously tolerant of him, as were the boys,
who regarded him, even when in their impatient teens,
with great pity and patience. He was, indeed, for a time

almost one of the family, and day after day we would talk, for he never could get away from himself and his problem. We would pray together, he would have a spell attending Church, drink innumerable cups of coffee or have a meal with the family, and I would hope. Then one day he would not appear and I would see him lurching along the street on another of his long lasting benders.

We had others too whose personality had been twisted by alcohol, whose jobs had been lost, whose marriages had eventually broken up, and though often disappointed in failure, fed up at our home becoming a "shelter," or downright angry at the waste of it all, we soldiered on, and now and again saw a twisted life straightened out, and a sub-human, weeping, weary, sodden sot of a man really overcome, sometimes with the help of Alcoholics Anonymous, sometimes by will power and the grace of God, and feel it was all worthwhile.

Mary's problem was different. That her mind had many twists and turns I realised at her first visit to me. She came when in acute depression and almost suicidal. She was an intelligent, well-to-do young woman in her twenties. She returned every week for nine weeks and quite early I realised there was one particular something which I could not understand, and which was remaining hidden in the dark recesses of her mind. She was not mentally deranged, only profoundly unhappy. No doubt a psychiatrist would have talked to her, and touched the hidden springs of her mind, but I was no psychiatrist, and like so many more she seemed to prefer a minister. So I could only as a person seek to care and help as best I could. There were, indeed, many, like Mary, who came, and whose life, at the time was, like Ivor Huxtable's cow, twisted and in need of straightening. Then one day for Mary it all came out. I felt that, at last, I had reached the bottom line. She had committed a wrong and felt she could not be forgiven, not ever. Very gently I pointed her to One who on the Cross had prayed "Father, forgive them," who had indeed died that we might be forgiven and like the twisted uterus of the cow straightening up to allow the new life to come forth like light after darkness, as I had thought that day at Ivor's, so Mary too went away with light in her face, a new life stretching before her, "ransomed, healed, restored, forgiven." No further need of the minister now, to my and her delight.

We did not have the same success with Trevor and Jeanette, husband and wife, but a story as twisted as a Devon lane, and constant new revelations at each turning of the road. They visited me together and singly, Jeanette haunted the Manse where Janet did her more good than I could, and in time we unravelled some of the facts. The basis of it all was that Jeanette had been brought up in the closed Brethren in Wales, a very narrow group of believers they appeared, had left them and, as she said "gone into the world." After a chequered career, she had married Trevor, and they had three children. But her parents had never forgiven her even though she was now back at worship, twice a week in prayer. Her complaint now was that Trevor was too friendly with a neighbour. I think the poor fellow was only seeking a normal household where he would spend an hour or two, usually playing Scrabble or just talking, for in his own home he was clearly an outcast, and Jeanette would openly tell their children he was bad. She herself had a massive guilt complex even though she had come back "out of the world," and in addition she could not forgive Trevor, despite her own past, for what she, quite wrongly, I am sure, regarded as unfaithfulness, and in truth resented him because she had married him in her wild youth. I would listen hour after hour to their talk, accusations of one another, claims and counter claims, try to advise, inwardly groaning for something "simple" like Swine Fever or a twisted uterus, and eventually stagger over from my vestry like a limp rag, for treating twists is an exhausting business!

I had a young couple one Thursday at my Vestry Hour, having a rehearsal for their Saturday wedding. As they left the Church the bride calmly announced she was away home to start to make her wedding dress.

"To *start*?" I gasped.

"Yes—I've been so busy making the bridesmaid's dresses."

The great day dawned bright and fair, the bridegroom and best man arrived, the whole congregation was assembled including the bride's mother, but at the scheduled time, no bride. Ten minutes late, twenty . . . thirty . . . forty still no bride. By now the groom looked like something left high and dry by the tide, was feverishly lighting one cigarette from another, and in general, not too happy! After forty minutes, I phoned the bride's home and got her father.

"This is the minister here. What's the trouble? I hope she hasn't changed her mind."

"No . . . nothing like that," he replied, "just a slight hitch. She'll be along in due course."

"When? How long?"

"Oh, about another half hour."

So I went into Church, told the wondering guests there had been a slight hiccup, but all would be well, and they might care to walk in the grounds for half an hour. The organist, Jim, who had been playing non-stop for an hour, was mighty glad of a rest too. Eventually the bold girl arrived, as cool as ice, an hour and twenty minutes late, and took her place beside her groom, who was in a state of near collapse. While they were signing the wedding certificate, I asked what had caused the delay.

"Oh," said the bride, "I was working on my dress to the last minute, and when I put it on, it burst!"

I was not feeling very gracious, but managed to say "So the hitch was a stitch!"

Ah well, I thought as I made my way back to the Manse, there's many a twist and turn in life, but the trouble is if you don't get them straightened out in time, there's liable to be an explosion!

The Impossible Takes Longer

TWENTY-TWO

I came out from my weekly visit to Raigmore Infirmary, Inverness, feeling very solemn. I had been the rounds of our sick folks in the different wards of the various hospitals in the ancient burgh, and as always, after sharing with the many each week who were ill or waiting for surgery, and trying to bring comfort and cheer, I was feeling drained and tired. I knew well what that verse in the New Testament meant when it said of Jesus "virtue had gone out of Him."

But it was the final visit which had really solemnised me, and a talk I had had with the Sister of Ward 15. My last patient was Gordon. He had been in hospital for a year, and every week either my Assistant of the time, Donald (now serving in Zambia) or myself had seen Gordon. He was a young man in his thirties, an exceptionally fine young fellow, a cheerful companion and friend, and in his long illness steady, brave, patient, a man, who lived for his wife and family and if what the Sister had said was correct, he would not have much longer to share with them. For about ten years Gordon had suffered from a heart condition which had slowly, progressively, become worse until now he was confined to a hospital bed, weak, weary, and if at times discouraged, who could blame him.

He had seen consultant after consultant, undergone all

sorts of tests and treatment, but his progress had been steadily downward. Now he was so weak, his heart so failed, that he could scarcely walk. He certainly could not have the least bit of activity for immediately heart pain would stop him. Occasionally he would be allowed home for a weekend, and when at home, he would struggle to Church and the family pew up in the gallery, stopping for a rest every few steps up the stairs. There was no doubt that Church meant much to Gordon, and it had been his quiet faith that had sustained him over the long, hard years, that and the love of his wife, Irene and their two children. I had baptised his children for him, his son about eight years before, and as a fervent Rangers fan Gordon had called him Colin Andrew after two of the Rangers heroes of the time. Many years before, when he was still half fit, I had occasionally golfed with him, for he was a keen and talented sportsman. Really I should say Gordon golfed. I just gave the worms a fright! All in all I had got to know Gordon and Irene well over the years, so that they were, as with so many of our congregation, not just members, but friends.

Of course I had seen his gradual deterioration, but had hoped for the miracle, but the talk with the Sister that day had dashed this hope. Quite simply, but with genuine concern, for Gordon was a favourite with the nursing staff too, she had said that it was impossible for him to live much longer, and there was, in addition, nothing possible that medical science could do for him.

Impossible! The word had sunk deep into my mind. It seemed so final and as I drove slowly the sixteen miles home two things came on the wings of memory. One was the slogan of a certain firm, "the difficult is our business, the impossible takes longer." Impossible! That too was the word Mrs. Murdoch had used nearly thirty years before when I arrived at the farm of Laigh Buccleugh to treat one of their cows. It had a prolapse of the uterus, a calf bed out as the farmers called it. Her husband and their workman (a German ex-prisoner of war who had

stayed on with them after the war) were both out in the
hay fields and too busy to come in. I was then a young,
inexperienced assistant vet, working with Ian Buchan at
Mochrum where I had grown up, and as Mrs. Murdoch
and I stared at this huge organ hanging down behind the
cow to its hocks, and then looked at the little hole through
which it had all to go back into the cow, I could well
understand her saying, "I would say you are trying the
impossible!"

For this is the big job in veterinary practice, the heavy
task, the one that vets of my era had nightmares about,
especially when there was no help available. Some pro-
lapses are worse than others, but all are difficult. What
happens is that the cow, straining to deliver her calf, then
the afterbirth, goes on straining till it expels the whole
womb, and having got rid of it, does not want it back.
Many were the ploys vets had used over the years to assist
in putting the uterus where it belonged, building up the
cow's stall at the rear, hoisting up the animal with a block
and tackle till its hind end was suspended in mid air,
wrapping the womb in a sheet and two or three men
lifting it to a horizontal position, slowly tightening the
sheet to make the organ smaller, at the same time pushing
hard, and a variety of other dodges. Normally there
would be several men to assist with the job, but that day
I was on my own. I shared the woman's view, it seemed
impossible, for that womb was swollen and engorged
with blood, big, flabby, slippery to handle, an ugly thing
as most parts of the anatomy are, when not in the place
the great Manufacturer put them.

The cow in question was standing chewing the cud as
if nothing had happened, and occasionally glancing
round at me as much as to say, "I've given you a corker,
young man. What do you think you're going to be able
to do?" Oh well, get started and try, I thought, can only
try. I stripped off jacket and shirt and got into my calving
coat.

"Could you please bring me a bucket of warm water,

soap, towel, an old sheet you won't need again, and oh yes, a pound of sugar."

"Sugar! Did you say sugar, Mr. Cameron?"

"Yes, a bag of sugar." Mrs. Murdoch went off shaking her head. Then followed the preliminaries to each operation of the kind, a bottle of calcium for it was believed then that calcium deficiency was involved in such cases, a shot of Phenergan to counteract the shock of handling such a large and vital organ, a jab of Pituitrin, an extract of a little gland in the brain, which helped to contract and shrink the womb and finally, an epidural or spinal injection of local anaesthetic to take away all pain and feeling, and hopefully to prevent the cow pressing and straining against me. By the time I had done all this, Mrs. Murdoch was back with my requests, and as she clutched the sugar was looking at me in mystification.

"What in all the world are you going to do with this sugar?" I grinned and tried to look cheerful, which I was far from feeling, and said, "A bit of black, or rather white magic!"

I got the bucket of water, poured in some disinfectant, and began to clean the pendulous uterus, for it had blood clots, dirt and bits of straw adhering to it. Then I took the sugar, slit open the bag, and shook the contents over the womb, like dusting a large cake. "What does that do?" enquired the little woman, utterly puzzled. "It's an old trick, Mrs. Murdoch, It helps to draw off some of the fluid and reduce the size of the thing. Just watch for a few minutes."

Sure enough, as we watched, the fluid started to pour off the womb, and we saw it visibly reduce in size before our eyes. But nevertheless it was still big.

"Well, that's a queer use for sugar, right enough," she said, "but I still can't see how you can get that big bag through that wee hole."

"I'll wrap it in the sheet, and gently squeeze. Do you think you could take one side of the sheet?"

She gave a howl and shook her head vehemently.

"Oh no, I couldn't touch that—that thing. It makes me feel queer to even look at it. I'm off." She muttered again, "Impossible, impossible," departed and left me on my own.

"The impossible takes longer," admitted the company in their slogan, and undoubtedly it took longer to replace the prolapse, working on my own. It also took me to the limits of my strength for the womb of a newly calved cow is a heavy organ, but slowly, with the sheet wrapped round it to prevent it continually slipping out of my arms and to apply extra pressure, it eased its way back in. Holding it horizontally in my arms and using my chest to give leverage, bit by bit it was "fed" back to where it belonged. Without the spinal injection, of course, it would have indeed been impossible, but with the whole of its rear end numb, the cow did not really know what was happening and although looking bored with the whole business, it made no comment! The final foot of uterus disappeared from sight with a plop, I dropped the sheet, and then inserting my arm made sure that the two legs of the V shaped organ were fully extended, and with a sigh of relief turned to the final short task, inserting three tape stitches through the lips of the vulva to make sure the whole thing did not come out again. One can have too much of a good thing and I had no desire to repeat the whole process, maybe at one o'clock in the morning! So while many vets maintained that if the job had been properly done, no sutures were necessary, I always played safe. Mrs. Murdoch had, by now, come back to the scene of the action to see how "the impossible" was progressing, and it gave me great satisfaction to see the disbelief on her face as she saw their cow once more outside in.

I left some sulphanilamide to dose daily and keep down infection, and told the still wondering Mrs. Murdoch I would be back in a few days to take out the stitches. Finally, after cleaning up in a fresh bucket of water, I was on my way to the next case, feeling a bit smug at the success of my one man "impossible" victory.

By now I had reached the Manse and after giving Janet a run down on the condition of our various patients, for she always wanted to know about our ill folks, I told her what the Sister had said about Gordon, and we that night again specially committed him to God in prayer. A few days later I learned he had been sent to some hospital in England where it was hoped something could be done.

Perhaps a month later, one May evening, Irene came to see me at my Vestry Hour. She clearly needed to talk to someone and I felt glad and humbled that so many of our folks knew they could come to me and share their problems, and know also their confidences would be respected. It transpired that the hospital Gordon had been sent to was Papworth, near Cambridge, which had become famous for the heart transplants carried out there by the brilliant surgeon, Mr. English. Gordon had been subjected to many tests, and the great surgeon discussed everything with both Gordon and Irene several times for he believed that the wife had a vital part to play in the post-operative care and way of life of the patient, and while many people needed a heart transplant physically, not all were psychologically suited to cope with the disciplined kind of life afterwards. They also needed to be able to handle the media, for in 1980 heart transplants were still big news, and indeed only one patient, Keith Castle, had lived for several years. Irene told me all about their experiences, their conversations, their impressions and I was able to reassure, just a little, for I too had been a patient in Papworth for six weeks, and had been greatly impressed by the hospital. Eventually, she told me that Gordon had been accepted for a transplant, when a donor became available, but meantime he would stay in Raigmore, Inverness, to have complete rest and quietness.

But she was clearly and understandably worried as to whether they had reached the right decision. She wanted a fit husband, of course, but at present she had a husband and who knew what would happen in the state of heart transplants then and the high mortality rate, and she was afraid, quite simply, after surgery, she would have no husband. A dreadful dilemma for the poor lass to be in! She also asked me earnestly not to mention to anyone the proposed transplant, for they did not want the pressure of publicity. So we talked, then it was the most natural thing in the world to commit Gordon into the hands of One, who, when He walked the earth, constantly made the impossible happen.

The weeks went past, and dragged into months, while Gordon waited with what patience he could muster. Then one evening in August, I had a phone call from Gordon's mother telling me that Gordon and Irene were at that moment in the air, being flown to Cambridge, for a heart had become available, in a few hours he would be on the operating table, and would I pray for him. I jumped into the car and drove down to the hotel Gordon's folks owned, and to my great surprise had to dodge reporters who thus early had heard the news and were plaguing the family for a story of Gordon's childhood, work, interests, sufferings and so on as well as looking for photographs. Newsmen have a difficult job to do but at that moment the family were not in a fit state to cope with this kind of extra pressure. I wondered how in all the world the reporters had heard the news and concluded that someone from Raigmore hospital, nurse, porter or perhaps someone from the airport had phoned the press to get a tenner.

I sat with the family for a while and we talked of all sorts of things as the time dragged slowly by and we waited for news. Again I found that my own experience of Papworth, though nothing like as serious a condition as Gordon's, proved to be a blessing and I was able to describe the layout, the lovely grounds, the calm of the whole place, and assure them of the skill and dedication of the staff. After a while we all gathered round, and committed Gordon and the whole family into God's hands for what was going to be a long night for them all.

The next day the papers hit the streets and there was Gordon on the front page, Supermac as they dubbed him, the first Scot to have a transplant at Papworth, I believe. In the Stop Press was the brief announcement that the operation had gone smoothly. Gordon made rapid progress and I had a long letter from him telling me of his experiences, and saying that to be conscious of a strong heart beating inside him was both exciting and a bit frightening, but rejoicing in how well he felt already after all these long years of illness. I was greatly touched by that letter. We rejoiced as a whole community for our lad and his family and I recalled that talk I had had with the Ward Sister telling me that it was impossible that Gordon should live. Looking back over the years, it was true, as the slogan had it, that it had taken longer, but the impossible had indeed happened.

I was no longer in Aldermouth when Gordon returned home fit and well, and there was great thankfulness in his family, friends and the whole community. But every Christmas I hear from him, and I have, in a return visit to Aldermouth Old seen him, Irene and all the family in their familiar pew upstairs, and had time for a few words with him. As I write this, nearly eight years later, Gordon is going strong, cycling, swimming, golfing, able to earn a living again, the longest surviving heart transplant Scot. He has been interviewed many times on radio and by the press and in this own quiet way has never omitted to testify to the strength and courage his trust in God gave him, allied of course to the love that surrounded him from family and friends.

That slogan about the impossible taking longer? Come to think of it, does the Bible not say with God nothing is impossible?

Family Matters

TWENTY-THREE

I was down in the depths, tired, sorry for myself, allied to a feeling of guilt, my health, to say the least, indifferent and generally a poor specimen of a minister that day in 1980. There was nothing wrong with the day, the very opposite, a glorious mid-summer day of blue sky and lazily drifting clouds, as if Nature was calling to one and all, "Come on out! There's a big, wide world out here waiting to be enjoyed."

I suppose my mood had started with the funeral, that of a young man with all his life before him, but who had been taken at eighteen. That was the age of our youngest, Alan, and while I had tried to bring comfort to the sorrowing parents in the funeral service and afterwards in their home, I had felt my words were empty things, imagining how I would feel if it had been our laddie, now down in Edinburgh studying for a BSc.

The house was empty when I arrived home, Janet out shopping and David, now twenty-one and on holiday away from Aberdeen University at his summer job of Life Guard on the beach, and enthusiastic about his work. David, a Life Guard and loving it! That seemed an unlikely thing, recalling how afraid he had been of the water years before, and how he had cried for days before he had to go to the swimming baths with the school for the first time. Neil, the eldest at twenty-five, was in Edinburgh, an honours degree in zoology behind him, but with precious little demand for zoologists and the outdoor life he craved, and which his friend Peter Archibald had found, was now a Computer Programmer in the Civil Service. Ian, number two son, had at least found his desired niche as an English teacher, and had also a highly successful career as a professional footballer, first, while a student, with Aberdeen and now with Kilmarnock, then in the Premier Division, a Scottish League Cap and his cherished blue jersey tucked away in a drawer. But whenever I thought of the boys, now men, and now all away from home, my guilt complex came back, that when they had needed him and wanted him, Dad had more often than not been too busy in the Lord's work. Janet told me it was nonsense, I was not aware of any criticism from our brood of four, but I had carried this sense of neglect with me for years, *the* one big regret of my life, that I had been a minister first, and father second, and missed so much in their earlier years, and now it was too late. Yet was that not the way it had to be? Had Jesus not said "he that loves father or mother, or son or daughter more than me is not worthy of me?" But it was hard, as all pathways of dedication can be hard.

Janet's footsteps sounded on the gravel and in she came, carrier bags in her hands, and, as always, her very presence seemed to cheer. She glanced at me, asked "How was the funeral?," then, with the intuition that twenty-eight years of marriage had given, she guessed that all was not well with her man.

"Poor Mr. and Mrs.—" she said, then softly,

"But you cannot carry everybody's sorrows all the time, my dear. Why don't you go fishing tonight? It would do you good to get out."

"I've a sermon to write," I retorted, none too gently.

"You'll write it better after a break."

In the end, we compromised. After tea, I went into the

study and tried to sermonise, but at 8:00 pm gave it up, gathered my tackle, and said, still far from gracious, "I'll away up to Lochindorb and see what's doing."

Lochindorb was a large loch twenty miles up in the hills, absolutely full of small, sweet brown trout, so that only a complete dud failed to catch anything. I managed to be a complete dud many times without even trying! But it was, more important, a place of peace, surrounded by its sentinel hills. In the middle of the loch were the ruins of a castle where Edward I reputedly had met the highland chieftains, the whole the scenario for one of Maurice Walsh's books.

I parked the car and made my way down to my favourite bay and patch of shingle. There was not a soul to be seen and all was silent save for the whirr of a startled grouse, the call of a sheep and the soft boom-boom-boom of Lochindorb House's electric generator, a lovely spot, a panacea for tired minds and handmade to help disgruntled ministers. But I did not become less gruntled easily that night even when I realised it was a hopeless night for fishing. The gentle breeze had died away, and its going was the signal for the midges to venture forth, millions of them and in the gathering dusk there was a plop-plop-plop all over the loch as the fish came up to feed. I tried all my favourite flies, Zulu, Blue Zulu, Silver Butcher, Black Spider, Heather Moth, Greenwell Glory, but gloomily thought that only a fish with a very low IQ would fancy my bait when all these midges were there for the taking, that is the ones that were not feeding on me, and who seemed to be wearing tackety boots or had specially sharpened their teeth for my coming! As I tried bait after bait, finally needing a torch to tie the line, I thought of John McEwan's story of a predecessor in lovely Stratherrick above Loch Ness. John was minister there and one of my closest friends and he had told me of this former minister, a widower, with two lovely daughters. One evening he was out walking, in mufti, a daughter on each arm, when he met a fisherman coming up from one of the many lochs in the parish.

"Have you had any luck?" the minister enquired.

"Not bad," said the fisher, showing his catch.

"Very good, I'd say," said the disguised minister.

"Are you a fisher yourself?" asked the angler.

"Well, . . . I suppose you could say I was, . . . a fisher of men." Looking at the two bonny girls, the other replied, "Ah well, you've certainly got the right bait!"

None of my bait was right, so at last I laid the rod aside, threw myself down on a bed of heather, tried to ignore the midges, and watched the last rays of the sun disappear in the west. I shone my torch on my watch, 11:40 pm sunset. Maybe it was midsummer madness, but I decided to wait in that soft, still night and see the sun rise again, and as I lay there, my whirling thoughts took over once more.

I sighed wistfully as I realised this would be my last summer at Lochindorb. My health had failed, an odd sort of condition that took a lot of diagnosing and caused much pain, the product, said the experts, of years of overwork and stress. If I wanted to go on working, or even living, I must find a quiet Church where the pressures would be much less than in Aldermouth Old. I did not want to go, indeed I hated the thought of it, for I loved Aldermouth, its people and my Church, but go I must and I had been accepted by two linked country Kirks in the lovely Border country, and was due to start in September. It would be very different in scattered rural parishes, but people's needs would be the same and the folks we had met had been warm and welcoming. Besides, after twelve years I felt I had given my all to Aldermouth, had seen the Church grow, and knew it to be in a satisfactory condition, and maybe it was time, for the Church's sake as well as my own, to make way for someone else. So, at any rate, I tried to convince myself.

One tangible thing I was leaving behind gave me great

satisfaction. I had been Presbytery Convenor of the Home Board when the new town of Culloden started to take shape, and I managed to persuade Presbytery that the Church should be there from the start. So we had bought an old tithe barn for £600. It was used as the first Church, elders were appointed, and while a Home Board Missionary, Jim Pettie, was put in charge for the day to day running of the Church, I was, at the beginning, minister in overall control and I felt highly honoured in taking the first Communion, first Baptism and first wedding in the old barn, round which eventually grew up a lovely Church served by a very fine minister in Peter Walker. Oddly enough, just before leaving Moorton twelve years before as Home Board Convenor there too, I had a little share in the erection of another new Church in the New Farm Loch area of Kilmarnock. I felt privileged that I had had a share in the erection of two lovely new Churches in large new housing areas.

So I mused as I lay in the heather in the dark of that summer night, but my mind kept swinging back to home, and my sense of guilt, the boys, . . . ah, the boys again! Once more their old Dad was failing them, for they too loved Aldermouth. There they had finished their schooling—there they had become men—that's where their friends were—there was home, and the stupid, weak, old man had not had the sense to pace himself or delegate work to others, and so cracked up. My mind went back over the years.

I remembered Neil, as a wee boy at Moorton asking one night, "Can you play with my fort tonight, Daddy?"

"Not tonight, son. I've got a meeting."

"Tomorrow night?"

"Sorry, another meeting."

Wistfully, "Next week?" and I realised my whole week's evenings were taken up. What am I doing to my family, I thought? I remembered the great George Duncan in Troon Portland saying one Sunday that early in his ministry he had *made* time from 5:30 to 7:15 pm each evening to be with his family, so for a time I did the same. But soon I slipped into my old ways and would be away out on a round of visits or attending an urgent call before playtime was over. Janet had often had to be both father and mother.

Another memory of Neil drifted like thistledown into my mind. It was Christmas and the boys at school were all pooh, poohing Santa Clause. So on the great night, when all were asleep, I dressed myself in my long gowns (not having a Santa suit), draped a towel round my head and hanging down like a beard, and put all his parcels on his bed. By the light of my little torch, he looked so serene and peaceful as he lay asleep, I stroked his forehead. He stirred and I fled for my bed, jumped in, gowns and all to hear an excited young voice call, "Mummy, Daddy, Santa's been! I saw a great tall figure beside my bed and felt an old horny hand on my head. There *is* a Santa!"

Then there was the time Neil had come off a bike at speed and landed on one knee which was gashed and lacerated right through to the bone. We shivered when we saw the extent of it, but all the poor wee lad could say through his tears was, "Sorry I've torn my new jeans, Mummy." That injury had kept him from running or footballing for two years and permanently slowed him up.

Another memory of Moorton came back to me. Ian had come running in saying there was a crowd of big boys hitting David at the swing park. Dad was out the door like a shot and soon at the scene of the mêlée. There was indeed a crowd of boys up to the age of fourteen hitting little David, mocking him and saying again and again, "Sweir boy, sweir. Come on, minister's son, we'll make you sweir!" In the midst was three year old David resolutely refusing to swear. I threatened some very un-ministerial things to that crowd if they ever laid a hand on my son again, and as they slunk away, put an arm round our wee lad, and feeling very proud of him, led him home.

I had tried to make it up to the boys with a lot of attention and playing on our annual holidays by the sea shore in our caravan and ancient tent. These were halcyon days when we built sand castles, searched in rock pools, fished off the rocks or pier, played Test matches at cricket and World Cup at football.

Football! That had been *the* great love of all our four, although they were all-rounders. Ian, for example, having a badminton medal and Neil a table tennis one. Even allowing for an old doting father's pride, they all excelled at soccer. I remembered David, young for the team at nine, chosen for the area schools' select, Alan at eleven captaining the school to victory in the cup final against the much bigger Elgin boys (who stoned the bus afterwards), and scoring the winning goal while John Duggie, Bill Barnett the Headmaster and myself bawled instructions and bit our nails between looking at our watches. I remembered Ian at fifteen making his senior debut for Aldermouth in the Highland League (having played also for the school in the morning) and in a mazy dribble, his speciality, as it was Neil's, beating six Hibs players in a friendly match. I recalled David as a ball boy, then later captain of the Youth team, on his eighteenth birthday playing a stormer of a game for the senior team at right back to win the Inverness Cup, in the same game Neil (who came late to senior football, having concentrated on his studies for his degree) scoring a scorcher of a goal from forty yards. I recalled my pride as young Alan captained the Northern Schoolboys in the annual national tournament. I had been at all these games yelling my head off. I remembered the Aldermouth manager and coach saying, "Alan will be the best of the four." But alas, a disability in his teens put paid to Alan's football for these vital years. Then all the excitement of football trials for Ian and Neil with, among others, Manchester United, Dundee United and Airdrie. Ian making it with Aberdeen, and Neil, who I am convinced could have also made it if he had started earlier, remaining in the Highland

League. They were twins in style, position and inherent ability, while David and Alan were likewise twins, initially, as doughty defenders.

They had played cricket, and all had captained the school team in turn (handing on their "whites" from one to the other), Ian and Alan being powerful sloggers, while Neil and David were all-rounders, handy with bat and ball. Happy days and a proud Dad!

Then golf. Our sideboard was covered with trophies they had won, Ian chipping the ball into the hole for an eagle three on the eighteenth to win the King Cup at the age of fifteen. Neil winning the big prestigious Open tournament in the handicap section at seventeen, his excited Dad caddying for him. David and Alan had their share of junior wins too, and both could hit the ball out of sight. It seemed no time since I had given them their first, old hickory shafted clubs and they had played with Dad, getting two strokes a hole. Now they all looked pityingly at the old man and asked, "How many strokes do you want?" I recalled David caddying for me in the only competition I ever entered, being quite excited as I went two ahead, then my caddy looking worried as I lost my lead and finally exploding with a loud groan "Oh Dad," as I chipped into the burn and lost the match two and one.

They had all worked in their summer holidays, Neil at the Golf View Hotel keeping the grounds and "hoovering" the outside swimming pool each day. Two days he was away and Ian took over. On the first day he lost a bit of the "hoover" and had repeatedly to dive for it, while on the second day, walking round the pool and watching some guests, no doubt pretty girls, he had fallen in, fully clothed. David and Alan had worked on the Golf Course, then with "the squad," the grass cutters and garbage collectors of the little burgh, before David became a Life Guard, a swimming medal to his credit.

Another memory, less pleasant, of Alan, drifted into my mind as I continued to lie in the soft, fragrant night

beside the loch. Alan had witnessed a boy vandalising a
drainpipe at school. The culprit was a fellow member of
the Academy school football team, and Alan, brought up
by us never to "clipe" or tell tales on a friend, had refused
to give the other boy's name, though he himself was
totally innocent. I had a letter from the Deputy Head
Master stating that if Alan did not spill the beans "he
would be invited to remove his presence from the school."
That made me see red. Whether Alan was right or wrong
is a moot point, and readers will form their own judgement, but the boy was merely carrying out the code we
had taught him. I had a stormy meeting with the Deputy
Head, reminded him that none of our four had ever given
the least bit of trouble, all had brought honour to the
school scholastically and in sport with never a "thank you"
or word of praise from the authorities, and to threaten our
son with expulsion for a deed he had not done was like
taking a sledgehammer to crack a nut. I did not succeed
in convincing the Deputy Head, but at least the air was
cleared and we heard no more about it.

So my thoughts drifted on, borne on the wings of
memory as I lay beside the loch, enveloped, embraced by
a silence that could be felt, till suddenly other wings
startled me as a gull swooped over me. I was startled, yes,
but also stimulated to recall our episode of the gull at the
Manse.

Ian had found a herring gull on the beach unable to fly
because of a damaged leg, and carried the bird home to
see if Dad could do anything for it. The leg was, in fact,
too damaged for any real hope, but I splinted it as best I
could, and the bird, dubbed Sinbad remained in the garden, a source of interest, but also eventually becoming a
nuisance to numbers of people. For a start it had to be
fed, so every evening I went to the river, returning with a
catch of minnows or small trout, which Sinbad consumed
speedily. Although it stayed around the garden for the
most part, in time it would fly short distances, and one

day, one of our elders, Bob Anderson came to the door and informed Janet the bird was sitting right in the middle of the road and thus a traffic hazard. So a posse of the boys went after it, and brought it back from the midst of tooting cars. Ian tried to teach it to fly better by throwing it out of his upstairs bedroom window, encouraged or derided by the others watching, or catching below. Sinbad's territory increased, and spotting a lovely patch of green turf from the air about 100 yards from the Manse, the gull landed there one day and produced chaos as it limped about! Janet was again confronted by an elder, little Bobby Sim who spoke rather quickly, and in his excitement was almost incoherent but Janet got the message,

"Mrs. Cameron! Ian's bird is sitting in the middle of the bowling green and upsetting all the games." Again the posse went out and brought Sinbad back. So it went on. Sinbad was the subject of a children's address in Church, and "Ian's bird" was known to the whole congregation. But things could not go on indefinitely as they were and eventually, though it was still a partial cripple, Ian returned the gull to its native element, thus ending the Sinbad phase in the Cameron history.

There would be no more such episodes, for now the boys were all gone from home. It was Darby and Joan at the Manse, but at least we had them to come home, not like the couple whose lad I had buried that day, poor souls. There seemed to be a strange light behind me and I looked round. It was the sun, rising again at 12:30 am, hardly any night in these northern climes, and my sermonic mind told me, "That's like life. Sunrise on the other side of the hill follows sunset in life here and hereafter." For that lad I had buried that day there was already the sunrise of the great beyond of eternity, life all of a piece, now and beyond the hills of time, and for us, with our unknown future, a Hymn came to me like an answer to all my yearnings.

"In Heavenly love abiding, *no change* my heart
     shall fear;
And safe is such confiding, for nothing changes
     here.
Wherever He may guide me, no want shall turn
     me back;
My Shepherd is beside me, and nothing shall I
     lack."

and the marvellously assuring last verse.

"My hope I cannot measure, my path to life is
     free;
My Saviour has my treasure, and *he will walk
with me*"

I rose from the heather and thought I would try one more cast, even though the midges were still providing a self-service restaurant, and lo! and behold, there was a splash, a tug, and I had my trout, even though it must have been a mentally defective one! Maybe there would still be fishing of all kinds for the minister in the Borders!